D1127898

THE
CHANGING FACE
OF THE CHURCH

EDITED BY
TIMOTHY FITZGERALD
AND MARTIN CONNELL

LITURGY
TRAINING
PUBLICATIONS

Acknowledgments

Most of the original Celtic prayers and runes cited in "The Celtic Legacy: Tool or Treasure?" by John L. Bell are found in *Carmina Gaelica*, published by Floris Books, Edinburgh. Also in Bell's article, "Jesus Dies" is from *Love Burning Deep* by Kathy Galloway, © 1993, by permission of SPCK; the extract from George MacLeod's prayer is from *The Whole Earth Shall Cry Glory* (Glasgow: Wild Goose Publications, 1985); the monologue, "The Wedding," is copyright WGRG, the Iona Community.

The text of "The Spiritual Storyteller" is copyright © 1998, Thomas Sparough; the text of "Waking the Church: Grief that Frees Us, Dreams that Compel Us" is copyright © 1998, Whitehead Associates.

The prayer by Paul Philibert in the chapter "The Changing Face of the Church in a Parish's Preparation for Liturgy" is © 1995 by the Order of St. Benedict, Inc. Published by The Liturgical Press, Collegeville, Minnesota. Used with permission.

Excerpts from *Plenty Good Room: The Spirit and Truth of African American Catholic Worship* © 1990, the United States Catholic Conference, Inc. (USCC), Washington, DC; excerpts from *The Order of Christian Funerals, Appendix II: Cremation, Pastoral Introduction* © 1997 USCC; and excerpts from *Reflections on the Body, Cremation, and Catholic Funeral Rites* © 1997 USCC are used with permission. All rights reserved.

Excerpts from the English translation of the *Order of Christian Funerals* © 1985, International Commission on English in the Liturgy, Inc.; all rights reserved; used by permission.

Excerpts from the English translation of *The Rite of Marriage* © 1969, International Committee on English in the Liturgy, Inc. (ICEL); excerpts from the English (draft) translation of *The Order for Celebrating Marriage* © 1996, ICEL. All rights reserved; used by permission.

Copyright © 1998, Archdiocese of Chicago: Liturgy Training Publications, 1800 North Hermitage Avenue, Chicago IL 60622-1101; 1-800-933-1800, fax 1-800-933-7094, e-mail orders@ltp.org. All rights reserved.

This book was edited by Martin F. Connell. Audrey Novak Riley was the production editor. The design is by Lisa Buckley, and the typesetting was done by Mark Hollopeter in Gill Sans and Sabon. Printed in the United States of America. The cover photograph is by Bill Wittman.

Library of Congress Catalog Card Number: 98-85452

1-56854-259-3
FACE

Contents

Timothy Fitzgerald

Introduction

I t was a happy coincidence of two anniversaries marking a liturgical legacy. In the summer of 1997, the Notre Dame Center for Pastoral Liturgy held its twenty-fifth pastoral liturgy conference on the campus. Since 1970 these conferences have drawn nearly fifteen thousand people as participants and have led to the publication of this and twelve other books, many audiotapes and even two videotapes. This volume features some of the presenters and presentations from the twenty-fifth conference. It is a tradition that has served the church well.

Summer 1997 also marked the fiftieth year of the liturgical studies programs at the University of Notre Dame. In June 1947, the Holy Cross priest Michael Mathis first drew together scholars and writers from Europe and North America for the academic study of the church's liturgical life and heritage. His summer institutes, held together by force of will, led to the graduate programs in liturgical studies at the university, the Center for Pastoral Liturgy (founded in 1970), the Center's summer liturgy conferences and much more. The dogged efforts of Father Mathis planted seeds that have formed and informed generations of liturgists and ministers, who in turn have helped to shape the prayer of the church around the world.

Fifty years of higher education intersects with twenty-five years of pastoral concerns and liturgical formation: It is a valuable convergence and those who read this book will surely agree. That academic concerns and pastoral practices inform each other comes as no surprise to those engaged in liturgical leadership and other ministerial roles. They know well that our liturgical practice expresses and shapes our liturgical understanding and that our understanding in turn influences our practice. Our understanding and our experience of liturgy intersect all the time.

The face of the church and its worship for this generation of believers is far different than what Father Mathis and his contemporaries experienced. Since his day, we have changed our liturgical experience—deliberately, steadily, profoundly. While much of this was initiated by Vatican Council II and its subsequent commissions which called for changes in our liturgical practice the consequent changes in our understandings have often come as a surprise.

Our liturgical life of the past thirty-five years has provided us with different images of the church than what Mathis knew; now we are at pains to decide whether this changing face of the church is to our liking or not. The Council's call for full, conscious and active participation in the liturgy conveys a different standard for our common life than some are willing to accept. The decentralized model of ministry embodied in the reformed liturgy has profoundly affected our presumptions about roles and responsibilities. The revision of our rites of initiation has revealed the long-forgotten centrality of baptism, and we find some of this 'new wine' is stretching the 'old wineskins' to the breaking point. The face of the church is changing, our understanding of the church is changing, in no small part because of liturgical changes we intentionally set in motion.

The papers in this collection address the pastoral and liturgical issues that animate, vex, challenge and comfort us on our pilgrim way. As the church, can we die to the old and rise to the new? Do we welcome as gift the growing diversity of the church and its practice, or do we resist it as threat? How do we deal with the changes that press in on us—a diminishing number of ordained ministers, the cry for more inclusion in ministerial roles and decision making? Preaching, preparation for marriage, initiation of adults in small parishes

Timothy Fitzgerald

with limited resources, the funeral of a Christian who body has been cremated, Sunday worship in the absence of eucharist: The living, breathing church changes and grows and moves along.

A generation after Vatican Council II, we are part of a process of change far more dramatic than the Council fathers ever imagined, and quite different from anything we Catholics ever dreamed. Though we have come a long way from belting out "Sons of God" as we gathered at the "turned-around" altars of the '70s, we are still grappling with what it means to be people of God, living out the radical equality of baptism into the body of Christ.

Twenty-five conferences later, this collection of papers is a good reflection of the life of the post-Vatican II church and the questions that engage us as we press ahead. The conference attempt to bring the best of pastoral practice, teaching and writing to bear upon the changing landscape. May you discover in these pages fresh evidence of the work of the Spirit among us, the Spirit that enables us to stand firm in faith, even as we learn to live with, to love and to welcome the changing face of the church.

February 2, 1998
Feast of the Presentation of the Lord

On Receiving the Michael Mathis Award

Dear Friends of the Center for Pastoral Liturgy:

Your applause gives me courage and a sense of solidarity with you. I thank Sister Eleanor Bernstein and the Notre Dame Center for Pastoral Liturgy for this great honor. I accept the Michael Mathis Award in the name of all liturgists who have worked so hard to produce the revised Sacramentary and revised New American Bible Lectionary. I think, in particular, of Dr. John Page and the International Commission on English in the Liturgy (ICEL) staff and Monsignor Alan Detscher and the U.S. Bishops' Committee on the Liturgy (BCL) staff.

There are parallels between Father Michael Mathis and myself. We both arrived on the liturgical scene somewhat late in life and at a time of liturgical backsliding, liturgical retrenchment. Father Mathis was sixty-two years old when he began to influence audiences beyond the Notre Dame campus. The American liturgical movement was already ten years old, but still a minority phenomenon. At that time, the liturgical movement was facing suspicion by mainstream Catholics and many bishops. Michael Mathis and other liturgists of his day struggled to make the church realize the importance of full, conscious and active participation in the eucharist. It was an uphill battle, but they knew the righteouness of their cause and they would, indeed, be vindicated at the Second Vatican Council.

Most Rev. Donald W. Trautman

Today, there is also suspicion and a sophisticated applying of the brakes to liturgical renewal. I recently saw on a college campus a T-shirt with the message: "Join the resistance — Support Vatican II." Are the liturgical achievements of Vatican II in jeopardy? Do we hear important voices in the church calling us back to a liturgical theology and practice prior to Vatican II? Is liturgical renewal becoming a dinosaur?

Serious articles and books have recently appeared, challenging the reform and restoration of the liturgy realized at Vatican II. I refer to a book by Monsignor Klaus Gamber, *The Reform of the Roman Liturgy* (1993), which stresses the reform of the reform. Gamber and his followers reject most of the actions of the post-Vatican Consilium for the implementation of the *Constitution on the Sacred Liturgy* and reject the changes in revised liturgical books.

Father Joseph Fessio and *Adoremus* also want a complete rethinking of the reform of the liturgy. Proponents of this movement to reform the reform — most notably the group CREDO — indict ICEL for distorting the Roman Rite and the vision of Vatican II. Monsignor Francis Mannion, writing in *America* (November 30, 1996), summarizes the views of those advocating the reform of the reform. He cites the Reverend Brian Harrison who advances the following:

> The restoration of the recitation of the canon in Latin; exclusive use of the Roman canon; the restriction of communion to one species; priest and people facing in the same direction during the eucharistic liturgy; the use of two scripture readings instead of three, and the exclusive use of men in liturgical ministries.

Monsignor Mannion comments:

> How widely shared these proposals are in this agenda group, I am uncertain. My impression is that they are widely shared by those who speak of reforming the reform. Cardinal Joseph Ratzinger has spoken positively of Harrison's proposals and the English Dominican, Aidan Nichols, has suggested a similar direction.

I find these proposals alarming: They are indicative that the liturgical advances of Vatican II are in trouble — advances which the vast majority of Catholics have received positively.

On Receiving the Michael Mathis Award

We do not need to reform the reform. We need to revitalize the reform. This is my thesis: *To revert to a liturgical practice and style before the Second Vatican Council, rather than to progress with vision for the millennium, sins against the reform and restoration of the liturgy accomplished at Vatican II.* I would like to use this occasion to enlist all of you in an effort to revitalize the reform. Liturgists need to stand together more than ever. You might ask: What can you do? Teach, teach, teach. Liturgists have missed opportunities to use the media. We may have communicated with one another through liturgical journals and theological position papers, but we have missed golden opportunities to reach the people in the pews. We need a new catechesis. We must give better instruction. With charity and patience, we must dialogue with those blinded to liturgical renewal.

We must become more pro-active, more aggressive, writing articles and speaking out in public forums, so that liturgical reform may be properly understood. Consider the state of the Catholic press and the Catholic presence on television in the United States. How many Catholic publications or television programs would you consider to be theologically balanced or moderate? When was the last time you saw a positive, objective article on horizontal inclusive language or the revised sacramentary?

The people in the pews are not receiving an accurate message. They are being influenced by many in the media who are biased and liturgically illiterate. The people are being alarmed by extremist voices which continue to blame all the ills of the contemporary church on the changes in the liturgy. Due to many cultural forces, society itself has changed radically since the 1960s. We must avoid simplistic approaches that call us back to an era that has passed. For Catholics, the eucharist as sacrifice, memorial and sacred meal is the absolute — not its external form, not the Latin language, not the rubrics of the sixteenth century, not the rubrics of 1962.

Father Mathis knew the importance of communication in promoting liturgical reform. Father Mathis was not a radical innovator or liturgical rebel. He was a pastoral person who knew the importance of reaching the people and catechizing them in their full rights as members of the assembly. He published a biweekly mimeographed flyer entitled "Preparation for Mass." Father Mathis published and mimeographed editions of his Vigil service with commentary. We need to imitate Father Mathis. Liturgists need to take their case directly to the people and we must gain access to them through publications and the electronic media.

I would like to challenge all here, who believe that a reform of the reform is not the answer, to revitalize the reform. If you believe this, then I challenge you to persuade others, especially leadership people of the church, to understand that when a faith community celebrates liturgy well, transformation can and does take place. That must be our driving force. The parish community that celebrates liturgy with full, conscious and active participation of the assembly will become a powerful sacrament of Christ, a leaven in our midst.

Father Mathis and liturgical pioneers of his day understood this and they have given us a magnificent legacy that we must not only protect but pass on. A renewed catechesis on the nature of the liturgy and its renewal is essential. In the course of the centuries, much of the vitality in the worship life of the church has been lost. But thanks to "the movement of the Holy Spirit" at Vatican II, a new beginning was made. We cannot forfeit these advances through a reform of the reform. We need to revitalize the movement of the Spirit at Vatican II.

Tomorrow [Friday, June 20, 1997], the United States bishops will consider the fate of the New American Bible lectionary. Problematic is horizontal inclusive language. I say to you, addressing women using male language denies women their own identity. When women are not named specifically, they are excluded from full participation and this diminishes the church. Those in opposition to inclusive language have persuaded many in leadership roles and many people in the pews that inclusive language is a sinister plot on the part of feminists to advance women's ordination.

Inclusive language is fundamentally a scripture question. In many instances, a more inclusive translation will actually be closer to the original Greek or Hebrew text. At times, inclusive language will be more faithful to what the inspired author wanted to say. For instance, Mark 8:36–37: "For what does it profit a man to gain the whole world and forfeit his life? For what can a man give in return for his life?" Not to render this text in accord with the Greek text, which speaks not of a male but of a human being, is a distortion and inaccurate translation.

Inclusive language is a sensitive issue which has ramifications far beyond the New American Bible lectionary. It has become the focal point for judging continued liturgical progress or retrenchment. It is a major pastoral concern for the church in the United States.

Those opposed to inclusive language argue that everyone in our culture understands that "man" is generic. If that is true, why are many chagrined when they hear this text from the Catechism of the Catholic Church: "Called to consecrate themselves with undivided heart to the Lord and to the affairs of the Lord, they [the ordained ministers of the Latin Church] give themselves entirely to God and to men"? Given homosexual behavior in our society, this is not the appropriate language to promote celibacy in the contemporary culture of the United States. This is an example of why exclusive language is unacceptable.

A new edition of a lectionary for the United States without horizontal inclusive language will be inferior to other biblical translations. This past year a new translation of the Bible was published by Tyndale entitled *Holy Bible: A New Living Translation.* This Bible is the work of conservative biblical scholars from the evangelical tradition (Southern Baptist Theological Seminary, Trinity Evangelical Divinity School, Southeastern College of the Assemblies of God and Denver Conservative Baptist Seminary, among others). This text boasts of the fact that it uses gender-inclusive language. If Bible scholars from the fundamentalist tradition, who clearly revere the literal interpretation of the Bible, employ gender inclusive language and our revised edition of the lectionary offers only tokenism, there is a serious loss to God's people. What was originally developed was a horizontal inclusive lectionary, in keeping with the best of English translations and biblical scholarship. What is now being presented to the bishops is much less.

I will cite for you two particular passages symptomatic of the whole. In Matthew's gospel (5:23), we read:

> If you bring your gift to the altar and there recall that your *brother* has anything against you, leave your gift there at the altar, go first and be reconciled with your *brother* and then come and offer your gift.

This passage reflects exclusive language and is not the translation originally approved by the bishops. Compare it with the following text from the New Living Translation:

> If you are standing before the altar in the temple, offering a sacrifice to God, and you suddenly remember that someone has something against you, leave your sacrifice there beside the altar, go and be reconciled to that person.

Another example where the text does not express the inclusive meaning of the original Greek is found in Matthew 10:41:

> Whoever receives a *righteous man* because *he* is a *righteous man* will receive a *righteous man's* reward.

This exclusive text will be seen by many as an insult to both women religious and laywomen. The proposed translation does not express the intent of the original Greek. It is no secret that many Roman Catholics are entering fundamentalist churches today. How can the Roman Catholic tradition fail to keep pace even with the evangelical tradition in offering inclusive language?

Liturgical and biblical translations have been evolving for centuries. We have been using inclusive language liturgical texts in English since 1976, in the Rite of Christian Initiation of Adults, the Rites for Anointing and Viaticum and the Order of Christian Funerals. These texts have been well received by our people. Why can't we have an inclusive language lectionary faithful to the original biblical text and equal to the best in the evangelical tradition? I suggest this is not so much a scriptural problem as an ecclesiological problem. Those advocating a reform of the reform have prevailed in high places; liturgists have been too complacent; liturgists need to retake the high ground. If we believe in the movement of the Holy Spirit at Vatican II, if we believe liturgical renewal and restoration came from an ecumenical council of the church, prompted by God's grace, then we should not be timid in defending our beliefs. There is a dismantling of the renewal taking place before our very eyes. The reform of the reform is attempting to reverse the renewal and restoration of the liturgy. We need to revitalize the reform. Only liturgists can give momentum to this revitalization. I call you to act before it is too late.

Liturgists today are going through what biblical scholars went through years ago. Father David Stanley, a Canadian Jesuit and biblical scholar, died recently. He once served on the Pontifical Biblical Commission. Father Raymond Brown, known to all of you as an internationally renowned Johannine scholar, commented that Father Stanley must be given a place of honor when the history of the American Catholic biblical movement is written. Father Brown noted that Father Stanley defended his ideas "with considerable courage" at a time when they were "considered dangerous, but now are taken for granted."

I can say the same thing about two of my professors at the Pontifical Biblical Institute, Father Stanislaus Lyonnet and Father Max Zerwick. They had been disciplined and deprived of teaching exegesis for a number of years. Today, their contributions to scripture are acclaimed. Why do we hurt our best and brightest?

By God's providence there are similarities between Father Mathis and myself: We are both latecomers to liturgy, we both hold graduate degrees in scripture, we both have taught and done pastoral work. Having read much of Father Mathis, I can say we both passionately believe what the great liturgist, Josef Jungman, once wrote: "For centuries the liturgy, actively celebrated, has been the most important form of pastoral care."

When I speak to you of revitalizing the reform, it is with this principle in mind. We owe it to God's people. I repeat once more: We do not need to reform the reform. We need to revitalize the reform. Thank you.

John L. Bell

The Celtic Legacy: Tool or Treasure?

There have hardly been three consecutive days in 1997 when some inquiry has not reached my colleagues or me regarding things Celtic.

There are research students doing theses on Celtic music, Celtic worship, Celtic spirituality, Celtic ecclesiology, Celtic theology who ask for opinions or information. There are composers of songs and writers of prayers offering their most recent products for authentication by the Iona Community which we represent.

There are self-appointed experts in Celtic knot-design, Celtic harp-playing, Celtic iconography and — doubtless still to come — Celtic hang-gliding seaweed cookery, who are keen to have knowledge of their expertise promulgated.

And there are books appearing every second week from academic, theological and New Age printing houses, offering the definitive word on what is actually indefinable.

Because "Celtic" can properly refer

a) to the tribes who occupied central Europe for millennia BCE,

b) to the peoples of western Scotland, Ireland, southwest England and northwest France who shared a common culture in the first half of the first millennium CE,

c) to the expression of Christian faith used in the evangelization of Great Britain, Ireland and parts of central Europe in the second half of the first millennium CE, and

d) to the devotees of two very different sporting organizations which have vied for the attention of the citizens of Glasgow and Boston in the current century.

But in the current year, because of the happy coincidence of the date of Ninian's arrival in Scotland (497) and Columba's death on Iona (597), it is the religious aspect of Celticicity which has attracted most attention. Yet even this is something of a mishmash.

For, if the legacy of Celtic Christianity is not some easily identifiable and homogeneous mass just ripe for the picking by interested historians, theologians or liturgists, the tradition or traditions as evidenced in Britain and Ireland are in reality quite untidy.

Irish Celtic Christianity as epitomized in Patrick, Scottish Celtic Christianity as promoted by Columba, Welsh Celtic Christianity as represented by David, English Celtic Christianity as found in Hilda . . . are more of a patchwork than a pattern, colored and confused by the historical, cultural and geographical dissimilarities of these and other regions.

Celtic Ireland may be best celebrated for its scholarship, Wales for its literary and cultural endeavours, Scotland for its missionary fervor and Celtic England for holding the disparate fruits of the other nations in the face of the conformist requirements of old mother Rome.

I am a Scot who was imbued with my Celtic heritage not primarily through study but through my mother's milk. My engagement with the Iona Community, whose retreat centers are on the place where Columba landed in 563, has increased my awareness of that legacy about which so many are curious today. Though within the length of this paper I cannot claim to do justice to what is a complex issue rooted often in pre-literate societies, I hope simply to share some of the insights culled from this inheritance which have proved themselves to be pertinent to the life of the church today.

I have little time for misty-eyed romanticism when it comes to Celtic Christianity, because those who developed its historical expressions were people who lived physically on the edge of the known world and had to espouse a tough faith in the face of the natural elements and foreign predators. In Britain at the present time we have enough parish churches masquerading as Elizabethan or Victorian theme-parks without adding to their number from antiquity.

But I do believe that there are deep insights and revered practices in the Celtic tradition which, if seriously pondered today, might show either how truly traditional our future needs will be or how deeply futuristic the past was. So let me identify some themes for contemporary variation.

The Celtic Community

One of the key distinctions between the classical expression of the Roman church in the first millennium CE and that of its Celtic wing was that, while Rome was organized on hierarchical lines, the Celtic expression was based on community.

The Roman church's missionary endeavors frequently mirrored the degrees to which Rome itself had influence on the princes and statesmen of different nations. When an area was deemed ripe for evangelization, a diocese was proclaimed and created, and those within it found themselves subject to a bishop.

But this was not the Celtic model, because Britain and Ireland were not so much nations as loose and sometimes hostile associations of tribes headed by clan chieftains and sharing a closely integrated common life. With great perceptiveness, therefore, the Celtic missionaries decided not to foist an alien hierarchical system of ecclesiastical discipline on lands which did not have a similar governmental infrastructure. Instead the monks would build a settlement beside already existing dwelling-places and thoroughly integrate themselves into the life of the local community, so that evangelization was done by friendship, persuasion and service rather than by spiritual tyranny. Thus Ireland, distinct among many nations, had no blood spilled as it changed from pagan religion to Christianity.

Thus it was also that — so unlike today — a woman could tell a bishop what to do. Because in the Celtic churches, the main figure was the abbot or abbess, a term which is derived from the Aramaic word *Abba* for father. The abbot was the *paterfamilias,* the one charged with caring for the extended family of the monastic and secular settlement. He or she recognized what operated for or against the common good, and he or she modeled the grace of hospitality, as can be recognized in the way Columba, the abbot on Iona, was keen to wash the feet of travelers whenever they arrived on the island.

The abbot or abbess ruled with firmness and gentleness the spiritual life of the local community, directed its outreach and safeguarded its worship. The bishop was a functionary who reserved the right to confirm and ordain, and as such was invited by the abbot not as the superior embodiment of visible unity, but as a fellow member of the body of Christ who had a particular function.

When the people of God met together in Celtic churches, they met as people who, following biblical precedent, worshiped beside those whom they knew because of bonds of common experience, mutual service and shared responsibilities within their local communities. Their worship was common prayer in the proper sense: It represented the shared aspirations and needs of a people who were bound to each other outside the confines of the sanctuary and outside the times of public worship.

How different today, when so many of our churches do not gather the community together for prayer, but bring together an unintegrated collection of people, the majority of whom will never see each other from one Mass to the next and may never want to. Yet, particularly in the Catholic church, we call this the "community" even though the people have nothing tangible *in common*. And we sing hymns such as "Bind us together" while we stand in such geographical or psychological isolation from each other that our mouthing of these words is a mockery to heaven.

There is, within the Celtic understanding of church, a prerequisite that—as in the primitive ecclesial gatherings of the Jews for the first Passover, as in the early meetings of the local synagogue, as in the first worship services of the New Testament church—common worship rises from common life. And common life cannot be established by the purchasing of electronic gadgetry, the refurbishing of pipe organs or even the employment of special pastoral ministers. Community is established, in the words of the founder of the Iona Community, only by participating in "a demanding common task" and in being both vulnerable and encouraging to each other.

In an age of social fragmentation, with people whose lives are in flux either through bondage to fashion or the need to change location for purposes of employment, rootedness is sometimes sought after by delving into family genealogy. Hence every year an invasion of tartan plaid-wearing Americans assault civic and parish registrars with questions about their ancestry. (We know that they are American because no one else wears tartan plaid in Scotland in the middle of the summer.) Such investigation of the ancient past might say where we or our forebears came from. It does not, however, quench the desire for belonging. That can only come from real, interactive and visible community to which the church is called and which was magnificently exemplified in the Celtic past.

Celtic Priesthood

The exact practice of priestly ministry in the life of the Celtic church is as much a matter of conjecture as is how and what they sang.

We are told that monks shared the Eastern tonsure, not a mandatory bald patch at the apex of the skull, but a shaved strip from one ear to the other. We are told that in Scotland and Wales, the office of priest did not entail obligatory celibacy, but that wives were permitted.

But, for me, the fascination which history and contemporary church life have with "what Bishop so-and-so said" and "what Father so-and-so did" is a means of obscuring that common priesthood to which all in Christ are called, and which is epitomized in the words of the first letter of Peter: "You (plural) are a chosen race, a royal priesthood, a dedicated nation, a people claimed by God for his own." (2:9)

This perspective on the church was one of the rallying calls of the Protestant reformers who espoused a belief in the "priesthood of all believers," which is sometimes now difficult to see enfleshed, so sacerdotal have our Presbyterian brothers and sisters become. And it is a doctrine which, in more recent years, was espoused by the Second Vatican Council, in whose documents and unique among many denominations, the pastoral and liturgical offices of lay people are detailed and approved.

However, just as the ordained priesthood sees its ministry as being to some extent derivative of the priestly ministry of Jesus, so lay ministries have been frequently regarded as derivative of or pale imitations of what the ordained minister can do.

Yet the exigencies of the life of the churches in the Celtic tradition of ministry could not be so derived. The life of the church could not depend solely on the ordained ministers. In the Celtic tradition we see writ large the priesthood of the laity, the liturgical and pastoral expression of priesthood expressed by those who were—like the first disciples—lay people. And part of that has to do with geography.

For if, in the fifth to tenth centuries, you lived on a Scottish or Irish island or in a remote region of the mainland, geography, weather and the uncertain perambulations of ordained priests required that faith should not be dependent for its weekly or daily celebration on the services of the professional religious. In a location where a priest might not physically appear for up to three months, the catechizing of children, the blessing of homes and vessels, the burial of the dead, the baptism of infants, had to go on regardless. And in places where the physical construction of a building set aside for the liturgical offices was an impossibility, prayer and meditation had to find their places in the midst of work and in the workplace, rather than after it was done and in a secluded chapel.

The catechists, the baptizers, the buriers and blessers in the Celtic church were women and men who tilled the land, tended animals, spun wool and suckled infants. Proof of this exists not in the histories or hagiographies that eighth- and ninth-century annalists were moved to write, but in fragments of poem, rune and prayer which were transmitted in the oral tradition from generation to generation and gathered by two independent chroniclers at the end of the last century, Alexander Carmichael in Scotland and Douglas Hyde in Ireland.

Thus we find a fragment of a baptismal rite coming from the island of Barra, which Carmichael chronicled:

John L. Bell

After the child is born, it is baptized by the nurse or midwife. She said:

When the image of the God of life is born into the world, I put three little drops of water on the child's forehead. I put the first little drop in the name of the Father, and the watching women say Amen.

I put the second little drop in the name of the Son, and the watching women say Amen.

I put the third little drop in the name of the Spirit, and the watching women say Amen.

And I beseech the holy three to wash and bathe the child and to preserve it to themselves, and the watching women say Amen.

Elsewhere, Carmichael notes the litany used for the launching of a boat. But it is not a naval chaplain or bishop who invokes divine blessing; it is the helmsman.

Helmsman: Blest be the boat!
Crew: God the Father bless her.
Helmsman: Blest be the boat!
Crew: God the Son bless her.
Helmsman: Blest be the boat!
Crew: God the Spirit bless her.
All: God the Father, God the Son,
    God the Spirit, bless the boat.

Now, note in these two examples, that we do not have not a simple, quaint homespun prayer, but rather poetic, participative and trinitarian liturgy. And this because we are dealing with a people who, whatever their poor material estate, had a sophistication of imagination and culture and lively intellects.

One of my favorite credal statements comes from this oral and therefore unattributable source:

I believe, O God of all gods,
that you are the eternal maker of life.
I believe, O God of all gods,
that you are the eternal maker of love.

I believe, O God and Lord of all people,
that you are the creator of the high heavens,

that you are the creator of the skies above,
that you are the creator of the oceans below.

I believe, O Lord and God of all people,
that you are the one who created my soul and set its course,
that you are the one who created my body from dust
   and from ashes,
that you gave to my body its breath and to my soul
   its possession.

Lord, bless to me my body;
Lord, bless to me my soul;
Lord, bless to me my life;
Lord, bless to me my belief.

In these present years, as before, liturgical development invariably progresses at a speed determined by the ordained priesthood whose knowledge of parish life and contact with parish people is arguably less than it was in previous centuries. It may be that the precedents set not for liturgical formation but for the formation of liturgies by our Celtic ancestors might just be examples we need today.

Is it beyond the wit of contemporary educated and cultured individuals who spend time and money decorating their homes and expanding their libraries to spend less money but perhaps more time in devising words and ceremonies by which, in homes and in churches, the life of faith might be expressed and God worshiped?

Celtic Worldliness

But if this were indeed to become the case, then it should not simply be the example of inclusive priesthood which is emulated, but also the determination not to divorce prayer from every other human activity. For, indeed, it is our engagement with the world in all its beauty and horror, tension and calm, which informs prayer and prevents it from becoming a barren ritual.

I alluded earlier to how for the Celtic peoples, as indeed for the Jews of the Old Testament and for Jesus, there was no curtain shielding the sacred from the secular. If you had no regular priest and no

John L. Bell

consecrated space, then everyone had to take on the priestly role and every space had to reverberate with holiness.

George MacLeod, the founder of the Iona Community, in his magnificent, crafted prayers for public worship, was keen to encapsulate this sentiment in such memorable phrases as:

> Invisible, we see you, Christ beneath us.
> With earthly eyes we see beneath us stones and dust and dross,
> fit subjects for the analyst's table.
> But with the eye of faith, we know your upholding.
> In you all things consist and hang together:
> > the very atom is light energy,
> > the grass is vibrant,
> > the rocks pulsate.
> All is in flux; turn but a stone and an angel moves.

The Celts would never balk at the nostrum beloved of twentieth-century preachers that "prayer should be as natural as breathing," because for them it was. Every conversation, every activity, every thought was present to God and should be presented to God, not through neurosis, but as normally as one would comment to a companion on whatever thoughts came to mind while sharing a walk together.

The Celts had a treasury of prayer which was filled by the wisdom and piety of their ancestors and to which successive generations added. Hence we have examples of prayers spoken in the work of weaving:

> Bless, O Chief of generous chiefs,
> my loom and everything near me,
> bless me in every action,
> keep me safe while I live.

Or again, a prayer of consecration for the sowing of seed:

> I will go out and sow the seed,
> in the name of him who gave it growth;
> I will place my front in the wind
> and throw a gracious handful on high,
> Should a grain fall on a bare rock,

it shall have no soil in which to grow;
as much as falls into the earth,
the dew will make it to be full.

Father, Son and Spirit Holy,
give now both growth and kindly substance
to everything that is in my ground,
till the day of gladness shall come.

Or for milking the cow:

Bless, O God, my little cow;
bless, O God, my desire;
bless thou the partnership
and the milking of my hands, O God.

Bless, O God, each teat;
bless, O God, each finger,
bless thou each drop
which falls into my pitcher, O God.

And finally a prayer for kindling the fire in the morning. Note here
the natural progression from the fire being kindled in the hearth to
the desire for God to kindle love in the heart.

I will kindle my fire this morning,
in the presence of the holy angels of heaven,
in the presence of Ariel and Uriel,
without malice, without jealousy, without envy,
without fear, without terror of any one under the sun,
but with the Holy Son of God to shield me.

God, kindle today in my heart
a flame of love to my neighbor,
to my foe, to my friend, to my family,
to the brave, to the servant and knave,
O Son of the loveliest Mary,
from the lowliest thing that liveth
to the name that is highest of all.

Admittedly, we cannot transfer the domestic or work piety of eight
centuries ago and expect it to be of anything other than curio value

today. Few of us operate handlooms, milk cows or kindle fires as part of our daily routine.

It therefore requires us to find equivalents if—and only if—we still believe that life cannot be compartmentalized into a religious segment which stands juxtaposed to every other activity.

Is it not conceivable that in the way we deal with money, in the processes of parenting, in the hospitality we share in our homes, in the attention we give to our gardens, in the time we spend with people who are ill or demanding and even in our daily association with manual or mental work, we cannot also find the means to affirm ourselves as being as present to God in these activities as we are in church, and thus present what we do for the guidance of God's Spirit?

For myself, before I rise in the morning, having thought about the day ahead and whether it will involve manual, social, emotional or intellectual energy, I pray slowly these words:

> God bless to me today,
> my eyes and my seeing,
> my ears and my hearing,
> my lips and my speaking.
>
> God bless to me today
> my hands and my holding,
> my feet and my moving,
> my body and my health.
>
> God bless to me today
> my mind and my thinking,
> my heart and my loving,
> my soul and my believing.

Keep this facet of Celtic spirituality, its prayer life, bound up with sheep shearing and wool spinning, and it will understandably remain quaint and kitsch. But take its fundamental assumption—that all of life is offered to all of God—and the need to develop contemporary expressions of this will become the more urgent.

Celtic Incarnational Theology

This understanding of prayer as all-pervading cannot be considered in the abstract. It is the necessary concomitant of a biblical theology which extols and celebrates the incarnation. For the Celts, as evidenced by one of the freestanding crosses outside Iona Abbey, the favorite gospel was that of Saint John. For in it there is proclaimed the truth that "the Word became flesh."

For the Celtic peoples, who lived with the awesomeness of the seasons and the language of evil and benign spirits, there was no difficulty with the transcendence of God. Their primitive and pagan faiths bore witness to heaven and heavenly beings long before their conversion to Christianity. What, in the deepest sense, was novel about Christianity was that the transcendent one had come into time, or—as one of their poems described it —

> This is the night of the great nativity,
> the soles of God's feet have touched the earth.

That Christ should have been incarnate of the virgin Mary, sharing our common humanity, being touched by human hands and being reared in a specific culture was a source of great hope and a reason for great celebration. And just as other primitive peoples have witnessed to the incarnation by putting their cultural forms and practices at the service of the gospel (such as African painters depicting Jesus in red rather than white) so the Celts did not domesticize him as much as affirm his oneness with them.

Thus, in Ireland or Scotland, Jesus would be referred to both as Jesus Christ and as Jesus MacMary. After all, if you were Fergus and your father was Donald, you'd be called Fergus Mac (son of) Donald.

Christ in the Celtic nations was given Bride or Bridget, a legendary saint, as his foster mother. And domestic practices such as the lighting of an evening lamp to welcome travelers was used in some places to indicate an open door for Jesus should he and his mother (as in his early years) be made to go on the run.

Here is a short rune which is repeated at the Welcome Service in Iona Abbey each Saturday evening. It indicates the desire that Christ, whenever he comes, will be the object of indigenous hospitality.

John L. Bell

I met a stranger yestreen.

I put food in the eating place,
drink in the drinking place,
music in the listening place,
and he blessed my home, my cattle and my dear ones.

As the lark says in her song,
often, often, often
goes the Christ in the stranger's guise.

Whatever the incarnation said about the proximity of God to human history, and the worth of human life being underscored by the presence of God in the flesh, it also said something about the need for human culture to cradle and celebrate the Word of God.

It was not simply first-century Middle Eastern culture that Christ had sanctified with his presence and in which Mary and Joseph had reared their Son. If he really was the Lord of All, every culture should similarly be sanctified by and serve him. What does this say to us today, whose religious culture may be a hundred years or a thousand miles away from authenticity? What does this say to us today who have foisted on the developing world Eurocentric evangelism, Western liturgies and antediluvian forms of ministry?

It is in the documents of the Second Vatican Council that we see the growing realization that the Western celebration of the Mass in which a priest stands more or less statically behind an ambo or altar while the congregation sings Gregorian chant might not be best suited to the Congo or to Botswana. In such places, to make music means to move, to dance, and in such places English or Latin are not necessarily the best languages for communicating the deepest truths most.

But the implications of the incarnation for ecclesiastical culture are not just a matter of releasing churches of the southern hemisphere from bondage to Elizabethan or Victorian language, norms and values. It is also about ensuring that in the West we do not allow the church to become a memorial to the past rather than a harbinger of the future.

This does not require the ditching of every sacred text, well-loved hymn and revered depiction of the Virgin with or without child. It requires the supplementing of them with contemporary images, hymns and practices which allow Christ contemporary culture to be a means of evangelism.

As an example of what is possible, I take a poem by Kathy Galloway, a Scottish writer and member of the Iona Community. This is one of her recent poems of the Stations of the Cross; it is entitled "Jesus Dies." It stands in stark contrast to the devotional piety even of thirty years ago, using terse language, a lack of conventional phrases or sentences, but rather a succession of verbs to illustrate the brutality of the crucifixion:

> Fingered
> Taken
> Stripped
> Spreadeagled
> Exposed
> Humiliated
> Whipped
> Mounted
> Violated
> Broken
> Jeered
> Handclapped
> Spat on
> Cursed
> Abandoned
> Dead.

And what is true for language is true also for other forms of cultural expression.

Some time ago, I walked through Saint Magnus Cathedral in Orkney. My attention became focused on two objects which seemed quite out of place. One was a pulpit fall, an innocuous piece of blue velvet with gold braid which I had seen in a hundred other Methodist and Reformed churches throughout Britain. Why, I wondered, in an island which had copious examples of indigenous tapestry and needlework in the windows of shops facing the cathedral's west door, was there no representation of native art work inside?

The other incongruous object was the seat behind the holy table on which the minister, as Christ's representative, sat. The Orkney islands, because of a perennial lack of wood, are home to highly prized Orkney chairs fashioned from a minimal wooden structure which is interlaced with straw. For the head of the household, there is a special chair with a high back and canopy. The chair that sat behind the Holy Table could be found in another thousand Presbyterian or Congregational churches throughout Britain. Why, if Christ was really Lord of this island, was its native and revered form of carpentry not put to his service? Why was he being kept at a cultural distance when he came to take on all of life and to redeem and be served by every human culture in every era, not just by the artifacts from dominant and sometimes plastic cultures in specific historical eons?

If we were to put our language, our architecture, our artifacts, symbols, our music against the grid not of relevance, but of relationship to the culture in the midst of which we worship, would they be found as wanting as the pulpit fall and communion chair in Orkney?

This is not to deny the efficacy of what has been handed down to us from the past; it is rather to question whether we are ossifying in the present.

The Celtic Bible

As the patterns of traditional Celtic design are interwoven and have no clear beginning or end, so the strands of their spirituality are intimately conjoined.

The community emphasis has its natural concomitant in the importance of lay ministry; the importance of lay ministry requires that the life of prayer be broadened beyond the confines and conversations of the cloister. This in turn is informed and buttressed by the realization that the incarnation put a value on all of human flesh and not just on the sacerdotal variety, and thus all of human work and culture should also be caught up in the praise of its Maker. And this activity informed the way in which scripture was transmitted and was influenced in turn by the relevance of the scriptures when properly broken open.

The Celts loved the Bible. Thus in the monasteries they lavishly and lovingly copied out and illustrated the biblical manuscripts both as an offering of human time and effort to God and as a means to educate an illiterate population. It is only in the present century that we have boldly and naively expected everyone to read and understand the scriptures individually. Previous centuries saw it not as private book addressing the individual soul, but as public truth to be claimed and read in public places.

And if people could not read, they could at least understand pictures or depictions. Hence we have high standing crosses in Scotland, Wales and Ireland with stories of the Old Testament carved on one side and stories from the gospels depicted on the other. Round these people would gather and pointing to these, monks would tell the narrative on which the faith of God's people is grounded.

For us today, the Bible is a boon of texts, an intellectual minefield for some, a devotional treasury for others. But for the Celts, the Bible was also God's picture book in which were depicted their ancestors in the faith to whom they were genetically linked in the Body of Christ. And if they could but get to know better these people who had encountered God in mystery and splendor, or who had been the table and walking companions of Christ, then perhaps these same biblical characters would enable them to come closer to their common Lord.

So they loved the saints, and felt surrounded with them, different ones on different occasions—Mary when a baby was due, James and John when they were fishing, Moses when a long journey lay ahead.

Some people may know the at times embarrassing experience of going home to your mother's house with friends she has never met before. And, in the course of conversation, mother reaches for a large biscuit or chocolate box, not intending to share any confection, but to bring out from within photographs of her son or daughter in the most regrettable of situations.

When that happens I like it best when we look at other pictures, not so much of myself or my known relatives, but of those who have gone before me . . . people like Jimmy Neil.

Jimmy Neil was my great-grandfather on my paternal grandmother's side. He died decades before I was conceived. But when I look at him and hear the stories about him I begin, curiously, to understand a bit more about myself. I discover that he had two great passions in life, whisky and hymn singing, and as his engagement in the one grew, so did his vocal commitment to the other. While I share these interests, I hope I do not have them in the same proportions!

But it is from looking at the pictures and hearing the stories that I understand and value my pedigree, and realize what is in my genes.

The familiarity of the Celts with the saints was part of the same process. They depicted them, and developed a close interest in them in order that their self-understanding might be deepened and their discipleship enriched by the friendship of the church in heaven.

Thus it is that we find this somewhat irreverent or (depending on your standpoint) appealing depiction of the saints in the poem of a twelfth-century Irish woman:

> I would like to have the men of heaven
> in my own house,
> with barrels of good cheer
> laid out for them.
>
> I would like to have the three Marys,
> their fame is so great;
> I would like people
> from every corner of heaven.
>
> I would like them to be cheerful
> in their drinking;
> I would like to have Jesus too
> here among them.
>
> I would like a great lake of beer
> For the King of Kings.
> I would like to be watching Heaven's family
> drinking it through all eternity.

What an image of heaven! (with due apologies to the Methodists.)

This practice of depicting God's people, seeing the Bible as God's family or picture album, has been particularly important for our work in Glasgow, particularly in what are known as "urban priority areas" — housing projects where books are not a common form of recreation and, therefore, the Bible is not often read.

We were aware that in doing biblical reflection, people sat dumb, waiting for the priest or minister to make what sounded like an intelligent statement and then nodding or grunting assent. It took us a while to realize that perhaps this model of biblical reflection worked well for those familiar with and interested in both written texts and intellectual discussion. But what about the others?

So, leaning on the ancient tradition of seeing the Bible as God's picture book, we began to gather a library of black and white postcards, depicting the world in its people in every possible guise. And when we came to look at, say, a miracle story, we would read the text aloud a couple of times and then ask people to look at all the cards laid out on tables and come back with the hemorrhaging woman, the demoniac or whoever. People began not just to talk, but to engage their imaginations in creative Bible study which allowed them to bring their observations on the life of the world to the truth embodied in the word of God.

Here is an example of the kind of insight which ensued from a conversation about Mary. Ask people to talk about what the mother of Jesus is or was like, and they will invariably go for the silent, anemic and servile Madonna beloved of a million souvenirs. But try to depict her as described in John's account of the wedding at Cana of Galilee, and a much more robust, defiant and gregarious Mary appears.

The Wedding

He was 30 when it happened.

There was no warning;
he had never done that kind of thing before,
though we had been at plenty of weddings.

But this was a really big wedding.
it was Isaac Morgenthaler's daughter
who was marrying a boy from the city,
and everybody in our village was invited.

So I says to him,
"Listen, Jesus,
there's going to be a lot of nice girls at this affair.
You're thirty and you're not getting any younger,
so don't be backwards at coming forward
just because your old mother's there.
I won't be watching you."

John L. Bell

Well, he just rolled his eyes the way his father used to,
so I said no more.

At any rate,
we got to the wedding
and into the reception,
and what a spread . . .

There was breaded octopus,
roast quail in pomegranate sauce,
pickled locusts . . .
and mushroom omelettes for the vegetarians.

Everything was magnificent . . .
except for the olives.

Now, personally, I don't like olives—they talk back to me.
But everyone who ate them said they were very salty.

So between that and the heat—it was about 78° —
there was a lot of drinking going on.

We must have been sitting at the table for well on two hours.
Everybody was talking at the top of their voice;
and then I noticed it got distinctly quieter, maudlin even.

So I turned to our Jesus and I says,
"I think that the wine's run out."

He just turned to me and rolled his eyes and said,
"Not all powers of observation are beyond me, mother."

But I knew from the way he said it
that he might be up to something.

So when I saw him rising from the table
and going into the kitchen, I said to one of the waiters,
"You see that man walking towards the kitchen? . . .
That's my boy.
Follow him and do what he tells you."

Well, exactly what happened after that I don't know.
There are about a dozen different stories.

According to Jesus,
he just asked for the big wine jars to be filled with water.

Then he lifted them one at a time,
gave them to the waiters,
and told them to take them to the tables.

Well, in no time the noise was as loud as ever,
and everybody was congratulating Mr. Morgenthaler
on the Beaujolais Nouveau (or Cabernet Sauvignon).

When he came back to the table,
I said to him,
"Jesus, how come with all the water jugs in my kitchen,
you've never turned your hand to the winemaking before?"

Well, he just rolled his eyes the way his father used to,
and then he said,
"Mother, I just wanted everybody
to be as happy at this wedding with wine
as you are in your kitchen without it."

Well, that was all in the past,
but ever since
there's been a constant flow of invitations
from people who would like Jesus to come to their wedding.

Celtic Connections

There are many other themes that emerge from the Celtic past which could be helpful in our contemporary context. I want to mention just two more. The first is associated with the impact the incarnation should have on human culture and in the understanding of the Bible as God's picture book. It has to do with the Celtic worldview, or, rather, with the way in which the Celts allowed themselves to be to be touched by other cultures.

Were I going to speak about the missionary endeavors of the early Celtic saints, I could cite how Columba and his emissaries from Iona evangelized remote parts of Scotland, and the English east coast and Midlands. I could recount the adventures of Brendan, possibly the first European to cross the Atlantic, or of Columbanus, whose evangelization of western and central Europe is evidenced to this day in the German city streets named after eighth- and ninth-century Irish saints.

John L. Bell

But that would be to provide a one-sided picture of the connectedness of the Celtic church to other parts of the world. It would be in keeping with previous Western missiology which looked at the effect the "sending" nations had had overseas, rather than appreciating the way in which the overseas nations could influence the church in Britain.

When we go back to our Celtic roots, we discover a church which was not isolated from the rest of the Christian or pagan world but influenced by it. And we know that through a variety of means. It is common knowledge that, in terms of spirituality, Patrick was deeply influenced by his mentor Saint Martin of Tours, while the Welsh saints were related in their monastic practices to the desert fathers and other luminaries of the Middle East.

The design work on ancient manuscripts includes flora and fauna which were not native to British shores but may have been seen or copied from Mediterranean or African sources. The style of singing even today of the Gaelic speakers in the Western Isles finds close parallels in the singing of North African Copts. And it has been conjectured that some of the blue tincture on certain illuminated manuscripts can only have been produced by crushed lapis lazuli rock brought from Afghanistan, at the Eastern end of the Black Sea.

Here we have a religious tradition which is healthily eclectic, which is not afraid to borrow or learn from other nations and continents and which exhibits thereby a bondedness to unlikes in the Body of Christ.

Is this not something which we need so desperately to rediscover as the new millennium dawns? Is it not time that we dropped the pretense of being the epicenter of Christian mission simply by dint of English tongue? Is it not time that, acknowledging how the Holy Spirit has given gifts to our African and Asian sisters and brothers (some of whose nations had practicing Christians long before ours), we should open our hands to receive from others rather than to continue to patronize them?

This was the plea of a pastor from Ghana who recently addressed the General Assembly of the Church of Scotland. He noted how the recipients of European-based mission were expected to take on the hymnody and prayer life of their Western "superiors," but now in an era in which the African church expands in inverse proportion to the European church contracting, there is no flow of spiritual gifts in the opposite direction.

If, within the Body of Christ, we were to lean on and learn from Africa and Asia in this era, we would not only be opening ourselves to new wells of spiritual nourishment, we would be emulating the practice of the Celtic peoples of the past and benefit as they did.

Celtic Ecology

Finally and cautiously, I suggest that a part of the Celtic legacy we would do well to draw on today has to do with the way in which the ancient peoples regarded and related to the natural order.

I speak cautiously because I am aware that New Ageism is both a reality and a charge sometimes levied against those who revere the Celtic roots of Christianity. Granted we are dealing in the first millennium with people who had emerged from nature religions, and with people who were much more intimately aware of the ravages and beauty of nature than twentieth-century city dwellers are. But their connection with and understanding of nature was neither romantic nor aesthetic in intent. It was deeply biblical and theological.

Here two fragments of poetry; the first from Ireland:

> Only a fool would fail
> to praise God in his might,
> when the tiny mindless birds
> praise him in their flight.

and, from Scotland:

> There is no plant in the ground,
> but is full of God's virtue;
> there is no form on the shore
> but is full of God's blessing.

> There is no life in the sea,
> there is no creature in the river,
> there is nothing in this . . .
> but proclaims God's goodness.

John L. Bell

On a first or casual hearing such fragments might well be dismissed as fanciful or pagan. But closer consideration reveals that they are not out of kilter with biblical sentiments from Genesis to Revelation which talk about hills skipping, valleys singing and trees clapping their hands.

For the Celts as for the Jews, nature was not pantheistic. Nature was ordained by God to be an arena in which worship was offered. Imperceptibly to us, but clearly to God, the regularity of tide and flow, day and night, the beauty of spring and harvest, the diversity of animal, vegetable and mineral life were all part of a litany long before Teilhard de Chardin coined the term the "Hymn of the Universe."

We live at a time in history in which the threat of global annihilation by nuclear war has receded, pray God, permanently. But the devil that has been driven off has quickly been replaced by other threats to the well-being of the earth, in terms of global warming, pollution, overfishing and the depletion of clean water stocks as much by human greed as by natural processes.

If the valleys cannot laugh and sing because they have been over-fertilized, if the trees cannot clap their hands because of unnecessary deforestation, if the rivers cannot roar their praise because of oil slicks, if the mountains cannot leap because they have been irradiated, if, as Hosea might say, "nature mourns her lost good," then humanity must stand accountable.

As a corrective to that fearful prospect on the day when the nations shall be judged before the throne of God, it is important that we learn from our distant forebears to have dominion over the earth rather than to dominate it; to safeguard the praise it imperceptibly to us offers God rather than to silence it.

For the ancient Celts and for us today, ecology is doxology . . . the care of the earth enables it to worship its Creator.

Michael Clay

Christian Initiation in the Small Non-Metropolitan Church

S ince 1974, when it appeared in English, the *Rite of Christian Initiation of Adults* has slowly found its way into the life of the Catholic church in the United States. Pastoral ministers in the urban and suburban church who possessed abundant human and material resources took the lead with its implementation. Their efforts have borne much fruit.

In many urban and suburban parishes, year-round catechumenates, adaptations for children of catechetical age and teams are commonplace. Innocently and with good intentions, these developments have been offered as models for others to imitate, including rural and small-town parishes in non-metropolitan settings. The intentions may have been good but the results have often been unsatisfactory. This is due to the fact that urbanites mistakenly think what works for them will work in the non-metropolitan setting. Thwarting the success of this intention is the fact that rural and small-town parishes are not miniature versions of urban and suburban parishes. They are quite different from their counterparts and awareness of this is necessary for effective pastoral ministry in the non-metropolitan setting, including the implementation of Christian initiation.

This article will address the pastoral challenge of implementing Christian initiation in the non-metropolitan setting. It will proceed by an examination of two dynamics. First, there are some general characteristics of rural life and ministry which are distinct from urban and suburban life and ministry. What is different about rural and small-town life and ministry? Identifying some of the major characteristics will be the focus of the first section of this article.

Second, how do these differences affect the way Christian initiation is implemented in these settings? This article will examine the liturgical and catechetical dimensions of Christian initiation as viewed through a rural and small-town lens. In other words, by placing the characteristics of rural and small-town life and ministry in a dialogue with the liturgical and catechetical vision of Christian initiation, some new insights might emerge which could help rural and small-town ministers more effectively implement the rite.

The Rural Ten Commandments

Volumes have been written concerning the differences between the urban and rural worlds. Sociologists and anthropologists have studied this dynamic for quite some time. An overview of the major differences between the rural and urban worlds will help us increase awareness. These characteristics are fairly set in stone in the classic rural setting and, because of the religious focus of this article, I dub them "The Rural Ten Commandments."

One opening caveat: There are over forty definitions of "rural." Southern rural will not be exactly like Southwestern rural. There will be similarities but there will also be differences. Rural and small-town Catholics in areas where they enjoy a majority will experience life a little differently from those who are a minority of the total population. Rural communities which are experiencing in-migration by urbanites will have different and additional issues to deal with than those who are experiencing a decline in population. It will be important to resist absolutizing the following characteristics attributed to rural people and settings thinking they apply to each and every rural individual and situation. These are general characteristics which apply in many, but not all settings.

The First Commandment:
"Thou shalt not introduce change or conflict."

Generally, in the classic understanding of the rural world, the present makes sense to the extent that it is consistent with the past. By distinction, urban people tend to view the present with a view toward its connection to and possibilities for the future. "We've always done it that way" is much more important for rural people than it is for urban people. Urban people tend to think in terms of progress and do not generally fret over the necessity of change for progress' sake.

Change is resisted in the rural setting because it leads to an unknown future in a community which often is fragile and limited. For the same reason, conflict is also avoided. Conflict tears at the fragile fabric of a rural community. Consequently, it is generally not tolerated. There *is* conflict in the community, but it often is expressed in ways that are not directly confrontational. For example, gossip and ostracism are used as vehicles of resolving tensions created by emerging conflict. Gossip is a way to ventilate the frustration or anger an emerging conflict may generate. Threats of ostracism keep conflict from escalating. A rural farmer may threaten to disinherit a son if he marries someone of whom the father disapproves. The same might be said if the son is thinking about switching religions, even "getting" religion.

The Second Commandment:
"I am the Lord thy God and I am mysterious, strict and the great judge."

In the book of Exodus, the commandments begin with a focus on God because one's relationship with God is considered more important than any other relationship. Here it is listed as the second commandment because of the importance of the first commandment described above. Ruralites, more than any other social group, see God in legalistic terms. This is due to many reasons, chief among them the fact that ruralites frequently have little recourse to right wrongs. Because of this limitation, God tends to be viewed by ruralites as strict, as the only one who can ultimately assure harmony. God is seen more as a just judge than a lenient lover in the rural setting. When wrongs are committed in the rural context, especially wrongs which cannot or simply will not be directly addressed by the one wronged to the wrongdoer, God becomes the dispenser of justice and correction. Ruralites are thoroughly imbued with this image of God over the course of their entire lives.

The Third Commandment:
"Thou shalt worship the Lord thy God in a transcendent mode and keep fellowship outside the church doors."

Studies indicate there is less social interaction among parishioners during Mass in the rural and small-town world than in any other social group in the Catholic church in the United States. A rural woman's comment on the relationship between Sunday Mass and fellowship typifies the thought of many rural people. "I don't come to Mass to visit with people. I come to visit with God." Fellowship in the rural and small-town context will precede and follow Sunday eucharist, but is less visible during the liturgy itself. The immanent dimension of God is harder for many ruralites to comprehend because of the need for God to be the just judge. Additionally, in a rural world where nature and its rhythms plays a significant role in life, a mysterious God makes a lot of sense to traditional ruralites.

The Fourth Commandment:
"Thy relationships shalt be ends unto themselves and not means to an end."

Relationships are everything in a rural context. In comparison with the urban and suburban settings, rural communities are smaller in population and that population is less mobile. As a result, relationships tend to be fewer in number and long-term. Because a sense of belonging is highly valued in the rural context, relationships are of paramount importance and generally are not utilitarian in nature.

Lifelong friendships are more commonplace in the rural than in the urban setting. Rural people generally do not cultivate a relationship in order to achieve a goal. They will tend to cultivate a relationship just to cultivate a relationship. Cultivating a relationship in order to gain influence, power or prestige is more reflective of the urban setting where relationships are more numerous and can more likely be impersonal.

The Fifth Commandment:
"Honor thy mother, father and all other members of the extended family, including in-laws."

The extended family is a normative feature of rural life. This type of family includes anyone who is related through blood or marriage. Knowing who is related to whom is very important. Intergenerational relationships are still common in a rural context. A minister may need to be particularly careful when commenting on parishioners or community members. Chances are the person spoken of is related to the person to whom the minister is speaking!

The Sixth Commandment:
"Thy sense of time shalt be daily and seasonal."

Rural people tend to integrate their sense of time to the rhythms of nature. Sunrise and sunset, planting season and growing season, the annual harvest: All reflect a daily, seasonal, annual sense of time. By distinction, urban people tend to view time on a weekly basis, with the weekend being a significant benchmark. Because of human resources and technology, the natural rhythm of the day in a rural setting is replaced with a notion of a 24-hour day in the city. Compare the hours of operation of grocery stores in small towns and suburbs! A 24-hour grocery store is virtually unknown in the non-metropolitan setting.

The Seventh Commandment:
"Thou shalt tell stories."

Notice the popularity of country music in the rural setting. It has been suggested by experts in rural culture that this art form is nothing more than sung stories that communicate the realities of rural and small-town life. In a world where direct criticism is frequently avoided, country music and storytelling become a way to describe and critique issues in an oblique fashion. Rural people seem to prefer oral forms of communication over written ones and communicate fairly complex ideas without footnotes or references through this form of communication. The small-town housewife who struggles with an unfeeling or unfaithful husband may find consolation in a country song that describes her pain which she may hum as she prepares dinner.

The Eighth Commandment:
"Thou shalt be more concerned with well-being than with getting ahead."

Traditional ruralites generally prefer to use their free time for fishing, visiting, woodcarving and so on, than to improve their standard of living by getting a second job to make more money. Having time to relax and visit, to cultivate relationships, is considered a normative dimension of rural and small-town life. By distinction, urbanites tend to interact with other people with a view towards accomplishing something, such as a task at work. In the classic rural context, success is measured by making it on one's own rather than by keeping up with the Joneses. Conspicuous signs of success—lavish home, fancy car, exotic vacation—are more likely to be in evidence in a locale inhabited by people shaped by an urban or suburban worldview.

The Ninth Commandment:
"Thou shalt respond to justice issues that are tangible, short-term and local."

It has sometimes been said that rural people have the most difficulty of any social group in dealing with issues of justice. Ironically, this is the same social group that has one of the nation's highest poverty rates, one of the highest levels of problems related to alcohol and drug abuse and one of the lowest levels of education. In fairness, it should also be noted that rural people do respond to issues of need but the need has to have a human face which is known to the community or individual. Global issues of justice, for instance, the plight of refugees, will generally find little enthusiasm in the rural and small-town setting.

Traditional ruralites tend to be more conservative and moralistic in their worldview. Consequently, they also tend to believe that people should be able to help themselves and see social issues, such as welfare or foreclosure, as signs of weakness. Some have difficulty accepting assistance because it is viewed as a sign of weakness and so will go to great lengths to make things appear normal when they are anything but that. Because change itself is difficult to embrace, issues of injustice which call for conversion are difficult to address.

The Tenth Commandment:
"Thou shalt keep everyone in their place."

This is somewhat of a variation on the first commandment. Keeping everyone in their place is important in the rural setting. It is a form of social control which promotes social harmony by distinguishing the acceptable from the unacceptable, the insider from the outsider. This helps keep things from getting out of control, something abhorrent in the rural setting. Stratification, gossip and ostracism are social techniques used to keep people and situations from changing, even from changes which objectively are for the better.

Christian Initiation

Having provided a cursory overview of some major features of traditional rural and small-town life, this article now turns to the liturgical and catechetical dimensions of Christian initiation, noting some connections that may be made in view of a rural and small-town context. Each dimension will begin with some general comments applied in a rural context and then will identify a few relevant issues for the liturgical rites and catechetical dynamics associated with Christian initiation.

Liturgy

The ritual text of Christian initiation proclaims that liturgy is a normative dimension of the entire formation of catechumens and candidates, beginning with the Rite of Acceptance into the Order of Catechumens or its parallel rite for the already baptized, the Rite of Welcome. In other words, liturgical celebration is a constitutive element over the entire course of formation for catechumens and candidates. Christian initiation is not a catechism class or a course of instruction. It is formation centered around the word of God, the community of faith, the foundational teachings of the Catholic faith and a life of discipleship. The liturgy is where these elements are expressed on a regular basis; hence liturgy's importance in the formation of catechumens and candidates.

Michael Clay

Christian initiation is initiation into the paschal mystery, the passion-death-resurrection of Jesus Christ. Foundationally, those who are initiated into the paschal mystery are initiated into a relationship with Christ. His passion-death-resurrection has relevance for each person as well as for the entire human family. Since relationship is important in the rural setting, a faith tradition that initiates someone into a divine (and human) relationship should find acceptance in that social milieu.

The Rite of Acceptance into the Order of Catechumens, the first public rite of Christian initiation, is a threshold rite celebrated as the inquirer completes the Period of Evangelization and Precatechumenate. As a threshold rite it may be difficult for some traditional rural catechumens because it moves them from a certain world (the present, connected to the past) to an uncertain one (the unknown future based on an invitation: "Come and see" [John 1:39]).

Remember that traditional ruralites struggle with a future-oriented view of life. In a community that tends to view its worship as transcendent and formal, it may be difficult for a rural community to exercise the option of going out from the body of the church to celebrate the initial welcoming rites with those seeking admittance (see RCIA 48) because traditional ruralites may view this as too informal for ritual worship. In a world where everyone knows everyone else and where there is a good possibility that those being welcomed are already part of the worshiping community, it may not be as critical for the catechumens to be kept totally apart from the assembly as part of the welcoming rites.

The crossing of the threshold is an important dimension of this rite. However, other options in the rite may be more appropriate in the welcoming ritual; for instance, welcoming them inside the door of the church. The assembly needs to be prepared for this rite. Because the Rite of Acceptance introduces something new to the order of worship ruralites are accustomed to, an explanation of the rite and possibly a rehearsal of the assembly's role in it may be very helpful in bringing the assembly on board for its celebration. In the Bible Belt, it may be important to present a Bible to the catechumen at the presentation of the gospel that follows the homily in the rite (RCIA 64).

Sunday Liturgy of the Word and Dismissal is understood to be a normative feature during the periods of the Catechumenate and Purification and Enlightenment (RCIA 83). The presumption is that catechumens and candidates for full communion are dismissed immediately after the homily and are sent forth with a catechist from the assembly for a catechetical session. Again, this may work well in a setting with multiple liturgies, facilities and catechists; something more commonplace in the urban and suburban church. In a rural context where there may be only one Mass, no meeting space and one catechist who wants to receive holy communion on a weekly basis, dismissal may prove to be unfeasible.

In communities that are yoked, it may make better pastoral sense to convene a catechetical session at some other time during the week and simply allow the catechumens to remain in the church for the entire Mass. One might infer this as an option based on the fact that this is presented as an option (usually "C") in all the major rites of Christian initiation (see RCIA 67, 116, 136, 155). Again, it is preferable to dismiss catechumens, who are unable to share at the table of the eucharist, after the homily. But in many rural settings, this may not be possible.

The rites of Sending and Election normally occur on the First Sunday of Lent. The Rite of Sending is a parish-based liturgy preceding the Rite of Election, which is a diocesan rite normally presided over by the bishop. In a parish rite, an opportunity is provided for the sponsors who have accompanied the catechumens to speak about them to the community (see RCIA 112). One option provides the opportunity for the sponsor to speak to the assembly about the candidate. In a traditional rural community, this may be construed as too informal and the catechumens may be very uncomfortable having more attention than necessary drawn to themselves. Likewise, the sponsor may also be uncomfortable speaking to the community in this fashion during the course of formal worship. If this is the case, the ritual responses provided in the ritual text may be the preferred way of celebrating this part of the rite. Presiders may seek the counsel of some parishioners and the sponsors themselves before deciding which way to present the catechumens to the community.

Michael Clay

There are three Rites of Scrutiny celebrated during Lent, the Period of Purification and Enlightenment. This rite ritualizes the reality of sin and grace. It admits the reality of sin so that the reality of grace, the power of God and the saving love of Jesus may have more meaning in the life of the elect, and by extension, the faithful. Because of the difficulty in the rural setting with publicly acknowledging and addressing sin, this rite may prove to be the most difficult to incorporate in the rural and small-town church. In a world where change and conflict are painful issues, a rite which publicly identifies the conflict that sin produces and calls participants to the change of conversion will need careful preparation and thoughtful celebration. In a world where keeping up a good appearance and keeping everything in place, whether good or bad, are commonplace, this rite may provoke a strong negative reaction if celebrated in a way that directly names sin, for instance, racism, farm crises, strip mining, gossip, ostracism and the like.

The rite calls for intercessions to be prayed on behalf of the elect (RCIA 153, 167, 174). Taking to heart the directive in these paragraphs that other forms of prayer may be used in place of the intercessions, some communities have begun to substitute a litany for the intercessions. This particular litany structure names sin and evil and asks for the Lord's mercy (for instance, "In a world parched by sexism and prejudice; Lord have mercy"). Naming sin directly, an increasingly popular adaptation for the intercessions used in urban and suburban churches, will probably provoke outrage in a rural setting where direct confrontation of wrongs and wrongdoing is generally avoided. Since the intercessions in the ritual text are ritually weak in addressing the reality of sin, an opinion shared by some leading initiation scholars, some form of litany may constitute a ritual improvement in the Rite of Scrutiny.

It is also suggested that this litany utilize a more oblique naming of sin which identifies sin but in a way less likely to result in outrage by the community. Perhaps a couple of examples may help illustrate the point.

Direct	*Oblique*
In a community parched by racism, Lord have mercy.	In a community thirsting for greater racial harmony, Lord have mercy.
In a community made dark through the sin of gossip and ostracism, Lord have mercy.	In a community seeking the gospel light of acceptance and tolerance, Lord have mercy.
For those bound by alcoholism, Lord have mercy.	For families seeking to understand the illness of of alcoholism, Lord have mercy.

Other sins or manifestations of evil may find almost universal acceptance by rural and small-town communities and might be named more directly in a litany naming sin. For example:

> For communities neglected by big government,
> Lord have mercy.

> For those who exploit our natural resources,
> Lord have mercy.

> For those who are filled with despair because of unemployment,
> Lord have mercy.

> For a lack of adequate health care in our community,
> Lord have mercy.

At the Easter Vigil, the celebration of the Sacraments of Initiation occurs. This is the liturgical highlight of the entire process of Christian initiation. Rural people take seriously the making of a promise. In this celebration promises made are now fulfilled and eternal covenants are established. Because the stakes are high, the fullness of the symbols becomes important. Rural people will readily identify with the natural symbols of initiation: water, oil, bread and wine. Full immersion — using a wading pool or other acceptable vessel common to the area — will be a powerful experience for those being baptized as well as for those witnessing the baptism. It is recommended by the rite itself (see RCIA 213 and National Statue 17). In the Bible Belt, immersion may be particularly significant, although some catechesis may be necessary for rural Catholics who might see full immersion as an accommodation to the evangelical traditions which they may have a tendency to disparage.

In some rural communities it may not be possible to celebrate the sacraments of initiation in one's home parish at the Easter Vigil because of the necessity of sharing a priest with other parishes. It may be preferable in such settings for the community to gather on Saturday evening for the Service of Light and Service of the Word (perhaps presided over by a pastoral associate or pastoral administrator) and then return the next morning when the priest comes for Mass to celebrate the sacraments of initiation with the community the elect have journeyed with for many months, perhaps even years.

Catechesis

In Christian initiation the ritual text presumes a catechesis that is appropriate for adults. This type of catechesis is holistic and comprehensive and forms adults spiritually, intellectually, emotionally, experientially and in the midst of the community. Authentic initiatory catechesis forms the whole person.

Some dynamics of the rural context are worth noting to facilitate effective catechesis. The traditional rural world is a narrative culture. Oral forms of communication are preferred to written forms. Storytelling is a significant expression of this oral communication. Storytelling would be a useful method of formation throughout both the Precatechumenate and Catechumenate periods. The scriptures, especially the gospels, are filled with stories. Using them as a catalyst for the stories of the inquirers, catechumens and candidates is a great way to bridge the storytelling dynamic of the scriptures to the lives of people who are predisposed to any and all forms of storytelling. This fits nicely into the presumption of the ritual text of Christian initiation which states that beginning with the Catechumenate period the catechumens are to experience the liturgy of the word on Sunday as the starting point for all catechesis which follows (RCIA 83). The scriptures are the building blocks of our faith and will find acceptance by ruralites.

Stories engage the imagination and help people build meaning systems. Consequently, stories of God, the church, the saints, the traditions and history are effective tools of catechesis in a narrative culture. In a society where direct confrontation is generally avoided, storytelling serves as a way to address issues obliquely.

It was noted earlier that the faith catechumens are initiated into is a paschal faith. Consequently, it is a relational faith. Catechesis which is aimed at the whole person and has as its goal helping catechumens understand the meaning of the relationship they are establishing or strengthening during the process of Christian initiation will be effective in a culture which is itself relationally based. Rural people are more concerned about relationships than with tasks. This is not to say that tasks are not important. It is simply to note a priority. Catechesis in a rural setting needs to reflect this priority if it is to be effective.

Catechists should strive to build on the relationship they have with catechumens and see the task of learning as important but secondary to the relationship being fostered. Catechesis should be noted as doing catechesis "with" rather than "for" the inquirers or catechumens. Doing catechesis "with" the inquirers or catechumens makes it clear that a peer relationship is being developed between the catechist and the inquirer or catechumen.

Ideally the catechist knows the stories of the community and is comfortable telling them and using them as a means to engage inquirers or catechumens in telling their own stories. The catechist who knows the stories of the community is judged to be an insider and worth establishing a relationship with. This type of catechist is a treasure for any rural or small-town parish. Again, relationship is everything in the traditional rural world.

Catechists should be wary of pre-packaged programs of catechesis. Most, if not all such programs have an urban bias and could become more of an obstacle than an aid in the formation of the inquirers and catechumens. Many of these programs emphasize a catechesis that is aimed primarily at the intellect. In a rural context, intellectualizing the faith may seriously inhibit the establishment of a relationship between catechist and inquirer or catechumen and between the inquirer or catechumen and the authentic life of faith.

Michael Clay

Another dynamic to watch is fundamentalism. Rural people tend to view the world in a more black-and-white manner than other social groups. To many ruralites God is awesome, fearful and possesses condemnatory power. They are also fearful of change. These dynamics contribute to a fundamentalist worldview where life is reduced to simple solutions. Because Catholicism is not a fundamentalist tradition, traditional ruralites will likely experience some significant stretching as they are invited into a worldview that is clear on some issues and diverse on others. Catechists need to be particularly vigilant to this issue in their inquirers and catechumens, in their catechesis and in themselves.

Conclusion

This essay has briefly sketched some issues which might prove beneficial to anyone attempting to introduce Christian initiation in a rural or small-town setting. The points are intended more to establish a big picture of initiation in this special setting than to treat the issue exhaustively. It is hoped that this overview has helped the reader gain a deeper appreciation of the unique dynamics operative in the rural and small-town parish which are quite different from a parish in the urban or suburban setting. Rural and small-town life and ministry have their own set of gifts and challenges. Those incorporating Christian initiation in this social context will likewise experience areas where convergence and disjuncture exist. To the extent that this introduction to initiation in the non-metropolitan setting has helped the reader identify and appreciate these dynamics, it has accomplished its goal.

Austin Fleming

Marriage Preparation and Wedding Liturgies

Several years ago, on an unhappy Saturday evening, I found myself at a victory party after a football game between Boston College and Notre Dame. The party was at a rectory outside of Boston; most of the guests were fans of the Fighting Irish but the majority of points had been tallied on the BC side of the scoreboard. Not all was lost, however. I found myself huddled in a corner, speaking with Kenneth Untener, bishop of the diocese of Saginaw, and the topic of our conversation was preaching.

The bishop was commenting on how seldom the accounts of the death of Jesus appear in the lectionary and the impact of that on us, who, as Paul wrote in his first letter to Corinth: "Preach Christ crucified, a stumbling block to Jews and an absurdity to Gentiles, but to those who are called, Jews and Greeks alike, Christ the power of God and the wisdom of God" (1:23–25).

I mentioned that a large crucifix hangs over the altar where I usually preside and preach and that its imposing, almost overwhelming presence had led me to refer to it and "Christ crucified" in my preaching more than ever before in my ministry. "Even at weddings?" the good bishop of Saginaw asked me. "How often have you *preached Christ crucified* at weddings?" My honest answer was, "Never."

Bishop Untener went on to say that until recently, he hadn't either, but that he was making a concerted effort to "preach Christ" and "him crucified" whenever he preached—even at weddings.

I share that story with you not to suggest a particular plan for preaching at weddings, but simply to get us within striking distance of what I want to look at in this essay. Is there something about our liturgical practice that shields the wedding celebration, somehow insulating it from the heart of the paschal mystery? Does our preparation of engaged couples for marriage invite them to a deepening of their faith? Does our celebration of the marriage rite speak what the church speaks in its ritual book? What is the greatest challenge we offer engaged couples? Is it the challenge of rethinking the makeup of the processional party in an effort to include the groom in the opening festivities of the nuptial event? Or is it the challenge of living the gospel under the outstretched arms of the cross?

If we were to begin to take the rite of marriage seriously, what impact would that have on the ways we prepare engaged couples for marriage, and what impact would that have on the ways we celebrate the liturgy of marriage with them and for them? By simply posing the question, I suggest that at some levels we do not yet take the rite of marriage seriously. (Our operating rite is the *Rite of Marriage* of 1969, while we wait for final consultation, revision and approval of the *Order for Celebrating Marriage* of 1991. This essay will refer both to the 1969 *Rite of Marriage* and to the ICEL draft translation of 1991 *Order for Celebrating Marriage*.)

The Praenotanda

We have been celebrating with our present *Rite of Marriage* for just over 28 years. The introduction to the rite begins with four extremely dense paragraphs of a theology of marriage. The language may be difficult but is worth the labor of translation in working with those about to celebrate the sacrament of marriage:

> (1) Married Christians, in virtue of the sacrament of matrimony, signify and share in the mystery of that unity and fruitful love

which exists between Christ and his Church; they help each other to attain to holiness in their married life and in the rearing and education of their children; and they have their own special gift among the people of God.

(2) Marriage arises in the covenant of marriage, or irrevocable consent, which each partner freely bestows on and accepts from the other. This intimate union and the good of the children impose total fidelity on each of them and argue for an unbreakable oneness between them. Christ the Lord raised this union to the dignity of a sacrament so that it might more clearly recall and more easily reflect his own unbreakable union with his Church. (*Rite of Marriage*, 1969)

How often, and to what extent, does our preparation of engaged couples include instruction on how the married couple is expected to signify the love which exists between Christ and his church? Is it not precisely this element that distinguishes Christian marriage from all other forms of marriage? Is it not this understanding of Christian marriage that justifies the union as a sacrament? How many newly married couples are prepared to articulate this truth which is meant to be the heart of their union? How is it that we regularly entrust this ministry — the work of signifying the love between Christ and his church — to men and women who have virtually no relationship to the church as individuals? Apart from the fact that the celebration takes place in a church building, what do engaged couples (and their ministers!) understand to be the truly ecclesial dimensions of the sacrament they are preparing to celebrate and to live? Can we fail to grapple with these difficult issues and run the risk that couples leave our sanctuaries bound together for life without any notion that Christ has raised their "union to the dignity of a sacrament so that it might more clearly recall and more easily reflect his own unbreakable union with his Church"? Apart from this basic understanding of Christian marriage, I see little in our own culture to otherwise help us argue for "total fidelity and unbreakable oneness" between a bride and groom.

Of course, such thinking demands faith! Thus, paragraphs 5 – 7 mark a change in tone and emphasis and give practical instructions for those who will prepare the engaged couple for marriage and, the text suggests, minister at the liturgical celebration:

(5) A minister should bear in mind these principles of faith both in his instructions to those about to be married and when giving the homily during the marriage ceremony . . . The bridal couple should be given a review of the fundamentals of Christian doctrine. This may include instruction on the teachings about marriage and the family, on the rites used in the celebration of the sacrament itself, and on the prayers and readings. In this way the bridegroom and the bride will receive far greater benefit from the celebration.

(7) Priests should first of all strengthen and nourish the faith of those about to be married, for the sacrament of matrimony presupposes and demands faith. (*Rite of Marriage*, 1969)

At what point in our preparation of engaged couples for the sacrament of marriage do we offer a "review of the fundamentals of Christian doctrine"? At what point do parish ministers "first of all strengthen and nourish the faith of those about to married," with the understanding that "the sacrament of matrimony presupposes and demands faith"? Where the *Rite of Marriage* clearly calls us to explore the paschal mystery with engaged couples (precisely because they are being called to witness and live that mystery in their marriage!) we are too often about the business of arguing through the liturgical niceties of wedding celebrations with couples who are often religious illiterates. That is not intended as a judgment but rather as a statement of fact.

Our teaching on marriage as a sacrament in general, and in the language of the *Rite of Marriage* in particular, involves the vocabulary of faith. Perhaps it is because so many of our engaged sisters and brothers speak this language only haltingly that we have failed to even try to communicate to and share with them the faith dimensions of the union they are preparing to enter. Part of our work as ministers with engaged couples is to introduce them to the language of the house of faith. To do so is not to impose some further requirement on the couple, but rather to share with them a gift.

The Introduction of the 1991 *Order for Celebrating Marriage* repeats and expands the 1969 text, ending with this beautiful summation, built largely on the words of Tertullian:

(11) . . . A marriage embraced, prepared for, celebrated, and lived out daily in the light of faith is the marriage that "the

Church arranges, the sacrifice strengthens, upon which the blessing sets a seal, at which angels are present as witnesses, and to which the Father gives his consent . . . Two are one in hope, one in the religion they practice. They are as brother and sister, both servants of the same Master; nothing divides them, either in flesh or in spirit. They are in very truth, two in one flesh; and where there is but one flesh, there is also but one spirit." (*Order for Celebrating Marriage*, 1991)

Where in our marriage preparation do we help couples to understand that the church stands ready to "arrange, bless and seal those marriages embraced, prepared for, celebrated and lived out in the light of faith"? Does the church know how to stand as witness to any marriage of a lesser kind? Some years ago, engaged couples asking to celebrate their weddings at Sacred Heart Church on the campus of the University of Notre Dame received a brochure which began by outlining the church's understanding of Christian marriage. Having described this sacramental union, the text closed with the line, "Please do not ask the favor of our house of prayer for marriages of a less astonishing sort."

It is interesting to note that in the introduction to the 1969 rite, and in the rite itself, there is no mention whatsoever of the bride and groom having any participation in the preparation of the liturgy for the celebration of their marriage. None. There is that business, however, of the bride and groom receiving a review course in the fundamentals of Christian faith. (A brief invitation to the couple to have a role in preparing the liturgy is tucked away in paragraph 29 of the new rite.)

I suggest we take some time out to consider how it is that we have in great measure ignored a substantial portion of the 1969 rite, and simultaneously have created a veritable cottage industry of trying to turn engaged couples into miniature liturgy committees charged with a task—preparing the celebration of a liturgy considerably more complex than the order for usual Sunday worship—for which they have no background or experience, while often lacking even the most basic level of articulate Christian faith we might expect of a regular Sunday worshiper seeking membership on the parish liturgical committee.

A quick response to all of this might be framed this way: We have rushed much too quickly and have made the rite (and its preparation) the center of everything, forgetting that while ritual is, in word and in deed, a sacred moment, it is also a moment in a much larger continuum. This is especially true of the sacrament of marriage, which is not only a liturgical act but also a lifetime Christian vocation. Liturgical ministers, myself included, are often quick to criticize brides and grooms (and their families and friends) for being so concerned about minor details that they forget "what's really important here." I wonder if in some analogous fashion, we pastoral and liturgical ministers have not also become so obsessed with liturgical and ritual details that we have forgotten "what's really important here."

A personal example: In my own ministry, I have been working for years toward establishing a parish practice in which the reception of the couple and the procession of ministers and wedding party resemble in some loose fashion what is envisioned by the *Rite of Marriage*. I make no apology for the concern and anxiety I experience over this issue. What bothers me, however, is that I am often more easily emotionally exercised by concern over the groom's placement in the entrance procession than I am over his faith life and spirituality as he enters a lifetime commitment in a Christian vocation!

We have looked at what the *praenotanda* have to tell us about preparing engaged couples for marriage; let's take a look now at what the marriage rite itself suggests for marriage preparation. Looking at the both the 1969 and 1991 rites, we see that there are seven basic components to our celebration of marriage, namely:
1. the reception of the couple at the church doors
2. the liturgy of the word
3. the preliminary questions
4. the consent
5. the blessing and giving of rings
6. the nuptial blessing
7. the eucharist (when celebrated as the context for the marriage rite)

The Reception of the Couple at the Door of the Church

What might this portion of the marriage rite suggest to us as we think about preparing engaged couples for the celebration of their marriage and their married life as a Christian vocation? First, we need to understand the rite itself.

There are four times in the liturgy of our church when the presider meets people at the church doors:

1. when those about to enter the catechumenate present themselves at the church doors, seeking entrance;
2. when parents arrive at the church doors asking for the baptism of their infant children;
3. when a wedding party arrives at the church doors to celebrate the sacrament of marriage;
4. and when mourners arrive at the church doors bearing the remains of a Christian who has died.

Two of these occasions are moments in the rites of Christian initiation, and another, the reception of the body at a funeral liturgy, vividly recalls the initiatory rites: sprinkling with holy water, clothing in a white garment and the presence of the paschal candle. To this list is added the reception of the couple about to celebrate the sacrament of marriage.

The origins of the minister meeting the couple at the church doors has less to do with initiation and more to do with the historical reality that in earlier times and ritual sequences, the minister met the couple at the church doors for a rite of betrothal, or even to receive the consent. In either case, the couple entered the church with a new status. Note that even though betrothal and consent are no longer celebrated at the church doors, the liturgical book maintains the custom of the minister meeting the couple there and, in the 1991 rite, the book replaces the regular introductory rites entirely with this special rite with the express and simple purpose of "greeting the couple (and the wedding party) with warmth and friendship, showing that the Church shares in their joy." The wedding party then takes its place, with the ministers, in the entrance procession.

What happens in this rite? As parents greet their children at the door, welcoming them home and leading them to the family table, so the church opens its arms to share the joy of children coming home (and very often, their wedding is a "coming home to church" after a lengthy absence) to celebrate their wedding feast at the table of him whose bride is the church and whose table is ours. The church is welcoming its own. There is something altogether ecclesial about this portion of the rite, and it very much has to do with the church's relationship to the couple and the couple's relationship to the church.

The introductory rite for the celebrating marriage suggests that the couple has chosen the church as the place, the community and the "way" (the ritual) through which they want to solemnize their union as husband and wife. The rite also suggests that in some sense the church has chosen the couple, that is to say, has agreed to stand as witness as they exchange their consent and become husband and wife.

The rite, then, suggests the formation of the couple in some ecclesial identity. Marriage preparation, then, needs to help the engaged couple in some way to understand their wedding as an ecclesial event:

- as a celebration of a church community that embraces them in love;

- as their celebration precisely because they are members of the church;

- and as a celebration of the church community in which they are, this day, ministers of a sacrament.

And if the minister understands the ecclesial nature of the introductory rites for the celebration of marriage, then he or she will be at the doors of the church fifteen or twenty minutes ahead of the scheduled time for the wedding:

- warmly greeting invited guests;

- welcoming the members of the wedding party as they arrive, especially the bride and groom and their parents;

- helping all to find their place in the procession;

- leading them to their places, as the entrance song is sung;

- gesturing for them and with them the sign of the cross of the crucified;

- greeting them with the love of God, the grace of Christ and the fellowship of the Spirit;

- welcoming all present to the celebration of this marriage;

- inviting all to open their minds and hearts to the word of God;

- and finally leading them in prayer for the couple to be married.

If the entrance rite thus described were to happen, and if the minister were gracious and knowledgeable in his or her role, then there would be no need for a wedding rehearsal the night before! No more than a gracious host on the night before a dinner party would hold a rehearsal for the guests on how to be seated and how to make their way from the front door to the living room to the dining room and back to the front door.

But all this will be a reality only if the minister, the engaged couple and the church at large have been prepared for this kind of ritual moment. This kind of procession is the church in action, the church at work, the church in ritual. This is the church's ritual movement, its dance. The church, in the person of the minister, moves, dances the wedding party from the door to their places for prayer. The minister and the couple and the church community must be prepared for this. This is what the rite suggests.

Envisioning the entrance rite for celebrations of marriage in these terms gives rise to other questions:

- How is the couple met, greeted and welcomed at the rectory door when they come to make arrangements for their wedding?

- How are they shown to the door as they are leaving?

- Does any part of the marriage preparation of the couple take place in the church building? at the church doors? in the aisle? in the sanctuary space?

- What kind of hospitality, welcome, do the engaged couple receive as they enter the church on a typical Sunday morning?

Austin Fleming

Of course, marriage is for a lifetime, not for a day. The couple's preparation for marriage then needs to bring to the surface the realities of hospitality and church relationship beyond the celebration of the wedding. The rite then suggests the following questions for marriage preparation and for the couple's consideration:

- What is the history of the couple's relationship with the church?

- What is the present reality of this relationship?

- What are their plans, hopes, goals, thoughts about the future of their relationship with the church community?

- How do they hope to serve the church community?

- How do they hope to be served by the church community?

- The church welcomes the couple for marriage with warmth, friendship and hospitality. How will the couple welcome others into their married life? children? their families of origin? old friends and new? new neighbors? the poor?

We can only come to know what the rite suggests for the preparation of the engaged couple if we understand the rite itself. There may be some liturgical practitioners who have yet to grapple with this basic task! And we cannot and will not come to understand the rite itself unless we do the rite.

And by doing the rite, I certainly suggest doing the rite in all its fullness, not holding back but pulling out all the stops, as one does when one invites friends into one's home for a special dinner.

In the RCIA we have come to understand the living, vital connection between the rites celebrated in the Sunday assembly and the spiritual formation taking place in the catechumenate experience. Nothing less than this needs to be at work in the preparation of engaged couples for marriage. The 1996 document from the Pontifical Council for the Family, "Preparation for the Sacrament of Marriage," makes this point compellingly and with authority, drawing us to see the faith-filled potential of marriage preparation that takes the sacrament, the rite and the engaged couple seriously. (See *Origins*, volume 26, pages 97 ff.)

Our preparation of engaged couples for their wedding day and for married life has centered on what a Creighton University study referred to as the six C's:

Communication
Commitment
Conflict resolution
Children
Church
Career (especially dual career needs)

(See "Effective Marriage Preparation" in *Origins,* volume 25, especially page 431.)

In the course of a typical marriage preparation program in my experience, the emphasis tends to fall on:

Communication (skills) — Conflict resolution
Finances
Career issues
Family of origin issues
Sexuality
Liturgy for the wedding celebration

Too often, the greatest investment of time, energy and interest goes into preparing the liturgy for the wedding — and in at least some cases, this is principally the time, energy and interest of the bride (and perhaps her mother).

What I find significantly absent from this list of topics for marriage preparation is prayer and spirituality.

All of these, of course, are important topics and issues for engaged couples to explore together as they prepare for marriage. And it certainly is good that such topics are pursued and perused under the umbrella of the church's ministry with engaged couples. But we have to ask: If it is a sacrament for which we are preparing the engaged couple, where is the spiritual formation in our programs? We do not prepare catechumens for initiation by inviting them to "plan the liturgy for the Triduum." Rather, we prepare them them for immersion by immersion: by immersion in the word, by immersion in the community, by immersion in prayer, by immersion in discernment. At its heart, the catechumenate is spiritual formation and spiritual direction. Along with the work of justice, spiritual formation rooted in the scriptures is the best the church has to offer. Should we offer anything else, or anything less to those who come to us seeking to celebrate the sacrament of marriage?

I call here on the rite of marriage to support this thesis. We have already looked at the reception of the couple and the introductory rites. There follow, then:

- the liturgy of the word

- the preliminary questions

- the consent

- the blessing and giving of rings

- the nuptial blessing

- and the eucharist (although not all marriages are celebrated at eucharist).

The Liturgy of the Word

That the word "liturgy" is a major component of the marriage rite is no accident. The liturgy always presumes that those celebrating a particular rite are:

- people of the word

- people hungry for the word, and in need of the word

- people who find in the word the very voice and presence of the Lord

- and people ready, or being readied, to preach and live the word.

How many engaged couples does such a description fit? Might this not suggest that some modest evangelization is in order here as we prepare couples for celebrating and living the sacrament of marriage? I'm not talking about a course in scripture study, or a mandatory Bible study, but simply looking for some ways, as we prepare couples for marriage, to evangelize, to bring the word of God to bear upon their lives, and to help them understand the sacrament of marriage in the terms of the scriptures.

Some possibilities:

- a Bible study based on the lectionary for weddings;

- beginning each session with the parish minister with a scripture lesson from the wedding lectionary;

- asking presenting couples in marriage prep programs to refer to the wedding lectionary as much as possible;

- seeking Sunday and religious education opportunities to high-light scriptures from the wedding lectionary;

- working with parish musicians to suggest and coordinate musical selections that work especially well with particular scripture texts;

- and looking to the background of partners from other Christian churches for scripture-based faith.

Address to the Couple, Preliminary Questions, Consent and Exchange of Rings

The next part of the rite of marriage includes the minister's address to the couple, the preliminary questions, the consent and the blessing and exchange of rings. Let's just review those texts for a moment:

> My dear friends, John and Mary, you have come together in this church so that before this community and the Church's minister, the Lord may seal and strengthen your resolve to enter marriage.
>
> Christ abundantly blesses your love.
>
> He has already consecrated you in baptism and now he enriches and strengthens you by a special sacrament, so that, forsaking all others, you may live in mutual and lasting fidelity and take on the duties of married life.
>
> And so, in the presence of the Church, I ask you to state your intentions.

Mary and John, have you come here freely and without reservation to give yourselves to each other in marriage?

Will you love and honor each other as husband and wife for the rest of your lives?

Will you accept children lovingly from God and bring them up according to the law of Christ and his Church?

Since it is your intention to enter into marriage, join your right hands and declare your consent before God and in the presence of the Church.

I, John, take you, Mary, to be my wife.

I promise to be true to you in good times and in bad, in sickness and in health. I will love you and honor you, all the days of my life.

I, Mary, take you, John, to be my husband.

I promise to be true to you in good times and in bad, in sickness and in health. I will love you and honor you, all the days of my life.

Mary, take and wear this ring as a sign of my love and fidelity. In the name of the Father, and of the Son, and of the Holy Spirit.

John, take and wear this ring as a sign of my love and fidelity. In the name of the Father, and of the Son, and of the Holy Spirit.
(*Order for Celebrating Marriage*, 1991)

Those who present themselves to the church announcing a desire for membership in that community are invited into the catechumenate to test and nourish that desire for communion. Children who present themselves to the church for communion at the Lord's table and teenagers who present themselves for confirmation are invited, indeed required, to prepare for those sacraments through a process designed to help them understand and discern how God is moving in their lives. Those who present themselves to the church announcing a desire to serve as deacons or presbyters, those who present themselves with a desire for vowed life in community—these, too, are invited into a process of discernment.

What do the preliminary questions and consent suggest to us with regard to how we prepare engaged couples who present themselves to the church for the sacrament, the vocation of marriage? When these couples come to us, we immediately "discern" their canonical status and readiness for the sacrament of marriage. What do we do to help them discern that marriage is their vocation, and that the partner each comes with is to be a life-long colleague (co-minister) in this vocation? I do not suggest here that we posit some doubt about their readiness for marriage. Rather, in my own ministry, I begin by presuming their readiness until something signals otherwise. What we can not presume is that the couple have had an opportunity to discern marriage as a Christian sacrament, and as a sacramental vocation. Look at the vocabulary in the address to the couple, the preliminary questions and the consent!

A Possibility

Many couples come to instruction and preparation for marriage thinking that they are going to be tested, that they might flunk, that the minister might deny them the sacrament. Suppose the minister begins by announcing:

"You are indeed canonically free to enter marriage; there appear to be no civil impediments to your marriage; the date for the celebration of your marriage will be November 15, 1998, at 2:00 in the afternoon here at St. Joseph parish. With that out of the way, I want to spend some time with you looking at the sacramental dimensions and implications of what we will be celebrating on November 15. God and the church invite and call you to understand and live the married life in some particular ways. I want to help you look at marriage as a sacrament, and to help you discern, discover, see how God is moving in your lives now as you prepare to enter married life. To help you do that, I want you to look at some of the words that you will be hearing and saying in your wedding in November . . ."

Here the minister hands the two parties each a copy of the texts above (minister's address, preliminary questions, exchange of consent and blessing and exchange of rings—with their own names in the particular places). The minister reviews the texts with the couple and uses them to help them understand just what it is they are going to speak, celebrate and promise to live on their wedding day. The individuals take the texts away with them, having been urged to review them, study them and pray over them every day. In this way we can begin to help a couple discern what their doing as a vocation and a shared ministry.

In addition to helping a couple discern their marriage as a sacramental vocation, the exchange of consent lends itself to and even suggests that the minister preparing the engaged couple use these texts to help the man and woman understand themselves as the very ministers of the sacrament of marriage, and to help them see that for the rest of their lives, they will be responsible for ministering to each other as husband and wife, to their children as parents and to their neighbors as brothers and sisters in Christ in justice and in charity. This is so much more than helping a couple decide between this statement of consent or that, between speaking the consent as a statement, or answering to it as a response to a question. This is nothing less than discernment of vocation for a lifetime of ministry.

The Nuptial Blessing

The two most basic elements of the rite of marriage are the exchange of consent received by the minister and the nuptial blessing. The nuptial blessing articulates God's relationship to the couple and their relationship to God. It is clear from these texts that the husband and wife are meant to depend on God for blessing, for assistance, for strength, for hope and for their unity and fidelity. Indeed, their dependency is ritualized in their kneeling for this blessing. No other part of the marriage rite more clearly reveals the spiritual relationship the couple is meant to enjoy with each other and with God.

Rather than simply handing the engaged couple the various texts of the nuptial blessing and inviting them to choose one, does the rite not suggest the opportunity here to explore with the couple their understanding of God, their relationship with God as individuals, their shared relationship with God, and their prayer lives (as individuals and as a couple). It is easy enough to critique the texts of the nuptial blessings (the 1991 rite offers better texts!) in terms of gender issues. It is a much weightier task to lead the couple through the blessings as texts for prayer and to help the engaged couple to enter into some shared prayer together. Helping the engaged couple to explore the possibility of praying together is the greatest gift the minister can offer them. This begins most easily if the minister is willing to pray with the couple, and to teach them to pray, in the meetings before the celebration of the marriage. Rooting this prayer in the scripture lessons and ritual texts of the marriage rite is an obvious and good place to begin.

The Eucharist

The Sunday assembly is the premier place to lift up the engaged couple in prayer in the general intercessions. Unfortunately, the Blessing for an Engaged Couple found in *The Book of Blessings* is not intended for liturgical use and is explicitly precluded from use with the celebration of Mass.

If the eucharist is to be celebrated as the context for the marriage rite, it brings with it a fullness and depth of ecclesial life and spirit that cannot be gained in any other way. It is to be hoped, of course, that the couple are regular participants in the Sunday assembly and because of this they desire to celebrate their wedding at the table of eucharist. Often, the impending wedding celebration occasions a couple's return to regular Sunday worship. Perhaps the best approach here is to meet each couple individually and to encourage them to whatever level of spiritual formation they can appropriate, remembering that they have a lifetime of marriage ahead of them in which to draw closer to the life and prayer of the church.

The preparation for engaged couples for the celebration of marriage and for married life is not primarily a short course in conflict resolution or liturgy planning! It is much more a matter of evangelization, catechesis, spiritual formation, spiritual direction, discernment of vocation and ministry, and prayer. This is much more work than many parish ministers presently take on and the scope of the work indicates clearly that this is a ministry to be shared by a team of hard workers. The minister who will witness the marriage, however, has a particular responsibility to see that the couple are afforded the opportunity for all that the rite itself envisions: growth in faith, deepening spirituality, an understanding of ministry and a greater relationship with Christ through the church.

Bibliography

A Book of Blessings (New York: Catholic Book Publishing, 1989), pages 96–101.

Catholic Household Blessings and Prayers (Washington: United States Catholic Conference, 1988), pages 236–244.

"Celebrating the Rites of Marriage," *Assembly,* volume 18, no. 4 (Notre Dame Center for Pastoral Liturgy, Box 81, Notre Dame, IN 46556).

Fleming, Austin, *Parish Weddings* (Chicago: Liturgy Training Publications, 1987).

Fleming, Austin, *Prayerbook for Engaged Couples* (Chicago: Liturgy Training Publications, 1990).

The Rite of Marriage in the collection *The Rites,* volume 1 (Collegeville, MN: Pueblo, The Liturgical Press, 1976).

Stevenson, Kenneth, *To Join Together: The Rite of Marriage* (New York: Pueblo, 1987).

Diana L. Hayes

Healing the Past, Claiming the Future: Naming and Welcoming the "Other"

Plenty good room
Plenty good room in my Father's Kingdom
Plenty good room
Plenty good room
Just choose your seat and sit down

Most Christians can sing this song but do we truly seek to live out its reality in our midst? What do we mean when we speak of the "changing face of the church" today? What are the changes involved? Who is affected by them? Why are these changes taking place? And do they frighten, threaten or challenge us?

My context in this paper will be that of the Roman Catholic church, of which I am a member, albeit as an African American woman, historically marginalized. However, the questions that I raise go beyond that church, impacting upon all Christian churches and, more importantly, all Christians.

If only it were true that we could simply "choose our seats and sit down," as the hymn recommends, but so often those seats for too many have been in the back of the church, on the margins, in the balcony, anywhere as long as it was out of sight and, therefore, out of consideration. For we tend, in the United States, to be fearful of change, wishing we could go back to the "good old days" of a fictitious past where everything was just right. And therein lies the problem. For in seeking to return, we eventually must realize that the past was never quite as we remembered it. Our efforts to return, therefore, are doomed before they have even begun.

An English journalist living in London provides us with the opportunity to share in this perspective as she reflects upon the changes that have taken place since the Second Vatican Council in the Catholic Church's celebration of the eucharist. She notes:

> Like many Catholics who reached the age of reason (in theory) before 1960, I often think I miss the Latin Mass. Something magical, dramatic and mysterious has gone; we are left with something un-grand, ordinary, proletarian, bald. . . . The present Mass in English is too workaday for God, who surely deserves something glorious; it is too workaday for ourselves, who need to make a break with the language of the newspaper and the bazaar.
>
> As the years pass, however, I am slowly changing my mind. First, I think I am wrong about Latin. . . . I mean the read Latin Mass we all knew and went to week by week, which was meant to last about 30 minutes but could be said, by an Irishman, in 20: "Father O'Grady really zipped through it today" is typical of the spiritual elation that resulted. Very little of this Mass could be heard by the congregation, who in any case scarcely counted. From the altar would come a low rumbling, like an approaching train, broken by a sudden burst of words which was the signal to kneel or stand; and most of my interest was to see whether the altar boys, whirling like dervishes from one side of the altar to the other, would actually crash together in the middle.
>
> A few years ago, having forgotten what so many of those Masses were like, I went to a church in London where a low Latin Mass was said on Monday evenings. It was a wet winter night; we were crammed in and steaming. And, once again, the priest and his server raced through, as if they were starved men late for their dinners. Yet it was not the speed that bothered me so much; . . . it was the fact that the priest had his back to us all

throughout, involving us only grudgingly, as if our intercessions did not matter. This was mightily annoying.

I came out into the night thoroughly disenchanted with Latin; but I was not yet reconciled to English, either. That has taken longer, and may have something to do with wanting something different out of the Mass. Mass is now a sort of oasis, a breathing space, in a mad day. . . . In that oasis, I do not want words to distract me; I want them plain and slow. The English of the modern Mass has no artifice, no rhythm, no conscious beauty; like a plain stone or a white wall, it gains beauty from whatever weight or meaning we wish to give it. . . .

When we, as English, hear these things, we are involved, we understand, and we get right through. There are no barriers to break down; the word takes us directly to the concept, and a great word (such as Love, or Justice) stands out plainly in all its force. The modern Mass, ordinary if you like, is also as clear and unadorned as a pane of glass; and through that glass we may sometimes glimpse God.[1]

In this brief viewpoint, the author, Ann Wroe, has gone to the heart of what I see as the issue confronting us today—the issue of change— in western society but, more importantly, in the Roman Catholic church and all Christian churches.

Mrs. Wroe looks back with a nostalgia to the "good old days" of the Latin Mass, imagining that they summed up the true glory and universality of the church. However, she soon realizes that those days were not really so good in many ways and comes finally to a realization of the vibrancy and vitality of the new liturgical shifts that have taken place which allow her and all parishioners to, as she notes, become "involved," to "understand" and to "get right through" to the elemental meaning of the Mass without having barriers to break through or unfamiliar language to decipher.

She is correct, up to a point. The point is, however, that presented with the Mass in her own language, in a style, custom and form which is in accord with her heritage and traditions, she finds (and again I quote her) that "the modern Mass, ordinary if you like, banal if you like, is also as clear and unadorned as a pane of glass; and through that glass we may sometimes glimpse God."

Diana L. Hayes

The truth of the matter is, however, that what may be clear as glass to one person may, to another, be as opaque as mud. This is especially true for those of us here in the United States where an incredible and rich diversity of cultures, heritages and traditions abound. These opening remarks about liturgy serve as the context from within which we can explore the question of the church of the twenty-first century and the challenges confronting it.

For just as our liturgy has changed, evolving in new and different ways, unimaginable in the past, so has the face and form of the Catholic church in the United States changed—becoming a global microcosm. Everything that we are, all that we stand for as church arises from our understanding of and celebration of the eucharistic liturgy. It is the symbol par excellence of the Roman Catholic church. Thus, it serves as a viable paradigm for the church as a whole and how it is changing as we enter upon the twenty-first century. Here I will focus on the Catholic church in the United States in its incredible ethnic and racial diversity, for we are the world church in a smaller scale. At the same time, it should be recognized that many of these changes are also taking place in other Christian churches as well.

The People of God

As church, the people of God, we are a eucharistic community, one which gathers to live out again and again the sacrifice of Jesus Christ. Without the daily offering of the eucharist, with its restriction or unavailability, with the loss of its meaning, its intelligibility, we are no longer the church we claim to be. We have, without a doubt, lost our way, failed in our mission to preach the good news—the bread and wine of life—to all who hunger and thirst for it.

In other words, if we can't get that right, if we do not understand the significance of liturgical inculturation, if the eucharist is not a reflection of all of us, old and young, black, white and every color and language under the sun, as various in its celebration as the sands of the seashore and the stars in the sky, then all else that flows from there will be of little value.

So what is liturgical inculturation? Simply put, it is the bringing to life of the liturgy in the cultures and traditions of the people celebrating. The 1991 document of the bishops of the United States, *Plenty Good Room: The Spirit and Truth of African American Catholic Worship,* notes that:

> Liturgy celebrates and evokes the divine reality that is at once remote and intimate, transcendent and immanent, beyond our reach and ever present. . . . Liturgy evokes a world that is at once shared with others and is at the same time beyond ordinary life. To borrow the words of Howard Thurman, liturgy "bathes one's whole being with something more wonderful than words can ever tell (Howard Thurman, *The Growing Edge* [Richmond, IN: Friends United Press, 1956], p. 117)." (PGR, 2)

Liturgy goes beyond our own immediate experience to celebrate mystery by means of symbols and signs. While signs have conventional meanings that have been established by a community (a *particular* community), symbols are ambiguous, capable of multiple meanings and associations that emerge from a "given historical, cultural, ethnic, and racial community" (PGR, 5).

> Certain realities become symbolic in particular circumstances and only in relation to a human community. . . . They can [then] assume levels of meaning that make sense of birth, life, and death—by means of tradition, community, and grace (Cf. Paul Ricoeur, *The Symbolism of Evil* [Boston: Beacon Press, 1967]). (PGR, 5)
>
> This is why people can participate in the same celebration of the Eucharist on Sunday and find different meanings in the Scriptures proclaimed, the hymns sung, the preparation of the gifts, the eucharistic prayer, the sign of peace, the sharing in the Body and Blood of the Lord. This is also why people of different ethnic and cultural backgrounds may have different subjective responses to the same objective symbolic activity. (PGR, 7)

We see this, for example, in the use of language—"man," "Lord," "brothers," etc., words which for many, male and female alike, are jarring and exclusive, while, for others, they present no challenge and raise no questions at all. For some, the spontaneous outbursts of

Diana L. Hayes

"amen" and "alleluia" can be disruptive as well, but for others it is simply an added affirmation of their own prayer and celebration.

Yet, while we may be gaining different meanings from the celebration, we are, at the same time, sharing as one community in the body and blood of Christ. It is this community, this body of believers, which makes us the church, the people of God, journeying towards that divine source from which we all have come.

Thus, we recognize that as a people of diverse races and ethnicities united by our Catholic faith, we live and work so that all people may be united with God and with one another and, as Jesus proclaimed, "All may be one as you, Abba, are in me and I in you. I pray that they may be one in us" (John 17:2). At the same time, it must be affirmed that there has to be room for the recognition of that already existing pluralism in the midst of our journey towards universality — for a false oneness, one imposed by some against the will of others, simply fosters dissatisfaction, distrust and eventually disunity.

True universalism must be able to embrace existing pluralism, rather than trying to fit every people into the mold of religion and culture generated from one historical experience. Only God is one and universal. Humanity is finally one because the one God created us all. But the historical mediators of the experience of God remain plural. To impose one religion — or one way of being Catholic — on everyone flattens and impoverishes the wealth of human interaction with God. In order to be truly Catholic, Christians must revise the imperialistic way they have defined their universality.[2]

In the liturgy, as in the church, Christ speaks to each person and each community in *their* lived condition. To be authentic, therefore, the liturgy must be presented and the church must see itself reflected in language, signs, and symbols which speak to those celebrating within it of their journeying with Christ.

It would be helpful at this time to take a brief detour through Christian history, for in order to see where we, as church, are today and where we, hopefully, are going as church tomorrow, we must also look back from whence we have come and call forth the memories — good, bad, and perhaps ugly — those memories which Johann Baptist Metz names as "subversive" because they turn our understanding of reality upside down, revealing truths not foreseen or understood when first experienced and helping us to look, with new eyes, at a past that was not as golden perhaps, as Ann Wroe noted, as first it seemed.

A Brief History Lesson

Christianity emerged in a time and place where cultures constantly merged and clashed, the crossroads of the Roman Empire found in the Middle East and Africa. Here, peoples of all nations, creeds and colors came together, rubbing elbows, exchanging ideas, learning from, teaching and influencing each other socially, economically and religiously.

For its first 100 or so years, Christianity had a Jewish context, gathering and spreading the message of Christ crucified through Jewish rituals, symbols, gestures and customs familiar both to Jesus and his original disciples, familiar yet at the same time in their new presentations subtly transformed and given a Christian meaning. Yet, today, many Christians, whether Catholic or Protestant, are not aware of this ancestry. Our young people especially, regardless of race or ethnicity, are rather stunned by the statement that Jesus was a Jew, not a Christian, as were the Virgin Mary and all of the first apostles and believers in the risen Christ.

They are further surprised to learn that the histories and cultures of other peoples also impacted upon and transformed the infant Christian church as those first disciples sought to live up to Jesus' command to "Go ye therefore and teach all nations" (Matthew 28:19) traveling to Greek, Roman and African territories where Christianity spread and evolved and encountered new and different peoples who themselves become devoted laborers in the vineyard and in so doing not only received much from their teachers but also gave much to them. They became teachers themselves and bearers of the good news in tongues and cultures that helped to broaden our understanding of Jesus' life, death and resurrection while, at the same time, enriching our liturgical and religious language with words and understandings from their own cultures. These cultural encounters gave us the Alleluias and Amens of the Jewish faithful; the language of epiphany, agape, advent, eucharist and eulogy from our Greek and Roman worshipers; new formulas for prayer and baptism and new forms of spirituality from the African churches as well as increasing ceremonial ritual from the imperial court. These influences shaped and formed Christianity as we have come to know over the passage of centuries.

Wherever the church traveled, wherever the seed of the gospel was planted, new and fertile growth took place; a growth always and everywhere established in and nurtured by the traditions and heritage of the peoples and cultures with which it came into contact. It was this ever-spreading cross-fertilization which nourished and sustained the church in its mission, a mission truly the work of the Holy Spirit alighting upon and anointing with tongues of fire the souls and minds of all, filling each and every one with the Spirit of God and enabling them to speak in the language of those with whom they come into contact and thereby inculturate the Christian faith within their midst. And so that mission continues to this very day, to bring the message of Christ to all in ways that speak not just to their minds but to their very hearts and souls.

Thus, as the church was not only Jewish but also Greek, Roman and African, it was historically always recognized, albeit often unconsciously, that cultural adaptation of the signs, symbols and language, of the liturgical rituals, of the very life of the faith, should and must reflect the culture of those participating or they would not be able to communicate the message of salvation that they carried within them.

A Shift in Vision

What we have come to realize today, however, is that this rich meshing of faith and cultures was eventually stifled and stilled. With the passage of time, the church continued to grow even further and further. It reached the very limits of the known world. Having converged with the world's manifold cultures and having adapted worthily to them, the church entered upon a period of "luxuriant growth" in which the liturgy was both reinterpreted and misinterpreted.

Many of us are familiar with the results, a shift from a liturgical style in which the entire community of faith came together in joyous celebration and *anamnesis* (remembering) to liturgies which diminished the "liturgical ministries coupled with an exaggerated piety toward the eucharist apart from the eucharistic action and the reception of the Holy Communion."[3]

> Equally unfortunate was the effect on persons: The Mass priest became dominant. Now, so long as he had a serving boy, he could dispense with deacon and other ministers; he could supersede the congregation also. With the disappearance of the sense of sacrifice there disappeared also not only the laity's communion but also the sense of its lay-priesthood. The ideal lay person was the boy who would serve the priest's Mass. Drill superseded worship and the Mass was commercialized. (Walter Howard Frere, *The Anaphora or Great Eucharistic Prayer* [London: SPCK, 1938], quoted in PGR, 19)

A rigor set in — some would call it a *rigor mortis,* a deathly rigidity and uniformity that almost proved fatal to the understanding of church and the eucharistic community as a living, enfleshed community, as beloved disciples joining with each other to commemorate and re-enact the sacrifice of the paschal lamb for the sake of all.

Unfortunately, this understanding of church and liturgy — rigid, unchanging, unadapting, uniform, robotic, often seemingly mindless, unfeeling and unfelt — was carried to the Americas to clash with peoples whose cultures were a total antithesis to this. The Catholicism of the French, Spanish and English missionaries who were instrumental in introducing the Catholic faith to the Native Americans as well as to those Africans imported against their will was so intimately wedded to their culture that many of them could not easily distinguish the gospel that they preached from their own particular expression of it. As a result, because of its links to Europe and its history, the church in America tended to assume that European cultures were the only viable cultures and found it extremely difficult to imagine, much less value, cultures other than their own.

Diana L. Hayes

What was not recognized or accepted was that these other peoples did have viable cultures containing customs which, "free of superstition and error . . . [could] be admitted into the liturgy" and thus into the life of the church (PGR, 24).

An African American Context

Using my own African American context as an example: Their ancestors, the peoples of western Africa—although few, if any, were Christian upon their arrival in these States—had a deep spirituality and religious understanding that was very much "in keeping with the true and authentic spirit of the liturgy" (CSL, 26).

> In African religion there is a high God comparable to the Christian concept of a one God. But just as there are many spirits in Christianity, angels and saints, each especially empowered (St. Michael for strength, St. Raphael for healing), so too in the African religions there are spirits for particular aspects of creation.[4]

Devotion to the Blessed Virgin Mary and the saints offered a rich context for syncretism with African understandings of the holy:

> The use of sacramentals (blessed objects), such as statues, pictures, candles, incense, holy water, rosaries, vestments, and relics, in Catholic ritual was more akin to the spirit of African piety than the coarseness of Puritan America—which held such objects to be idolatrous. Holy days, processions, saints' feasts, days of fast and abstinence were all recognizable to the Africans who had observed the sacred days, festivals, and food taboos of his gods.[5]

The religious cultural matrix of African peoples who, upon coming to these shores, were transformed into a new people (African Americans) includes several key concepts:

- "religion is an all-pervasive reality; (Cf. John S. Mbiti, *African Religions and Philosophy* [New York: Praeger, 1970])"

- "a sense of the holy encompasses the whole mystery of life, beginning before birth and continuing after death; (Cf. for example, ibid., pp. 100–162)"

- "to live is to participate in a religious drama; (Cf. ibid., p. 108)" and

- "African people see themselves as totally immersed in a sacred cosmos (Cf. J. S. Mbiti, *Concepts of God in Africa* [New York: Praeger, 1970], pp. 1–154)" (PGR, 47).

What the Africans were not prepared for, within the Catholic church especially, was the denial of the full expression of their new faith in ways indigenous to their culture, with song, dance, extemporaneous prayer, shouts and the attendant celebratory reception of the Spirit within their midst.[6]

Yet, the continued existence of African Americans in the Roman Catholic church is evidence of their having "contextualized their faith—that is, adapted it to their social, cultural and personal situation."[7] Rather than passively accepting the meanings given to them by slave owners or others, they "rechristianized Christianity" for themselves, providing new meanings for the symbols of Christian faith which emerged from their own experience of their humanity and their own encounter with God. What they did was also done and is being done today by Native Americans, Hispanic Americans and others. Again, what they have done is not new but is a response to a people's encounter with Christ that dates back to Christianity's very beginnings.

New Beginnings

Today, we must begin anew—retrieving what was good, rejecting what was not, which is not an easy task at any time but especially today when changes are taking place oftentimes too quickly for many.

In truth, I see that God shows no partiality. Rather, in every nation whoever fears him and acts uprightly is acceptable (see Acts 10:34–35). These words of Peter, written almost 2000 years ago, still ring true for us as the people of God today. For we are, I believe, on

Diana L. Hayes

the threshold of a new beginning, one that we are coming to realize, however, is in actuality not so new after all, but is both a return to and a continuation of the journeying in faith of those who have come before us and who will follow after us.

Indeed, as church we have changed especially in the last 25 years and are continuing to change. Words and actions, signs and symbols, music and celebration, histories and cultures once looked at askance, thought to be unsuitable, incapable of bearing the weight of the gospel, have processed down the main aisle of our churches and cathedrals, bringing with them new rhythms, new songs, new visions, new signs, new symbols of what it means to be church throughout. The Catholic church is truly becoming, at least in content if not yet fully in style or form, the universal church it has always claimed to be. In dioceses and parishes large and small, both in the United States and around the world, we have begun the process of returning to the place where first we started from and truly recognizing it for the first time.

The liturgical renewal that came about in this century and was brought to fruition at the Second Vatican Council is one from which there can be no turning back, for it has recalled us to the purpose and meaning of liturgical celebration as a church catholic. As the Sacred Constitution on the Liturgy notes:

> Liturgical services are not private functions, but are celebrations belonging to the church, which is the "sacrament of unity," namely the holy people united and ordered. (26)

In other words, no individual group or people owns the Mass but each one of us has co-ownership through our baptism in the celebration of the sacred eucharist and can rightly expect to be able to so celebrate it in a manner and style which is a part of who and whose we are, people of every race and nation within this one nation who believe in the resurrected Christ. It is only today, almost 25 years later, that the fullness of understanding and implementation of this renewal is beginning to take place. It is happening because further changes are taking place in our nation and, therefore, in our church which is reflective of that nation. These changes make it incumbent upon us to look with newly opened eyes at the emergence of voices and visions that are calling for the inculturation of the church's rites and rituals into the cultures of people heretofore voiceless and invisible in our land.

The Changing Face of Church and Nation

Many Catholics are already aware of these shifts to a certain extent but perhaps have not fully thought out their implications for all of us as a church. The 1990 census has revealed that major changes are taking place across the nation and within our dioceses and parishes.

Nationally, the face of the nation is changing:

> Already 1 American in 4 defines himself or herself as Hispanic or nonwhite. If current trends in immigration and birth rates persist, the Hispanic population will have further increased an estimated 21%, the Asian presence about 22%, blacks almost 12% and whites a little more than 2% when the 20th century ends. By 2020 . . . the number of U.S. residents who are Hispanic or nonwhite will have more than doubled, to nearly 115 million, while the white population will not be increasing at all. By 2056 . . . the "average" U.S. resident will trace his or her descent to Africa, Asia, the Hispanic world, the Pacific Islands, Arabia — almost anywhere but white Europe.[8]

For some, these statistics may be rather startling but at the same time they are a reality nearing fulfillment especially within the Catholic church in the United States, for many of those people of color who will reach maturity in the twenty-first century will be Catholic. Whether immigrant or first-, second- or third-generation, whether of Hispanic, African or Asian ancestry, many of the new and challenging voices being raised in our church today are the voices of Roman Catholics who are calling upon the church not simply to recognize their presence but to recognize the validity and legitimacy of their unique, valuable and much needed contributions to the catholicity of our church.

But let us look beyond the statistics. They're fine in their place but they are only numbers, which can be used in many different ways to support or deny particular theories, particular ideas. Statistics don't reveal the human face of those whom they represent; they don't reveal

Diana L. Hayes

whether or how those different peoples who are in our schools, not just in the inner cities but in the suburbs; who are moving from urban to suburban parishes; who are calling for a home in a church in which they have lived as "visitors" for too long a time are being welcomed and received.

Where are the people behind these numbers? What are their dreams, their desires, their hurts, their pains? How can we, as church, as the people of God in all of its forms, help them to become vibrant and valued members of the body of Christ with their gifts welcomed and the changes they inevitably bring joyfully rather than grudgingly received?

We must go beyond the numbers to see what they really symbolize. For they too are more than just signs, they are symbols which reveal more than they seem, which are mysterious, puzzling treasures to be unwrapped, explored and hopefully enjoyed by all. The numbers in themselves are insignificant; the question is how do we — whether as teachers, DREs, members of pastoral teams, vocation directors, social justice groups, clergy — build community? How do we welcome people of color into parishes that are predominantly white and vice versa? How do we overcome our own fear of change and our prejudices, whether conscious or not, against those who are different from us so that we can come together to break bread as a truly eucharistic community? How do we welcome older ethnic working-class Catholics into transformed black or Hispanic parishes that are younger and middle-class? How do we build bridges that link us rather than barriers that limit us?

These old but, to many, seemingly new Catholics (blacks, Hispanics, Asians) bring gifts of joyful celebration, of holistic gatherings, of welcoming communion, of a deep and abiding spirituality which have enabled them to get through the "rough places and the straight." They bring a challenge for they are the ones that knock on the door at midnight saying: "I am here; I cannot be turned away; I will not be turned away. Feed me, nourish me with the body and blood of Christ and realize that I do not come empty-handed, a clean slate to be written on by others but come with hopes and fears of my own that need to be shared, that need to be lifted up, that need to be blessed by the church as true and authentic ways of being Catholic." For if we don't do this, if we repeat the mistakes of the 1860s, when the Baltimore Plenary Council voted against a special evangelizing effort among the freed slaves; and of the 1960s when we too often forcibly integrated schools and parishes by closing and tearing down those of blacks and other non-Europeans, requiring them to enter schools and churches where for years they had been barred, which led many to abandon their faith.

If we continue to require that they become aliens in their own cultures, within their own families, in order to become priests and religious, we will destroy those whom we should be aiding. We will become once again churches "full of sound and fury signifying nothing"; we will become symbols empty of meaning and signs that are completely ignored.

This is the task and the challenge for all of us today as church, to "tend to the spiritual and temporal needs" of our neighbor; to see ourselves as "called and consecrated" to mission among all persons but especially those who are poor, marginalized, voiceless and invisible.

As church, we have recognized in our studies and workshops, sadly, that racism still persists, both in our nation and our nation's churches—but we also affirm that justice is a constitutive element of the gospel message. We have affirmed that our efforts toward unity rest on reconciliation, a reconciliation which requires that we become both giver and receiver, persons in need of being evangelized, even as we ourselves are being evangelized. It is long past time that we act upon these affirmations and beliefs.

This is so very important for peoples who have been the unequal and unwanted receivers in our church for too long a time, never permitted to set forth their own rich and unique gifts on the altar but having constantly to accept what, too often, they did not need or want, while having their own contributions rejected or seen as inappropriate and unsuitable.

It is for this and other closely related reasons that Hispanic and African American Catholics are abandoning the church in which they were born but have had to live restricted lives, for other Christian churches and other faiths where they feel more at home and more welcomed, where they have leadership roles and responsibilities that are meaningful and where, most importantly, they do not feel as if

Diana L. Hayes

they are in a strange land singing songs foreign to them, celebrating rites and rituals that have no meaning for them because they have not become incarnate in their midst.

This is also why we are losing too many of our youth of every race and ethnicity to the streets and secular associations where they too feel free to express themselves, unrestricted by rules and regulations forced upon them without explanation or opportunity for understanding.

And here we women must also speak of our own failures as women to recognize the gifts of other women, simply because of their ethnicity, race or class. In seeking to respond creatively to the developing needs of people, to see what miseries exist and how we might address them ourselves or remedy them in collaboration with others, we, as women of the church, must recognize not only the patriarchal church's sins of racism, sexism and classism but the sin of racism that has existed in our religious orders as well as in our seminaries and chanceries.

Those who have historically but incorrectly seen themselves as the personification of the Catholic church must not, however, be shut out or ignored, for that would be to repeat the mistakes of the past. They too have gifts which have been nurtured and sustained over the years of their presence in this land as well. We can, indeed we must all learn from and of each other, the old sharing with the young, the married with the unmarried, the men with the women, to overcome the sickness that plagues our nation and world today with its emphasis on cheap gratification and disposable cultures and people, especially the unborn, the poor, the crippled and the old.

We can do this; we must do this but only if we are willing to put a human face on the other, to name people rather than seeing them as faceless threats to our positions and authority. We must recognize and, hopefully, welcome the changing face of the church, globally, nationally and locally. Catholics of all races and ethnicities must be introduced to other ways of being church, ways that may be different, yes, but ways that are also truly and authentically Catholic.

We must learn new ways of celebration, new ways of worship, new ways of praying, new ways of being church, new yet in reality ancient ways of being Catholic while, at the same time, retaining what is beautiful, just and right in our present liturgies, in our parishes, in our religious congregations and seminaries and in our dioceses as they are presently constituted.

In other words, I am not calling for a complete upheaval, the throwing out of the old and its replacement with everything new, but for a meshing of visions and ways of being church, a true discernment of the movement of the Holy Spirit in our midst which will enable us to forge local churches that are viable vehicles of faith for the future, where liturgies are celebrated not in competition or opposition to each other—9 AM in Spanish, 11 AM in the gospel tradition, 2 PM in the "traditional" format—but liturgies that build community, that serve as the foundation for vibrant parishes where the people, regardless of race, ethnicity or gender are alive with the Holy Spirit and worship "in Spirit and in truth" in community and unity with each other. For it must be repeated that it is through our liturgical celebrations that this unified community can and should be expressed and celebrated.

Repeating the statement quoted at the beginning of this article:

> Liturgy celebrates and evokes the divine reality that is at once remote and intimate, transcendent and immanent, beyond our reach and ever present. . . . Liturgy evokes a world that is at once shared with others and is at the same time beyond ordinary life. (PGR, 2)

It is through symbols which point beyond themselves and signs that we celebrate the mystery of the eucharistic feast.

Worship lifts people up and moves them into the soul-stirring, the awe-inspiring, the transcendent and the inciting so that, ultimately, they may worship in spirit and truth (John 4:24), so that they may not honor Christ in worship clothed in silk vestments, only to pass him by unclothed and frozen outside.

Our celebration must extend beyond the sanctuary to the streets, offices and business centers, the shelters and schools, both Catholic and public, where our people work and live. We must once come together in solidarity for the good of all, reclaiming the positive aspects of ghetto Catholicism, for example, while taking it to newer heights. We have to come out from behind our walls and fences, cross over into neighborhoods unlike our own, challenge ourselves and those around us and revive the soul of our church once again. Take risks!

As the faithful change, so must our understanding of the church, its ritual, vowed life and community life, change, recognizing that we will be participants through our lived out inculturations of our faith, in a new creation. This "new creation" must today be one that arises from Christianity's encounter, not just with the culture and traditions of European-Americans but with that of African, Native, Hispanic and Asian Americans as well:

> Through Christ, the non-repeatable historical event becomes actual and Christ continues to be actively present in the world. The extent of the church's incarnation in various roles and cultures will be the extent of Christ's universality. The Incarnation is a historical event, but its universality lives on wherever the church assumes the social and cultural conditions of the people among whom she dwells. . . . The church must incarnate herself in every race, as Christ has incarnated himself in the Jewish race.[9]

As this is true for African American Catholics, so it is for other Catholics who seek to sing the Lord's song in their own language, using signs and symbols rich with meaning for them albeit new and perhaps at first strange to us. In concrete terms, this means teaching each other the words to our songs, building church together wherever we are gathered, in large numbers or small, learning each other's recipes, sharing in each other's festivals, growing with each other in each and every way.

The Future of Catholic Liturgy

As we look ahead to the future, what can we, what should we expect? There is an ancient Chinese curse that says: "May you live in interesting times." I believe that we are today living in such a time, a time of seeming turmoil and upheaval, chaos and disarray but also a time in which the Holy Spirit is surely moving across the land gracing us with the sweet and reviving breath of God. It is a time of *kairos,* God's own time, when new opportunities are being opened to us, new challenges being set before us. We can look straight ahead, with our eyes and hearts set on the road to heaven, ignoring these challenges because they come from places and peoples we don't or won't recognize and thereby continue our fall into sin, or we can take up the challenge, God's challenge, to truly love God and our neighbor as ourselves, seeking the union of ourselves and all people with God and one another by opening our hearts and minds to the many changes that are taking place in our nation and our church today.

We can cry out against innovation, adaptation, inculturation, opting for the status quo and holding fast to stereotypes and prejudices and watch our church slowly die the death of an institution starved of the life-giving spirit of innovation, of exploration, of expansion, that spirit which has kept it alive for almost 2000 years, or we can throw open our doors to the new and challenging voices and visions of church which are already in our midst and are persistent in their cries for life, recognizing that all of us image God in God's infinite diversity. We can fall into a state of death, a *rigor mortis* once again, from which we may never emerge and watch as our young people of all races and ethnicities flee from us and turn to other more prophetic voices or turn away from God completely, or we can confuse the minds of the nay-sayers and confound those weak in faith by being a church renewed by the life-giving transfusion of faith's lifeblood that is richly diverse and healing.

As we continue in our journeying in our parishes and dioceses, we must persist in opening ourselves to the healing and transforming grace of God, allowing that grace to enable us to recognize God's image reflected in all the colors of the rainbow, in men and women, girls and boys, poor and well-off, in all walks of life. For male and female God created us, in God's own image and likeness have we been molded. That is the greatness and the mystery of God.

May we be blessed with the ability to discern the Spirit of God as a living flame in the hearts of all humankind, recognizing and accepting that, as God's creation, we are finally all one body in Jesus Christ.

Diana L. Hayes

1. Ann Wroe, *The Tablet* (October 30, 1993).

2. Rosemary Radford Ruether, *To Change the World: Christology and Cultural Pluralism* (New York: Crossroad, 1981), page 39; also see Diana L. Hayes, "Emerging Voices, Emerging Challenges: An American Contextual Theology" in David Schultenover, ed. *Theology for the Third Millenium* (Lewiston, NY: Mellen Press, 1991).

3. See Anscar Chapungco, *Liturgies of the Future: The Process and Methods of Inculturation* (Mahwah, NJ: Paulist, 1989).

4. Clarence Rivers, *The Spirit in Worship* (Cincinnati: Stimuli, Inc., 1978), 4.

5. Albert J. Raboteau, *Slave Religion: The "Invisible" Institution in the Antebellum South* (New York: Oxford, 1978), 4.

6. Although within most Protestant churches, especially the Methodist and Baptist churches, the celebratory was not an issue, the lack of ceremony and austerity of or lack of forms of ritual celebration was often a problem for African converts accustomed, as noted, to elaborate ritual and ceremony in their traditional religions.

7. Preston Williams, "Contextualizing the Faith: The African American Tradition and Martin Luther King, Jr.," in Roy O. Costa, ed., *One Faith, Many Cultures: Inculturation, Indigenization, and Contextualization* (Maryknoll, NY: Orbis Books, 1988), 130.

8. William Henry, "Beyond the Melting Pot," *Time* (April 9, 1990), 28.

9. Anscar Chapungco, *Cultural Adaptation of the Liturgy* (Mahwah, NJ: Paulist Press, 1982), 59.

Theresa F. Koernke, IHM

A Generation after the Council: What is the Spirit Telling Us?

The liturgies of the sacraments, especially the eucharist, are the lightning rods for every issue of consequence in the life of the church. For this reason our attention to our worship raises key issues of ecclesiology and theology. In this essay we will consider seven areas in which liturgy and theology are closely connected: theology and behavior in the liturgy; the correlation between our experience and our worship; the origin of the church; leadership; ritual behavior; the eucharist; and the relationship of the Catholic church and other Christian churches.

Liturgical Practice and Liturgical Theology

We know from our history that attitudes shape liturgical behavior and that liturgical behavior, in turn, shapes attitudes and expectations on our part about the meaning of the liturgy. Hence, how can we appreciate our concerns and questions? For example: How can it be that persons of good will can have such different perceptions of liturgical practice and devotional practice?

Theresa F. Koernke, IHM

Hans Georg Gadamer — and Cardinal Newman and others before him — spoke of subjective expectations. And so, we may ask: How have our *subjective expectations* about the meaning and practice of our public worship been shaped? For example: How have our expectations about who does what, about our bodily actions (kneeling, standing and the like), about worship space and so on, been shaped? Why has anyone ever asked, "What is the most important point at Mass"? How did the practice of exposing the reserved sacrament come to be? Why would anyone have ever thought that praying the devotion of the rosary during Mass was a good thing? Why has there been such discussion about the placing of the tabernacle in our churches? Each of these concerns is an expression of "subjective expectations" about the significance of the liturgy.

The Correlation between Experience and Liturgy

Throughout history, persons have engaged in the process of correlation when faced with new challenges regarding practice. The process of correlation (a) raises the issue or concern and regards the culture out of which the question arises; (b) searches the lived experience of Christians in the history of the church for clues about how the issue was handled if it has arisen in the past; and (c) evaluates the past as well as the current question according to the best means of interpretation available. For, quite simply, it may be that either the past practice and theology or the current question may be skewed. Perhaps both may be skewed.

For example: The desire for lengthy exposition of the blessed sacrament, when examined in the light of the unfortunate reasons for the development of the practice in the past, may well indicate that the desire for retrieval of the practice in the present needs serious critique. Might it be that valid devotional expectations are misplaced?

The Origin of the Church

Throughout history, Christians must see their life and ministry in relation to that of Jesus the Christ. That is: How is what we do today an expression of the life and ministry of Jesus the Christ? Hence, whatever one thinks constituted the origin of the church will determine what one thinks about dealing with all other issues. It's that simple.

For centuries, and because of the influence of neo-Platonic philosophy and a pyramidal image of reality, the church imagined that those at the top of the pyramid on earth were directly related to twelve men whom they thought Jesus had directly chosen and ordained, to whom he gave seven rites and on whom he sent the Spirit. This model of the origin of the church presumed that all grace was channeled solely through these persons and those whom they would ordain.

This model of the church appears to have worked for a long time. Entire lives have been given to sustaining this model. However, with the rise of both the biblical and liturgical movements, historical-critical study of the texts of the scriptures and church documents enables us to see that the pyramidal model is not consistent with the origin of the church. So we are in the position to engage in the process of correlation. We need, by means of the best scholarship available to us, to evaluate critically this notion of the origin of the church (really a sixth-century construct), as well as to evaluate current desire to perpetuate that model in our practice. Clearly, there is a tension between this model and the image of the origin of the church available to us today.

Today, we would do better to understand the origin of the church in this way: The Spirit—by whom the Word of God was knit to human flesh and the matter of the universe in the womb of Mary, and who enabled Jesus to live his life and offer his life back to God on the cross—is the same Spirit that Jesus bestowed upon all the disciples. In this way, the Spirit bestowed by Jesus draws the church into being and creates an unbreakable unity between the members of the church, among all of the members to Jesus, and through, with and in Jesus the risen Christ, to God. This same Spirit is continually bestowed upon those who are initiated into the church, and the church then is the instrument by which we share in the mission of Christ to proclaim mercy and peace to all creation.

The eucharistic prayer proclaims that the church lives in the self-offering (sacrifice) of Christ for the peace and salvation of all the world. The church is a communion of persons, each called to live out the mission of Christ.

Modes of Leadership

The early absorption of the patriarchal social structures of the neo-Platonic (and later Aristotelian) philosophy into church practice and theology would lead to the unfortunate sense that the only kind of leadership in the church was that of male ordained ministers. For centuries, that social construction of reality supported monarchy in societies and monarchy in the church. For increasing numbers of historically conscious persons today, that patriarchal social system is recognized as no longer capable of making sense of human experience. Indeed, throughout the world since the eighteenth century, monarchies have given way to various forms of social democratization, or social processes that take the experience of all the persons involved in a social group into account in governance.

Today, we can see that a monarchical social structure was rather uncritically absorbed by Christians. So, while the earliest documents in the New Testament scriptures suggest acknowledgement of the radical equality of females and males, we now see that later scriptures—such as the pastoral epistles and the Letter to the Ephesians—demonstrate the fact that the church engaged in an unfortunate form of inculturation and allowed itself to be tamed by patriarchal social structures. We may ask: Is the Christian church so tied to the patriarchal social construction of reality that the faith can only be lived according to a patriarchal mode of governance? Is the Christ event, while surely to be lived in historical social structures, contrary to a mode of governance that regards the full humanity of both women and men? Why is the maleness of Jesus made more significant for his identity than his Jewishness or his age? Granting that every explanation of social structures has a bias, who stands to gain from recognizing that the risen Christ is bound to both males and females by the power of the Spirit? And who stands to lose if both women and men are recognized as competent to image the risen Christ in our public worship?

Given the retrieval of the origin of the church as the continuation of the bestowal of the Spirit by Jesus from God, ordained leadership continues to be essential to the ongoing life of the church for a healthy life and ministry. Indeed, there are various kinds of leadership within the church. While ordained ministers have the responsibility to convene the assembly for its public worship through the chief rites of the church, the Spirit also raises up leaders of other kinds. This will continue to be a key issue in correlating our theology and practice.

Ritual Behavior

Ritual behavior is repetitive, interpersonal and value-laden. That is, what a social group does over and over again, and in relation to each other, carries the values of that group and in turn reinforces those values. There are any number of these kinds of behaviors that come and go in the history of a group. We might think of such things as various devotional practices. While devotional practices are important means of expressing religious sentiment and, if they are not contrary to the faith of the church, are good, some of them could pass out of practice and not endanger the well-being of the church. On the other hand, there are other corporate ritual behaviors that, if they were not done, would jeopardize the very health and existence of the church. These latter are the chief rites of the church that we call sacraments.

Because these kinds of ritual behaviors are essential to the very existence of a social religious group, every world religion intuits the need to depute specified persons to convene the group for their celebration. Hence, the church has called forth persons whose lives are outstanding models of living in Christ to convene the church for the celebration of the liturgies of the sacraments. While others may be deputed to witness marriages, and in case of emergency to baptize, the meaning of the eucharist is so intimately tied to the universal existence of the church that persons are deputed on a stable basis to convene the church for its celebration.

Again, because of the absorption of the patriarchal social system into which the church was born and because of the uncritical absorption of that social system, it has been assumed that only males may represent Christ the Head of the church in the celebration of the eucharist. However, if one takes seriously the meaning of the resurrection of Jesus the Christ as now intimately united to all the members of the body of Christ, the church, then we can understand the current questions that are put to the centuries-long exclusion of women from the call to the orders of bishop and presbyter. For if it is true that corporate ritual behavior expresses and, in turn, reinforces values, then male-only colleges of bishop and presbyters may well be seen as reasserting a value that is inconsistent with the natural resemblance of Christ in the time of the church: male and female. And here is the crux of the tension: The patriarchal construction of reality which is, for the most part, operative in pastoral-theological papal and curial statements cannot imagine the ecclesiology of communion described above.

The Full Celebration of the Eucharist

It is our conviction in faith that, by the power of the Spirit, it is Christ who draws us into his saving self-offering on the cross to the glory of God in initiation. This renewed awareness about the meaning and consequences of initiation leads us to question long-standing attitudes and practices about participation in the celebration of the eucharist.

If for centuries all theological explanation and catechesis focused upon the action of the ordained minister and on what happened to bread and wine, then it is understandable that the re-appropriation of a communal ecclesiology into our celebration of the eucharist would create tensions and a certain degree of trial and error. For we cannot underestimate the influence of the former theological and practical over-emphases on the actions of the priest and on the bread and cup

What is the Spirit Telling Us?

in our current struggles to make sense of "full, conscious, and active participation" in the liturgy. This is so either for those who would preserve the liturgy of Trent or for those who presume to be promoting the liturgical renewal encouraged by the Second Vatican Council. Presuming that all are persons of good will, what insights might we gain from a civil exchange of ideas?

Contemporary retrieval of the origin of the full celebration of the eucharist as a celebration of the risen Christ among us for our consolation and judgement certainly asserts the fact that the primary mode of participation in the liturgy is the presence of the assembly, the corporate body of Christ in history. Thus, we hold that the Spirit who gave rise to the scriptures enables us to hear the word of God today, indeed, to hear the risen Christ speak to his body, interpreting our corporate lives to us. It is Christ who tells us who we are and who, in the light of the cross, gives meaning to every joy and sorrow of our lives. And in the eucharistic prayer, the ordained minister addresses God—through, with and in Christ by the power of the Spirit—in the name of the assembly.

Further, in retrieving our current understanding of what Jesus did at a ritual meal sometime near his death, it becomes unnervingly clear that the body to which he referred is the new corporate body brought into existence by his life, death and resurrection. To eat this body is to eat the church, to take into oneself those to whom one belongs. And to drink the blood of the new covenant is to re-give ourselves to Jesus' response to God into which we have been baptized. We are not denying the reception of the body and blood of Christ; we are retrieving the fact that, in the time of the church, the body of Christ is both head and members, and to drink the cup of blood is a profound metaphor for saying that our identity as church is configured to Christ in the act of redeeming the world. And so, if we hold this to be true, then we can say that we live in the justice of God and are bound by the ethical demands of that relationship.

From this perspective, doing what is right is not simply a consequence of receiving communion; the very celebration of the eucharist is an expression of doing what is right for the sake of renewing our resolve to do what is right beyond the celebration. We can no longer regard the sacrament received at Mass, or the reserved sacrament, as an object that we get for pure private devotion, although devotion it demands. The tabernacle ought not be the center of focus upon entering a house of the assembly, but the assembly ought be recognized as the reality of which the sacrament is sacrament: Christ and his members. This perspective does not necessarily preclude prayer in the presence of the sacrament, nor of the exposition of the sacrament. It does question the assumption that lengthy periods of exposition are to be preferred over the vigorous Sunday celebration.

Ecumenism

As the Vatican Council II document *Lumen Gentium* asserts, the one church of Christ subsists in the Catholic church . . . and elements of the church exist beyond the visible boundaries of the Catholic church. The elements that we hold to be essential to what makes the church what it is are the preaching of the faith expressed in the scriptures, the celebration of the sacraments, especially the eucharist, and stable ordained leadership.

Historical studies have enabled us to see again the common origin of all Christians and to note similarities in attitude and practice. We have been encouraged to take opportunities to pray together according to forms of prayer that are common such as the Liturgy of the Hours and scripture services. And yet, in our desire to overcome the painful separation among us, it is important that we respect, first, that there continue to be serious dogmatic differences among us—about the value of creation, for example, about the value of human nature and the role of the humanity of Jesus in salvation; and, second, that we are members of a corporate reality. It is easy to have remarked the many similarities between various Christian groups. Yet, is it possible that at least one reason for the apparent lessening in ecumenical activity is the discomfort we might experience in facing the responsibility of saying that the Catholic/Orthodox tradition has not always behaved as if it is the repository of the preaching of the Word, the celebration of the sacraments, and that its stable ordained leadership has not always served the good of the whole church? Our personal and corporate holiness falls short of the treasure we offer to the world.

Clearly, then, as individuals we have the physical ability of engaging in table fellowship in one of the reformation churches or other Christian gatherings. And yet, if half of all Catholics and Protestants were to partake of communion in each other's assemblies on a given Sunday, that fact would not bring about the union of the churches, would not restore the visible unity of the one church of Christ. Ecumenical effort does not deny serious theological and pastoral differences; it does call for the willingness to critique whatever, in any Christian group, is inconsistent with the gospel according to our best lights. In this way, we may no longer honestly speak of Christian groups "coming back" to the church of Rome. Rather, we would best speak of all of us examining our corporate conscience to remove those obstacles that inhibit the healing of the one church of Christ around the bishop of Rome.

Conclusion

Given the social function of religious ritual, we ought not be surprised by the goals yet to reach, for in the assembly of the church the presumed meaning of life is proclaimed, a matter of no mean significance for human experience. Granting that this side of the *parousia* the church will never get things completely straight, it remains a sacred challenge to be sure that what we do over and over again, and in relation to each other, bespeaks justice in the church for the sake of humbly proclaiming to the world that right relationship to God in which we live and move and have our being: Christ crucified and risen to the glory of God by the fire of the Spirit.

Carolyn Osiek, RSCJ

Discipleship, Equality and the Bible

We are on a journey toward the creation of a church that is yet to be, whose face we can only glimpse now. How has the face of the church changed with regard to a new vision of discipleship and equality, and where might we be going with this challenge? Does the Bible play any role or have anything to say about this quest?

Equality

First, the bad news, the interpretive difficulty. There is a popular assumption that a few biblical texts and the example of Jesus presume *in their historical context* that the authors or Jesus himself believed in an essential human equality *as we understand it today*, that is, an equality that must flow into equal access and equal treatment on all sides, a full social equality. We have learned the lesson that "separate but equal" does not work—for us. Cross-cultural social analysis suggests that this is not the way the people of the New Testament world thought, however. They saw society in terms of right relationships across social boundaries, so that everyone was treated with appropriate dignity, which is not the same as equality. This brings us immediately to a fundamental point of biblical interpretation: Fidelity to the Bible does not mean attempting to go back into the mentality of its authors, playing what Krister Stendahl calls "first-century Bible land," but doing what its authors did: making the best use of the means at our disposal to incarnate the saving presence of God in our own world. Therefore I would argue that striving for the vision of equality as we attempt to do today is in fact the best way to be faithful to what our ancestors in the faith intended in their own day.

The understanding of human equality that we try to live — usually without success — has been very slow to develop. Even the American founding fathers, in asserting that "all men are created equal," of course meant that more literally and more restrictively than we imagine: They were talking about themselves against their English overlords, and they did not intend to include either men of lesser status or any women in their vision of equality.

Yet the beginnings of the vision were there. Our understanding of equality is based on the philosophical foundations of the Western Enlightenment that were not present in the philosophy or culture of the ancient Mediterranean world. All the same, there are some remarkable discussions preserved from that world in which philosophers and others take up questions like the same education in philosophy for both sexes based on the same capacity for virtue, or equal consideration with regard to sexual fidelity in marriage. As we shall see, Paul, so often accused of misogynism, is among the best on this account. The ancient way of thinking about human society was not in terms of equal treatment but of right relationship. Ancient writers took their cue from contemporary philosophy and experience, just as we do.

The saying is attributed to Teilhard de Chardin that once a truth is seen, it cannot be taken back and must inevitably work itself out. That is probably true, but this does not mean that this truth cannot have a tortuous route on which it takes a very long time to arrive. There is no guarantee that truth will progress quickly while its real implications are being worked out. Perhaps the test of authentic insight into truth is the degree of resistance encountered in its implementation.

Carolyn Osiek, RSCJ

Christians yearning for equality and justice have rightly centered on Paul's prophetic text in Galatians 3:28: "There is no Jew or Greek, slave or free, male and female, but all are one in Christ Jesus." As Mary Daly wisely remarked many years ago: "In Christ there is no male and female. The trouble is, everywhere else there is." There is still Christian anti-Semitism, and more widely, racism and classism. Our own century has been the worst yet with regard to racism, so we can hardly claim to have overcome the division between Jew and Gentile in the church.

It took many centuries for the early church to renounce and outlaw slavery, that is, for Christians finally to accept the truth of its evil. As late as the sixth century of the Christian era, there is evidence of ownership of slaves not only by Christians but by church officials. Then with the discovery of the New World and convenient doubts raised about the humanity of its inhabitants and those of sub-Saharan Africa, slavery and racism combined to create in the seventeenth through nineteenth centuries three of the five true slave societies of world history in Brazil, the Caribbean and North America, the other two being classical Greece and early imperial Rome, in which the New Testament was born. So the phrase "no slave or free" has been very recently in process, too.

If we look with the eyes of history, it should come as no surprise then that the equality of women and men has not been exactly the most pressing issue in the church, nor is it the only equality or justice issue. Yet a society's treatment of women is always the last frontier. Beyond racial and class tensions, the relationship of women and men is at stake not only in city and neighborhood, but in family and bedroom, and it is axiomatic that the way a society treats its women is the litmus test of how it looks on the value of the human person.

Our contemporary Catholic understanding of church is based on the creative interpretation of scripture through the lens of tradition. The scriptures are the font and source of inspiration to which we return for nourishment and new insight in every age. Yet they are always to be interpreted by the living community that has formed its tradition over the centuries, an organic composite of the lived experience of faith. But of course, scripture was not written in an experiential vacuum. At a certain early point in the history of the faith community, these writings were executed to express and preserve the faith already being lived. The scriptures are thus part of the flow of tradition. They set standards and ideals, but they do not impose limits. That is the difference from biblical fundamentalism, which sees in the Bible the outside norm for Christian life, the limit beyond which the theological imagination should not go. This imposition of biblical limits only creates boundaries and reinforces divisions.

The Catholic starting point for change, as I understand it, is the conviction—in the light of biblical revelation, tradition and reason— that what is true and what is right ought to be lived. The process is therefore highly contextual. A first-century Christian would give different answers to the same questions about this process, yet with the same set of fundamental values incorporated into the answer: the central importance of the person in the community of Jesus Christ before God. In some contexts, including the first-century one, the order may be reversed: the central importance of God, acclaimed by the community of Jesus Christ, in which every person participates.

Individual in Community

The position of individual persons in society is a linchpin in any social system and the cause of endless debates and headaches in any legal system. In the United States, we live in the most individualist society the world has ever known, in which the development of the individual and the rights of the individual are stretched to capacity—some would say too far. It was very different in the ancient Mediterranean world that produced the New Testament. There the only approximate notion of social equality as we understand it was among freeborn males of the same social class and status. There was no *social* equality between men and women, even though some philosophers proposed a metaphysical equality, and the good of society or its smaller unit, the family, was paramount, not the rights of the individual.

Yet something different was happening in that ancient world, not only among Christians but before them among Jews and participants in many of the unofficial popular religions that we now call

Carolyn Osiek, RSCJ

"mystery religions." In this highly patriarchal society, political philosophy since Aristotle affirmed that the household is the microcosm of the state: As goes the (elite) household, so goes the state. If the household is not well ordered, neither will the state be.

Well ordered here means patriarchally ordered, in spite of some interesting evidence of households run by women (to be taken up later). We know next to nothing about how that worked precisely because it was not the conceptual norm, and so was never discussed, but we have some of the best evidence for households run by women in the New Testament. This political ideal of the household as microcosm of the state is echoed in 1 Timothy 3:4–5: One who aspires to be *episkopos* must show that he runs a good household. If he can't manage a household, how will he manage the church? The church is now modeled on the household, which means that it is seen, even in this small uninfluential group called Christians, as the microcosm of the state. Christian political theology has been born.

The religious norm is that the male head of the household dictated even which gods were to be worshiped by the family and when. Plutarch, for example, advises that a new bride should forsake her family and personal gods and worship only those of her husband, so that she would be well incorporated into the family religion of her husband. Above all she should avoid any religious activity conducted by women, which is never approved of by any god![1] This is part of what anthropologists refer to as the way in which women are "embedded" in men in such a culture. Women function as appendages of male honor and strategies, and can be used to further those ends.

The unusual thing that was happening, however, among Jews, Christians and the other forms of popular religion was that these groups were admitting free women and slaves into membership independently of their patriarchal head. The reverse was also happening: Male heads of households joined the church while their wives and slaves did not. Christians were doing this very early in more romanized settings like the Roman merchant colony of Corinth: "If any brother has an unbelieving wife and she agrees to live with him, he should not divorce her. And if any woman has an unbelieving husband and he agrees to live with her, she should not divorce the husband" (1 Corinthians 7:12–13). This passage is familiar from discussions about

Discipleship, Equality and the Bible

divorce in the early church, and it follows Roman law in which women as well as men could initiate divorce. But the passage carries other information that is seldom observed: It assumes separate decisions about religious affiliation on the part of both husband and wife. It means that the Corinthian Pauline church was taking the new way, rather than the traditional patriarchal way, of treating persons as capable of making their own religious decisions.

The same is seen in 1 Peter 3:1–2: "Wives, be subject to your own husbands, so that if some are not believers in the word, they may be won over without words by the conduct of their wives." (I will return to the submission theme later, but note that here it is a missionary strategy.) In subsequent centuries, we get the same picture. For instance, Tertullian in Carthage at the turn of the third century wrote a treatise *To His Wife* to urge Christian women to marry Christian men. He details what their lives will be like if they do not. Their husbands will constantly attempt to thwart their fasting, praying at home, going to all-night vigils in church and visiting the sick.[2] Hippolytus' rules for baptism, written at Rome around the same time, specify that a slave who seeks baptism must have his or her Christian owner's testimony of good conduct, but if the owner is an unbeliever, the slave must be taught to please his or her owner so as to avoid scandal.[3] In all of these instances, we can read between the lines that both wives and slaves were making their own decisions about religion.

This granting of personhood to subordinate members of households was not unique to Christians, but it was characteristic of them, and stood in marked contrast to traditional political ideology. Actually, this granting of personhood is continued in the infamous "household codes" in which wives, children and slaves are admonished to submit to a male authority. While such submission sounds unacceptable today, let us hear these texts as they may have been heard in the first centuries of the church.

The origin of these ideas is in the Aristotelian and later discussions of household management.[4] The usual form of discussion is that the patriarchal head is instructed about his role and about how the others subject to him are to respect and obey him. All discussion is addressed to him. Of the three categories, wives, children and slaves, we tend to dismiss the third because, fortunately, legal slavery has

Carolyn Osiek, RSCJ

been eliminated in Western society and we would rather forget about it. (It does still exist in many parts of the world, and it could be argued that there are other kinds of slavery still active today in the West through drugs, prostitution and so on.)

With regard to children obeying parents, we think the ordinance still applies. When these passages are read in church, parents cast smug glances at their minor children in the same way that slaveowners probably did to their slaves in the early church, and that sometimes husbands do to wives. What we do not realize is that it is not minor children but adult children who are being addressed here, in a society in which obedience was owed by law to one's father as long as he was alive. Thus the admonition to children to obey their parents is today no longer interpreted the same way either.

The submission of wives to husbands was presumed in the prevalent model of marriage, which was not a romantic choice of two persons for each other, but an arrangement between families for the social advancement of each family and the production of the next generation. At first marriage, the wife was usually younger than the husband, and ideally less "worldly wise" than he, which enhanced her dependence on him.

In the New Testament forms as found in Colossians, Ephesians and 1 Peter, the subordinate groups—wives, children and slaves—are actually addressed, and addressed first: "Wives, be submissive to your husbands; husbands, love your wives; children, obey your parents, parents, do not provoke your children; slaves, obey your owners, owners, do not treat your slaves unjustly" (paraphrase of Colossians 3:18–4:1). This practice stands out as entirely different from its literary contemporaries.

There was a concerted attempt in ancient male ideology to make women socially invisible. Public language reinforced this ideology. In Acts of the Apostles, for instance, most of the public addresses of Peter or Paul begin, *Andres, adelphoi,* "males, brothers." This is not because Luke thought women were not present. He knew they were there in the marketplace, both buying and selling. But public ideology dictated that the public forum was that of men, while the private aspect of family and house was the domain of women. Thus, the presence of women was not to be recognized in public.

Both 1 Corinthians and 1 Timothy pick up this theme and cast the assembly of the church as a public occasion. In First Corinthians, women should keep silent in the assembly and ask questions of their husbands at home, since it is shameful for a woman to speak in the assembly (14:34–35). Though this passage appears in a genuine letter of Paul, there is sufficient reason to suppose that it is an interpolation by another author. Even if it is not, however, it is not counter-revolutionary or excessively repressive, but merely an assertion of a common societal attitude about women's public role. First Timothy too enjoins that women should learn in silence and subjection, and that women should not teach men, which would imply a public setting.

Two thousand years later, it is difficult for us to see that an important step forward was taken in the household codes, where women became socially visible by being addressed, even though subordinate. They have a recognized role to play and a degree of personal dignity not usually granted to them in the public discourse of their culture. The New Testament authors, while keeping the principle of submission, have in fact subverted that submission by personalizing the characters. The relationship is not imposed from a centralized authority figure, but enjoined on persons as persons, so that by their behavior, they must give consent. *To encourage persons to think for themselves and voluntarily cooperate in a system is to undermine the autocratic authority of that system.*

Still more startling in its granting of personhood to women is Paul's discussion of marriage in 1 Corinthians, chapter 7. Here Paul answers questions posed by the Corinthians about several points on this topic: temporary celibacy within marriage for the sake of prayer (1–7); what to do in a mixed marriage when faith is the obstacle (8–16); the relative advantages or disadvantages of being circumcised or in slavery (17–24); the relative value of marriage or celibacy in eschatological perspective (25–35); the difficult passage which may be about a daughter to betroth, a fiancee to marry or a "spiritual marriage" (36–38); and finally, remarriage of widows (39–40).

If we bracket verses 17–24, which are not about male-female relations, only verses 36–38 are androcentric in perspective; that is, the thought is expressed only from the standpoint of the male, who may be a father with a marriageable daughter or a man about to

Carolyn Osiek, RSCJ

enter into betrothal. In every other discussion in this chapter, Paul gives equal weight to both the man's and the woman's situation, and in verses 39–40, which refers only to a female widow, probably because that is the one concrete case of widowhood referred to him by the Corinthians. For instance, in verses 1–7, Paul answers those who advocate sexual continence in marriage that this is only to be done temporarily, because "the wife does not have authority over her own body, but the husband does, and likewise the husband does not have authority over his own body, but the wife does" (verse 4). Such equal attention to women's experience is nearly unheard of in the literature of the time. It is further evidence of the tendency in early Christianity of which I have been speaking, of treating women and men if not equally, then at least in full complementarity.

What effect did this tendency produce in early Christian ministry? A central conviction held sway: that "all are one in Christ Jesus" (Galatians 3:28), that is, as it would have been understood at the time, that all, regardless of sex or rank, have full access to salvation in Christ, not through any powerful human mediation, as the patron-client social system would otherwise have set it up, but directly. This does not mean such access is individualist and isolated, however. Rather, it is embedded in the praxis of the believing community. The whole effort toward the formation of Christian community was and still is based on that central conviction. All Christian life is an attempt to incarnate it. There have been points all along the way when persons in power have tried to abrogate this conviction.

One example of these attempts to undermine that central conviction of enhanced personhood for all occurred already in the Pauline corpus of the New Testament. First Timothy 2:15, after enjoining silence upon a woman who may not teach or have authority over men, concludes that "she will be saved by childbearing, if she remains in faith, love, and holiness with moderation." This is an astounding and retrogressive statement: Women will be saved not by baptism or faith or good works, but by using their reproductive capacity. With all due respect to the joy and dignity of motherhood, this is not how salvation comes about in Christian theology. The allusion is probably to Genesis 3:16, where the first woman is told that part of her punishment for transgression will be pain in childbearing: The cure is where the pain is. For the author of 1 Timothy, biology is destiny, and the implications are devastating.

Of course the Genesis narrative goes on to make two more relevant points. First, part of the woman's punishment is that her husband will dominate her. The subordination of women to men is thus seen not as intended by God but as the effect of sin. Second, there is also a devastating punishment for the man: The ground is cursed and will yield food only with hard labor. For both the man and the woman, mortality is introduced: "From the earth you were taken, and to the earth you will return" (Genesis 3:17–19). But as in 1 Timothy, the curse is not applied evenly in the history of interpretation. As always, it is not the text that is the problem but the interpretation of the text, even when done by another biblical author. The same continues to be true today. It is not the texts that are the problem, but selective interpretation. It is an axiom of modern reading theory and biblical interpretation that the question must always be asked: Who benefits from a particular interpretation?

Ministry Initiatives by Women

In spite of the social embeddedness of women in men in this culture, and in spite of the prevalent ideology that split life into public male and private female domains, the literary remains of the early church give evidence of some surprising initiatives on the part of women. It all begins with the ministry of Jesus. In spite of the likely historicity of the twelve as an identifiable group around Jesus, they are not the only ones in his inner circle. For Mark, for instance, there is a group "with the twelve" who are with Jesus on the inside and who hear his private explanations (4:10). In Mark's narrative of the final supper of Jesus with his disciples, Jesus arrives with the twelve, having already sent two other disciples to prepare the room (Mark 14:13–17). When Jesus has predicted that one present will betray him and they begin to ask, Who?, he answers that it is one of the twelve, a superfluous comment if only the twelve are present (Mark 14:18–20). The Passover meal, which for Mark the supper is, was a family celebration, not one

Carolyn Osiek, RSCJ

for men only. All the disciples of Jesus traveling with him must have been present, and their presence assumed by Mark. Meal customs of the time and place suggest that the women would have been sitting together at another place in the room, while the men reclined closest to Jesus.

At the cross, the believing witnesses are many women who had followed him from Galilee (Mark 14:40–41). Given the principle of the social invisibility of women that precludes mentioning them except under special circumstances, their presence at the cross and later at the tomb stands out as an extraordinary narrative that underlines their importance in the community.

Luke is also explicit about the presence of women among Jesus' disciples along with the twelve. Early in the Galilean ministry, he includes with the twelve "some women who had been healed and exorcised, among them Mary Magdalene, Joanna wife of one of Herod's officials, and Susanna." Elisabeth Moltmann Wendel, in her charming book *The Women around Jesus,* wonders about the mysterious Susanna who never appears again in the gospels, and about Joanna, a married woman moving in the company of someone of whom her husband would surely not have approved![5] These are women who move with a certain independence.

Later, at the cross, all those who knew Jesus, including the women who had come from Galilee, see from afar (Luke 23:49). The women continue to be part of the gathering of disciples after Jesus' death (Acts 1:14) and are therefore assumed to be present at Pentecost (Acts 2:1). Whether or not these passages are historical in their details is not relevant. The point is to show that the authors believed, found credible and wanted to convey that Jesus had a significant group of female disciples.[6]

Women were the social glue of the early church. Second Timothy, whether authentically from Paul or not, evokes the faith of two generations of forebears in recalling the faith not of his grandfather and father but of Timothy's grandmother Lois and mother Eunice (2 Timothy 1:6). The house of Mary, mother of John Mark in Jerusalem, was the natural gathering place of the Jerusalem community in time of crisis; it is there that a large group had assembled when Peter was arrested, and it was there that Peter unthinkingly went when freed (Acts 12:12). This is only one instance in which the New Testament records a "church in her house." Another is that of Nympha in the letter to the Colossians, probably hostess of a house church in nearby Laodicea (Colossians 4:15).

We wish we knew more about such women as heads of households. The literature of the Roman period is almost completely silent on this point because it was against the patriarchal norm. Yet we know that it happened with a certain regularity. What we don't know is just how it worked in a very patriarchal and hierarchical society in which the well-ordered household was the microcosm of the state, or soon in Christian thinking, also of the church (1 Timothy 3:4–5).

When a meal was held in someone's house, the host was the normal "presider," that is, the leader in sharing food and conversation. The texts are silent on how that worked in a woman's household, but the supposition is that she would then be the normal "presider" at any meals, both of the family and when guests were present. This would especially be true when she was socially prominent, and in more Romanized settings, in which the custom of women reclining alongside men at meals instead of sitting next to the dining couch or in a separate place was just coming into vogue in the first century.[7] The issue of presiding is of course loaded with extra meaning for us, for modern reasons that it did not carry in antiquity, at a time when a sacramental, cultic approach to the Christian community meal had not yet taken shape.

The evidence for women in responsible positions of leadership in the New Testament church is clear. The best example is Phoebe, patron and deacon of the church of Cenchrae, one of the seaports of Corinth (Romans 16:1–3). Her patronage of Paul and others tells of her superior social status and places her in the well-known category of women patrons, powerful women who used their wealth and social power to influence events and even politics.[8]

Phoebe is a *diakonos* of Cenchrae. We do not know what this office entailed in the first century. As understood from the use of the word in other contexts, it could be representation of the community and its leadership and administration of goods and resources. It is customary to trace the rise of the diaconate to the story in Acts 6 in which the twelve settle a dispute by appointing seven hellenized Jewish

Carolyn Osiek, RSCJ

men to administer the social service program of the church. In fact, these men are never called deacons, though their work is understood to be *diakonia* of the table parallel to the *diakonia* of prayer and word performed by the twelve (Acts 6:1–6). In the entire New Testament, only one person is named as deacon of a particular church, and that is Phoebe. The role of *diakonos* is unlikely already at this time to have been understood as church office in the way it was later. However, if Phoebe did not hold church office, neither did the seven men of Acts 6. Ancient grammatical rules call for masculine forms when the sex of referents is mixed or uncertain. Because of Phoebe, do not assume that references to deacons, presbyters or overseers *(episkopoi)* in the early church (such as Philippians 1:1) refer only to men.

Phoebe is also called a *prostatis,* which in its masculine form, *prostates,* is known to have the meaning of one who presides at a meeting. In the context of the passage ("She has been a *prostatis* to many including me"), it is unlikely to carry that meaning here. More likely, it has another meaning of the word, "patron." In the culture of the time, this meant far more than what it means for us: someone who donates generously. A patron was a person of higher social status on whom one depended not only for funding but also for social protection and advancement. "Patron" is what Paul calls Phoebe with regard to himself.

Then there is the case of Evodia and Syntyche in Philippians 4:2–3. Paul takes time in his letter to the whole community to ask these two women to settle their dispute with the assistance of an unknown third person. This does not reflect well on Evodia and Syntyche, but it does tell us how significant they were in the Philippian community. They must have been important leaders, perhaps of two house churches, whose disagreement was adversely affecting the whole of Christian life in the city to such an extent that Paul had heard of it and felt it necessary to intervene and even appoint a mediator.

Finally, Romans 16 is a gold mine of references to women active in Christian ministry beyond Phoebe, who was discussed above: the couples Prisca and Aquila and the apostles Andronicus and Junia (verses 3–5, 7), and the women Mary (verse 6), Tryphaena and Tryphosa (probably sisters, perhaps twins), and "dear Persis," all of whom have "worked hard in the Lord" (verse 12). The texts reveal a vast network of companions in ministry, many of whom were women.

The married apostle Junia (verse 7) has had an adventurous career in the history of interpretation. The name as it appears here in the accusative could either be the common woman's name Junia, or the possible but otherwise unknown man's name Junias. John Chrysostom in the late fourth century is the first interpreter of the passage whose thought has survived. He clearly considers this person to be a woman apostle. By the twelfth century, however, she had become Junias, a man—because a woman could not be an apostle. In recent years, she has once more been reinstated as a woman.[9]

These glimpses of the life of the early church reveal the central importance of women in the work of evangelization and worship. Our foremothers in faith and ministry point the way.

Today's Questions

Few need to be convinced that there is an inconsistency in the institutional church's attitude toward women: It does not seem to know how to treat us as women without our being cast as "woman"—the other, the fatal attraction, the paradox of unclean and all-pure, the reminder of dependence and mortality. The traditional way for Christian women of earlier centuries to escape the ambiguity has been to become "virile women" by celibacy and asceticism. That way, they were able to retain some control over their lives. In some ways they were immersed more deeply into ecclesiastical control, but they escaped the most obvious form of male control, that of a husband in the patriarchal institution of marriage.[10]

I had mentioned earlier that women were socially invisible in the ancient world, but not only there. A few weeks ago, I was again in the Church of the Annunciation in Nazareth, standing before the large mural behind the altar of the upper church, finished in 1969. It depicts Christ, Mary and the church triumphant, heavy on ecclesiastical figures, gathered in groups processing toward the throne. Other than Mary, who looks like a cross between a blue birthday cake and a potted plant, there is not one woman among the throngs of the faithful. (The same, I note, is true of the "Touchdown Jesus" mural here at Notre Dame.) Invisibility and objectification continue. Mary is the one woman who escapes the curse of "woman."

The same basic inconsistency has continued in the institutional church's attitude toward women, with insistence on the one hand on the eternal sameness of "feminine nature" that is fulfilled in nurturing and in motherhood, and on the other hand, glorification of celibacy and even the revival of the consecration of virgins as spiritual fulfillment of the same nature. Social change does not happen in the church from within, but always as a response to outside forces of philosophy or social development. The modern institutional church attempts to keep pace with the evolution of women's consciousness in the modern world, by asserting our full dignity, full equality with men and freedom to pursue happiness, but with very little willingness to look at what that must entail in the church itself. Now with the rapid decline of priests in the developed countries, the secularization of society, the growing consciousness of women and the movement toward postmodern consciousness, we are beginning to see what these assertions might mean in the church.

The Changing Face of the Church

In light of this survey of women in the New Testament evidence, let us ask "Where are we going?" and reflect on some key issues.

Inclusive Language

Linguistic theory and empirical research have shown time and again that language both reflects *and creates* reality. As I write, we are faced with an unsatisfactory temporary solution to the lectionary standoff that has been going on for several years. The facts are simple: To speak of persons as if all were male is to continue the social invisibility of women; to speak of God as only male is to deny the theological assertion that both men and women are equally created in the image of God. Moreover, this is now a question of liturgical inculturation in those countries where significant numbers of people see the truth of what this linguistic symbolism is doing. All-male language is a distortion of reality, as one woman put it to me, "a foreign occupation of our natural resources." Mary Daly named it long ago: "If God is male, the male is God."

Women in Ministry

Increasing numbers of women and lay men in ministry is an inevitable trend. With the decline in priests that will get worse before it gets better, and with present practice with regard to ordination, the choice is being made to desacramentalize the church through decreasing availability of the sacraments. Will a desacramentalized church remain Catholic?

The Human Person in Christian Experience

A new Christian anthropology is urgently called for to reflect the changes that are happening all around us, not one about the "nature of woman" but about recognition of the full humanity of women as well as men. I have long thought that this is the root of the problem. The ancient and traditional way of thinking could affirm equality of nature without equality of treatment and participation. "Equality" is not Roman language. It is reluctantly adopted in nonthreatening contexts as a concession to modern thinking. It is a dangerous concept because it is not comparative: One cannot be more or less equal. "Some are more equal than others" is used in jokes and clever advertisements because we know it is a laughable non sequitur.

The Roman way is to talk about "dignity," which is the language of social status. The term is a direct descendent of the ancient Roman *dignitas,* an indicator of social rank and status. Unlike equality, "dignity" is a comparative word: One can have more or less dignity. In institutional church usage, the concept has been democratized to a certain extent by being extended to all persons and joined to the language of equality, but the term cannot be completely divested of its connotations of comparative worth.

We need to probe what "personal dignity" and "equality" mean in a modern and postmodern world, in which the institutional church is still catching up with the former, even as the world moves on to the latter. Church documents in the second half of this century have tried to combine the two concepts, thus:

> It cannot be forgotten that the church teaches, as an absolutely fundamental truth of Christian anthropology, the equal personal dignity of men and women, and the necessity of overcoming and doing away with 'every type of discrimination regarding fundamental rights' (*Gaudium et spes*, 29).

But to give an idea of how this is understood, the same text later says: "Diversity of mission in no way compromises equality of personal dignity." There is still room in this terminology for distinctions to be made on the basis of sex or other qualifications.

Equality in the Western world means more than equal access to salvation. It must also mean equal access on the basis of baptism to *participation*. That is the issue, not authority or ordination or power. But participation is not real without participation in leadership. It is time to call the institutional church to account on this issue of fundamental equality that it asserts. When women and lay male parish employees serve at the will of the pastor with no recourse while priests do not; when there are no women in key diocesan and curial positions, especially, but not exclusively, those that affect the lives of women directly; when the exercise of canonical expertise by women is severely restricted, in spite of their professional qualifications, women's fundamental equal human dignity is being violated in the church. It is time for the institutional church to practice what it preaches.

The Church

With all this in view, we need a new ecclesiology in which the model of the "People of God" from Vatican II is taken seriously. New images must arise to reflect the reality of what is happening, new images not like the one I recently heard from a new bishop: "The church is like a football team, in which all the players must follow the coach's orders to win." No, the church is not like a football team. Winning and losing are not the point.

The best result of last year's restatement against the ordination of women may be, in view of how leadership is really happening in our parishes, to break the long-established link not only between ordination and decision-making power, but between ordination and leadership, a link that did not exist in the earliest church and which is not essential. The present restrictions on ordination will make it increasingly difficult to find suitable candidates. Leadership positions will therefore necessarily continue to be filled by the non-ordained. One of the positive effects of these restrictions on ordination has been in recent years the flowering of many varieties of ministry in the church, something that was considerably less evident or possible in the ages when all leadership roles were filled by the ordained. But must this be at the cost of desacramentalization?

It is time to think more broadly and envision new ways in which we will of necessity in coming years be able to see each other as fully equal and fully complementary in the church. It will come by the catholic way of slow evolution rather than by administrative decree. It is time to dream dreams but not to lose the pulse of "the folks." Some reforms and revolutions have not prospered because to some extent they lost touch with what the people really wanted. Among them, I would count some aspects of the liturgical reform and of feminism. This time, let us not make the same mistake.

Not long ago, I was standing on Mt. Nebo in Jordan, which according to Byzantine tradition is the place from where Moses looked on the promised land that he was not to enter (Deuteronomy 34:1–4). Being there is always a reminder to me of being in a position to see what we will never see realized in our lifetime. Can we do that? Even as we see on the horizon the change that we long to see fulfilled, we must face the fact that perhaps we will not live to see it. Then let us work to pave the way for those to come after us, even as Mary Magdalen, Joanna, Susanna, Lois, Eunice, Mary, Nympha, Phoebe, Evodia, Syntyche, Prisca and Aquila, Andronicus and Junia, Tryphaena and Tryphosa and Persis did for us.

A literal interpretation of either scripture or tradition gets us nowhere and is not Catholic. To be faithful to our ancestors in the faith, we must act on our own convictions in the light of today's insights. That is what they would expect of us.

1. Plutarch, *Advice to the Married* (Moralia 140D [19]).

2. Tertullian, *To His Wife* 2.4–6.

Carolyn Osiek, RSCJ

3. Hippolytus, *Apostolic Tradition* 15.

4. For more, see David L. Balch, "Household Codes," *Greco-Roman Literature and the New Testament,* ed. David E. Aune, Society of Biblical Literature Sources for Biblical Study 21 (Atlanta: Scholars Press, 1988) 25–50.

5. Wendel, *The Women Around Jesus,* (New York: Crossroad, 1982) 133–138.

6. Similar things could be said about Matthew and John. See C. Newsom and S. Ringe, *The Women's Bible Commentary* (Louisville: Westminster John Knox, 1992).

7. For more on this and many other aspects of this discussion, see Carolyn Osiek and David L. Balch, *Families in the New Testament World: Households and House Churches* (Louisville: Westminster John Knox, 1997) 16, 60, 228, n. 31.

8. For the participation of aristocratic and imperial women in Roman politics, see Richard A. Bauman, *Women and Politics in Ancient Rome* (London/New York: Routledge, 1992).

9. For more of the story, see Bernadette Brooten, "'Junia . . . Outstanding among the Apostles' (Romans 16:7)," in *Women Priests: A Catholic Commentary on the Vatican Declaration,* ed. Leonard Swidler and Arlene Swidler (New York: Paulist, 1977) 141–144. See also the comment on Romans 16:7 in *The Catholic Study Bible,* 250, and any good contemporary commentary on the Epistle to the Romans.

10. This understanding of the early Christian asceticism of women is now generally accepted. Especially helpful are Elizabeth A. Clark, "Ideology, History, and the Construction of 'Woman' in Late Ancient Christianity," *Journal of Early Christian Studies* 2:2 (1994) 154–84; Kerstin Aspegren, *The Male Woman: A Feminine Ideal in the Early Church,* Uppsala Women's Studies. Women in Religion 4 (Uppsala: Almqvist & Wiksell, 1990).

Lois Paha, OP

The Changing Face of the Church in a Parish's Preparation for Liturgy

The title of our conference, "The Changing Face of the Liturgy," reminds us that the church and its prayer, the liturgy, are not finished products. The liturgy is alive and therefore subject to reform and revision as the needs and expressions of the people change. Historically, the liturgy has imitated the ways of society. Familiar examples include the way in which some elements of the Latin rite still carry vestiges of the imperial court of the Middle Ages. The Baroque period of history fostered a new wave of art and music not to be excluded from the sacred halls of worship. Even the architecture of buildings for worship mirrored the palaces of royalty to some degree.

Thus, the reforms of the liturgy promulgated by the Second Vatican Council are no exception. The beginnings in the late 1960s and early 1970s fit the times of life in the United States. And just as the faces of the presiders, planners and liturgical ministers of those days have changed in these three decades, the face of the liturgy has also changed, and continues to change. But humanly speaking, a changing face does not always indicate a distant, unfamiliar heart. The externals may change and the inner spirit may grow stronger, but we generally continue to recognize the basic elements of the person whose face we now see anew.

Lois Paha, OP

With the liturgy and preparation for the liturgy, the same holds true. The liturgy remains the same in its dynamic structure of praise and petition, word and response, but the many ways in which the local community expresses the great prayer of worship in the space, the music, the language and related customs shows us the face that changes and grows with wisdom and grace.

Likewise, the preparation that precedes the celebration of the liturgy takes on many different faces. From the faces of those who do the preparation, to the faces of those who have specific roles, especially the face of the assembly, there has been considerable changes over these years.

In his recent book, *Bodying Forth: Aesthetic Liturgy*, Patrick Collins reminds us that

> while the first two decades of reform and renewal brought forth
> new rites, spaces and ministries, the third decade calls for even
> deeper change in ministers and assemblies. Liturgical renewal
> was never primarily about turning altars around, or even prin-
> cipally about getting laity into liturgical ministries (19).

He goes on to remind us that the purpose of liturgical reform was to teach us how to be better at being church in the world today. (See the *Constitution on the Sacred Liturgy*, 1.) The task of the renewal is transformation. He continues:

> Renewal of rites is primarily about "turning people around" —
> turning toward God by turning toward one another and also
> turning toward the inner reaches of oneself (19).

As the liturgy is celebrated, the assembly is formed. The worshipers themselves continue to become a people that can once again be inspired to feed the hungry, clothe the naked, shelter the homeless, heal the brokenhearted and comfort those who mourn.

How is this goal of liturgy related to our topic? Everyone has the responsibility of full, active and conscious participation in the liturgy, but we all know that a few people help to make it happen with reverence and respect for the rites being celebrated and for the people praising God.

But the means toward the end are very different from place to place. It's not likely that we could find two parish liturgy committees that are identical in make-up, process, resources—even their goals. Clearly, we are working toward the same ultimate goal, to help the people pray, but we can only do that in the context of the human conditions in which we find ourselves. Those very conditions are the ones in which we will recognize the Christ who dwells in our midst.

The tasks related to liturgy preparation for any given occasion will obviously vary. Preparation for the installation of a new ordinary of a diocese will certainly require more detailed preparation than the weekday liturgy at the local parish church, yet the essential elements of liturgy preparation are present.

Here I would like to review some basic elements of liturgy preparation and explore some of the ways in which the society calls us to implement those elements.

Some Considerations

You've heard the phrase of frustrated parents that goes something like this (you may add your own inflections): "What do you think you are doing?" This inquiry is issued as a result of any number of circumstances in need of clarification. Likewise, we ought to ask ourselves that question: What do you think you are doing here in this liturgy? I believe that liturgical ministers, liturgy leaders throughout the country have done a pretty good job of quoting the pertinent paragraphs of the *Constitution on the Sacred Liturgy* to get the assembly involved. Paragraph 14 has what has become almost a mantra of the renewal:

> The church earnestly desires that all the faithful be led to that
> full, conscious and active participation in liturgical celebrations
> called for by the very nature of the liturgy.

In an attempt to answer the "what do you think you are doing" question, the response is generally, "Gee, I don't really know, I was only trying to . . . " Unfortunately, we are asking the wrong question.

Sociologists reminds us that when we first answer the identity question, we can then answer the task-driven question. You will know what to do when you know who you are.

The first question for the liturgy preparation group in a parish would then be the question, "Who are we?" This will give better direction for the "What are we doing?" question.

Our collective experience will verify the reality that, when the liturgical reforms first came to the parish, they arrived at the desk of the pastor, whose task it was to implement them. Pastors and bishops had help from those who had for years been doing the research, scholarship and rationale for the changes. The laity, however, were at that time unaware of the necessity of their role of participating in the liturgy in any way other than as the "silent spectator" and occasional dialogue partner ("And also with you"). Some people still remember how rapidly and without explanation the external changes were given to the people.

But the generosity with which Catholic parishioners built the churches, the schools, the hospitals and orphanages of the pre-conciliar period initiated their involvement now in the "new liturgy." So we need to ask ourselves continually: What has changed in the liturgy preparation process over these decades? Nothing? A few things? Is the process still at work? Are the people changing? Is the liturgy itself still changing?

As I see it, the business of liturgy preparation calls for two essential ingredients. First of all, knowledge of the liturgy, the ritual that we pray, and, second, knowledge of the assembly, the people of God who gather in prayer. It is everyone's responsibility to know those two essential elements, but it is the responsibility of a few people at a time to see that the particular services are prepared and prayed Sunday after Sunday.

Parish Liturgy Committees

When forming a parish liturgy committee, always begin where you are. Assess the situation. A 200-family parish in rural Texas may involve the majority of the parish in its planning process and liturgical ministries, while a 4000-family parish in the Metroplex may never be able to gather the entire parish in one place for one celebration. Circumstances of the assembly differ, but in both of these parishes, efforts to unify the parish through the Sunday celebrations can be enhanced by the work of good liturgical preparation.

In some places it is a given that the pastor will chair the committee and be present for all meetings. But this is not always possible in other places, and in other situations the pastor cannot be present. But the pastor, the presiders and the deacons do need to be informed about the decisions of the committee. The committee has a responsibility to offer information, formation and education to the assembly and to the ministers.

When preparing for any liturgical celebration, we must bear in mind that the starting point is always the worship of God, and knowledge of the rite unifies our prayer when we understand the intent of this ritual and find the ways this community can express it. A careful study of any rite includes the introduction, the ritual itself and the options and pastoral circumstances that need to be considered.

Conversation, then, over that information brings forth a healthy process for bringing about the best celebration possible for the community. Some members of the assembly take on specific roles in order to bring life to the prayer we celebrate. The reformed liturgy calls on the whole body of the church to share in the ministries of the liturgy. Paragraphs 26–30 of the *Constitution on the Sacred Liturgy* teach us that "liturgical services are not private functions, but are celebrations belonging to the Church . . . " (26). That level of participation requires preparation and formation in ministry. Thus, the tasks of liturgy preparation may also include the preparation of the ministers. Well-trained and well-prepared lectors, altar servers, eucharistic ministers, presiders, musicians and greeters can and do help the people pray.

From the opening convocation and liturgy of the Second Vatican Council to the daily Mass in a rural parish, the changing face of liturgy preparation matches the changing face of the parish membership. Culture and the changing needs of the community become ingredients for consideration. Look beyond the rubrics on the page to the assembly seated. Consider the members of the assembly who choose not to attend. How well do the laity and clergy work together? Who is the advocate for the children and youth who have a right to gather around the table? Who is attentive to the recent immigrants who come quietly and often invisibly for fear of being sent away? What new insights are necessary when the assembly ages or declines in number, or when that enthusiastic volunteer folk choir starts sounding old? And who will speak for those who cannot speak for themselves, the developmentally disabled, the physically handicapped?

We cannot be at liturgy without being with the whole body of Christ. Adolescents are also members of the assembly, even though they often do not believe that of themselves. Are they given opportunities to be liturgical ministers? or do we just ignore them until they get to be our age?

When planning liturgies with and for children and youth, we must continue to be mindful that we assist them in finding their suitable forms of praise of God. In its ritual books, the church is mindful of children, yet are we as attentive when implementing those rites? We must not be fooled into thinking that children and adolescents are not able to sing familiar hymns or carry the lectionary or preach from the ambo or be a cantor. They will respond to the reverence that is shown them.

Upon leaving the Office of Divine Worship in the archdiocese of Chicago, Father Ron Lewinski reflected on the ongoing reform of the liturgy from a systems perspective. He included issues of dialogue between parishioners and pastor, the vitality of community worship, the need for good preaching, the importance of attention to the cultural adaptation of the liturgy and more. He makes a very important point in relation to children and those who pass on the faith to them, the catechists:

> It's time for liturgists and catechists to work together. Where these two ministries are not working in tandem, the liturgist and catechist will be less effective. . . . Catechists have to be freed of seeing themselves as "Sunday school teachers." Catechists are liturgists who lead their flocks in prayer. They cultivate an appetite for liturgical prayer and offer a mystagogical catechesis that flows from the liturgy. Liturgists need to break out of the sanctuary and join their colleagues in catechetical efforts. The

catechumenate has taught us to see these ministries in a new relationship. (*Liturgy 90*, August/September 1994, 10)

There is hardly a parish in our North American dioceses that is not faced with cultural issues. It is not only issues of ethnicity, but differences of philosophy and ideology, of age and interest, of education and economics that invite us to be mindful of the planning process. The blueprint for planning is to know the rites and to know the people, then to roll up your sleeves, get to the drawing board, to the computer, to the sanctuary and choir area and let the prayer be celebrated.

We must "lift the liturgy off the planned page into an energized celebration" (Collins, *Bodying Forth*, 136). The liturgy committee that is running out of steam may be just what the liturgy doctor ordered. There will always be room for the organizational pieces of the liturgy planning process, but what may have been lacking, perhaps to a greater degree than we would like to admit, is the presence of the liturgical artist, someone who has knowledge of the liturgy along with some aesthetic sensitivity. Knowing how to move in the sacred space can be a real challenge, but if some things are not thought out in advance and even "choreographed" in the simplest way, the liturgy is compromised, the assembly is distracted and we haven't helped the people pray.

Some further advice that can give us new energy is basically "slow down." Think about what can and should be done. If you get a brilliant insight or have a beautiful experience that you are dying to try on your community, think about it within your context and present it to the liturgy committee. It may turn out to be a square peg that won't fit into the round hole of your parish's worship.

All changes must be rooted in the rites of the church, in their history, theology and pastoral development. In the rites, we see we see what is expected in our celebration of the liturgy. Observe the liturgical calendar without ignoring the calendar of the people. Be attentive to culture, but unafraid to invite growth or change within that context as well. I am reminded of the words of Bob Duggan on the responsibility of the liturgy committee:

Most of all, the liturgy committee must be the place at the heart of the parish where the deep spirit of renewed worship of God is fostered. If the links between liturgy and life are not understood by committee members, what is there for the parish at large? If the committee members see no connection between Eucharist and social justice, who will challenge a parish's tendencies to self-absorption? If the liturgy committee has no sense of the beautiful, or of the importance of an environment that invites worship, then how will we ever attract artists to beautify our celebrations? If parish liturgy committees abandon the effort for renewal, then and only then will the reform of Vatican II have failed. ("Liturgical Renewal and the Liturgy Committee," *Church Magazine,* Spring 1994)

The business of liturgy preparation is the business of keeping the heart of the liturgy beating at a pace that reminds us that as the people of God we are alive!

The heart of the prayer of the liturgist is the life of Jesus Christ through whom we pray in our celebration of the eucharist. Meditation on and celebration of the paschal mystery in our lives animates every moment of every day.

Let us pray:
Holy mystery beyond our vision,
beyond our reach,
Beloved God,
stay near to us.

Our days unfold in ups and downs,
joy and weariness, hopes and fears.
Redeem our waiting for your glory to be revealed,
and bless every action, thought and desire as we wait.

Reach into the circle of days so like one another
and speak to us clearly of your love and of your will.
You are the Lord of time and space,
the gracious one who saves us from confusion and despair.

Lord of history, have mercy on us.

(Paul Philibert, op, "Redeeming the Time," in *Seeing and Believing: Images of Christian Faith* [Collegeville: The Liturgical Press, 1995])

Basic Resources for Parish Liturgy Committees

Liturgy Documents:

The Roman Missal (Lectionary and Sacramentary).

The Liturgy Documents: A Parish Resource (Chicago: Liturgy Training Publications, 1991), containing these documents: Constitution on the Sacred Liturgy, General Instruction of the Roman Missal, Environment and Art in Catholic Worship, Music in Catholic Worship, Liturgical Music Today, Ceremonial of Bishops, Introduction to the Lectionary.

The Rites of the Catholic Church (Collegeville: The Liturgical Press, 1983), containing these documents: Rite of Christian Initiation of Adults, Rite of Infant Baptism, Rite of Marriage, Rite of Penance, Pastoral Care of the Sick: Rites of Anointing and Viaticum, Rite of Confirmation, Order of Christian Funerals.

Book of Blessings

Planning Aids:

Sourcebook for Sundays and Seasons (Chicago: Liturgy Training Publications). A practical, carefully organized tool for presiders and all who work with the preparation of the parish liturgy. Published annually.

Workbook for Lectors and Gospel Readers (Chicago: Liturgy Training Publications). Published annually, this resource is helpful for the lector, deacon and priest. It contains a pronunciation guide, introduction to the ministry of lector and gives instruction about good proclamation. (Available in Spanish as *Manual para Proclamadores de la Palabra.*)

Children's Daily Prayer for the School Year, by Elizabeth McMahon Jeep (Chicago: Liturgy Training Publications). Published annually. Daily prayers for the school year, also weekly prayer for the religious education program.

To Crown the Year by Peter Mazar (Chicago: Liturgy Training Publications, 1995). Solid suggestions for seasonal decoration without the gimmicks. Especially useful for liturgy committee, sacristans and all who work with the environment of the assembly.

Celebration: An Ecumenical Worship Resource, William J. Freburger, ed. (Kansas City: National Catholic Reporter Publishing Company). Published monthly, this resource contains numerous articles, scripture study, music suggestions, clip art, and more.

Periodicals:

Liturgy 90 (Chicago: Liturgy Training Publications)

Catechumenate (Chicago: Liturgy Training Publications)

Plenty Good Room (Chicago: Liturgy Training Publications)

Environment and Art Letter (Chicago: Liturgy Training Publications)

Aim: Liturgy Resource Magazine (Chicago: J. S. Paluch)

Today's Liturgy and *Liturgia Y Cancion* (Portland: Oregon Catholic Press)

GIA Quarterly (Chicago: GIA Publications, Inc.)

Modern Liturgy (San Jose, CA: Resource Publications, Inc.)

Selected Annotated Bibliography:

Preparing for Liturgy by Austin Fleming (Chicago: Liturgy Training Publications, 1997). The author states simply and accurately: "The church plans the liturgy, we prepare it." This volume is an excellent review of the depth of the theology and spirituality of liturgy. Fleming's clear understanding of the role of all liturgical ministers brings the preparation of liturgy to the pastoral art that it is.

Catechesis for Liturgy: A Program for Parish Involvement by Gilbert Ostdiek (Washington: Pastoral Press, 1986). Ostdiek's book embraces the theology of participation on various levels, drawing special attention to the preparation of liturgical ministers, liturgical space and the entire action of the liturgy. It can serve as an excellent formation resource for all those who prepare the liturgy in the parish regularly.

Bodying Forth: Aesthetic Liturgy by Patrick W. Collins (Mahwah, NJ: Paulist Press, 1992). With emphasis on the artistic aspects of liturgy, this collection reviews the roles of liturgical minsters as well as criteria for preparing liturgy with the eyes, ears and hands of the poet, musician, artist and believer.

In Heaven There Are No Thunderstorms: Celebrating the Liturgy with Developmentally Disabled People by Gijs Okhuijsen and Cees van Opzeeland (Collegeville: The Liturgical Press, 1992). Accounts of liturgies celebrated with residents of institutions for the mentally disabled in the Netherlands.

The Welcome Table: Planning Masses with Children by Elizabeth McMahon Jeep, et al. (Chicago: Liturgy Training Publications, 1982). This collection of practical and informative implementation of the liturgy with children as the primary liturgical assembly will assist all who work with children and take seriously their formation in the liturgical prayer of the church.

Why Go to Mass? Reasons and Resources to Motivate Teens by Greg Dues (Mystic, CT: Twenty-Third Publications, 1994). The author's experience as catechist, father and lay minister gives a forum for some some good liturgical teaching to the youth. His theology and liturgy are sound and presented in a palatable way.

From Age to Age: The Challenge of Worship with Adolescents by the National Federation for Catholic Youth Ministry, Inc. (Washington: January 1997). The purpose of this document is to explore the issues of liturgical participation by adolescents primarily between the ages of thirteen and nineteen. It offers suggestions for assessment, evaluation and an invitation to youth ministers, youth leaders and the youth to help them to do the work of "Gathering Everyone around the Lord's Table."

How Can I Keep From Singing? Thoughts about Liturgy for Musicians by Gabe Huck (Chicago: Liturgy Training Publications, 1986). Musicians are often given much responsibility for liturgy planning and preparation as well as the prayer itself. Huck offers many essential liturgical teachings that can be incorporated into the work of the musicians and thus foster stronger liturgical understanding and participation.

Guidelines for Multi-lingual Liturgies. (1986 BCL Newsletter, Volume XXII, June/July). This document is a result of a collaborative project between the Instituto de Liturgia Hispana and the Federation of Diocesan Liturgical Commissions. Its purpose is to assist parishes and other communities faced with multi-cultural and multi-lingual

Lois Paha, op

celebrations of the eucharist. The guidelines are based on the experiences of many parish liturgists, priests and diocesan worship offices in the planning and celebration of such liturgies.

Federation of Diocesan Liturgical Commissions Publications. Bulletin inserts are available on a number of liturgical topics. Check with your diocesan liturgical commission or diocesan worship office for the catalogue or topics on hand.

Paul J. Philibert, OP

The Maturing Faith of the Church: Signs of Development and Promise

The Roman Catholic church is living through one of the most profound transitions in its history. Theologians commented at the beginning of the Second Vatican Council that, at last, through its return to a biblical vision of the church and its concern to speak sympathetically to the emerging world of a new millennium, the church was finally leaving behind the era of Constantinian Christianity, that "compromise" by which the church became the privileged religion of the Roman Empire.[1] The real challenges of Vatican II had to do with interiority: awakening people to a mature faith, acknowledging that true religion arises out of spontaneous love, building communities of intentional mutual service and awakening to the evangelizing power of faith in a post-modern world. This new openness contrasted with an ecclesial complacency which had divided the world into Catholic and non-Catholic factions and had limited its concerns largely to internal sacramental administration in the Catholic world. In addition to neglecting the cosmic reach of the church's evangelization, this preconciliar attitude also tolerated a neutral or passive attitude on the part of laity.

This change of focus was concerned then with evangelization, creating a shift from ecclesiastical self-preoccupation to concern for the world, from ecclesiastical maintenance to world mission. Such a

Paul J. Philibert, OP

sudden new vision of church life meant that tensions were inevitable. Contradicting forces hoping to control the soul of the church have been in tension from the announcement of the Council until the present. There are more than a few who think that the Council was a mistake; some of these are among the most eminent figures in the hierarchy. We need to try to understand why this struggle was inevitable and how we might hope to get beyond it. Is there a path beyond stalemate?

The North American Church Today

Recent work by a team of sociologists led by Dr. Jim Davidson of Purdue University has produced an analysis of Catholicism in the United States that helps us to understand the pastoral predicament of the church. They speak of "three generations of Catholics" in the church.[2] Typically we presume that what is important in our theological argumentation, preaching or pastoral conversation is the authority of our message and the logic of our argument, if not the power of our rhetoric. Yet Davidson and his group are convinced that we are basically dealing with three "churches" and that our first pastoral priority must be learning how to address and communicate with them. The three cohorts (or groupings of people of a certain age) are so distinct as to provide three discrete mentalities. What are these three groupings?

According to this analysis, Catholics may be divided into "pre–Vatican II Catholics," "Vatican II Catholics" and "Post–Vatican II Catholics." These divisions are based on the effects of the life cycle that the groups find themselves in as well as by the events that have shaped their understanding of the world. Let us examine these groups one by one.

Pre–Vatican II Catholics

Pre–Vatican II Catholics were born in the 1910s, '20s and '30s; their teenage and young adult years were lived out in the 1930s and '40s.

They matured well before Vatican II. Their education was predominantly grade school and high school, with only twenty percent receiving some college education. Because the world at that time was much more divided culturally than it is today, Catholics of this group were in large part segregated from the culture at large. They also did not know television in their childhood years. This group remains today more closely attached to the church than the other two. They tend to prefer the hierarchical model of church that is familiar to them from their childhood years.

Vatican II Catholics

Vatican II Catholics were born in the 1940s and '50s and experienced the council during their formative years. Davidson says "they have one foot in the 'old church' (before Vatican II) and one in the 'new church' (after Vatican II)."[3] They are more highly educated than the pre–Vatican II group. Forty-eight percent had at least some college. Typical Vatican II Catholics are 35 to 54 years of age and similar in many ways to their pre–Vatican II counterparts. Yet they prefer a more democratic model of church life, to which they were exposed by the teachings of Vatican II and by the church's responses to the council, an influence which sets them apart from the generation before them.

Post–Vatican II Catholics

Post–Vatican II Catholics were born in the 1960s and '70s and came of age in the '70s and '80s. They have never known any other experience of church except the church as transformed by the reforms of the council. They don't know very much about the church before the council and they don't comprehend the "war stories" that their elders tell them about the church before the changes and during the struggles to change. Post–Vatican II Catholics have the least institutional idea of what it means to be Catholic. They attend Mass less regularly, don't feel a great obligation to support the church as a social institution and are less devotional. They have, like their parents, a solid education, but most likely less opportunity to do well in the present economy than their parents had.

Paul J. Philibert, OP

The Pluralism of the Three-Generation Mix

Davidson claims that these generational differences account for a great deal of the pluralism in the church today. These three groups experience the church differently and have different feelings about the church. (See Table 1.)[4]

TABLE 1

Religious Commitment among Three Generations of Catholics

COMMITMENT ASPECT	PRE−VATICAN II (%)	VATICAN II (%)	POST−VATICAN II (%)
Church is important	59	48	29
Would never leave the Catholic church*	83	58	50
Attend Mass			
Once a week or more	63	45	24
Almost every week	10	16	17
About once a month	9	18	22
Less than once a month	18	21	36
Pray			
Daily	90	67	53
Weekly, occasionally	6	25	30
Seldom, never	3	7	15
Know of pastoral letter on			
Women	60	51	29
Economic justice	26	24	11
Peace	24	21	12

*THESE PERCENTAGES REPRESENT THOSE WHOSE RESPONSES WERE AT POINTS 1 AND 2 ON THE 7 POINT SCALE, WITH POINT 1 BEING "I WOULD NEVER LEAVE THE CATHOLIC CHURCH."

In Table 1, there is a comparison among the three generations relative to the question, "Would you ever leave the church?": 83% of pre−Vatican II Catholics said they would never leave; 58% of Vatican II Catholics said they would never leave; but only 50% of post−Vatican II Catholics indicated that they would never leave the church.

On another telling question, "Can you be a good Catholic without going weekly to Mass?", 60% of pre−Vatican II Catholics said yes, 74% of Vatican II Catholics, and 80% of post−Vatican II Catholics said that you can be a good Catholic without going to Mass weekly. (See Table 2)[5]

TABLE 2

Belief among Three Generations of Catholics
that You Can Be a Good Catholic

PERSONAL RELIGIOUS PRACTICE	PRE−VATICAN II (%)	VATICAN II (%)	POST−VATICAN II (%)
Without observing church strictures against birth control	59	73	82
Without going to Mass weekly	60	74	80
Without observing church strictures against divorce and remarriage	50	64	67
Without observing church strictures against abortion	40	53	67
Without marrying in the church	53	65	64
Without donating to the parish	55	51	63
Without helping the poor	57	41	58
Without believing in infallibility	42	51	55

These responses represent a number of factors, including the growing secularization of our society and the successful communication to Catholics after Vatican II that their own conscience must be the judge of right and wrong in their moral and religious behavior. In addition, many U.S. Catholics today have horizontal expectations of the liturgies on Sunday; that is, a desire to be welcomed, included and addressed in relevant terms. The Davidson study does not explore these expectations directly, but other studies do.[6]

The post−Vatican II Catholics have a more tenuous relationship to the institutional church than their grandparents. It strikes me that the three generations can described impressionistically as follows:

- Pre−Vatican II Catholics have an a priori sense of the authoritative role of the church in their lives. For them, the church's authority is taken for granted.

- Vatican II Catholics grew up with a strong sense of the church's claim of authority in their lives, but that authority has come to be nuanced by reason of new attitudes of religious freedom and the influence of secularization in the culture at large; and

- Post–Vatican II Catholics are people for whom the church must make a case for itself; they do not take it for granted. The church in their lives has the same possibility of convincing them of its importance and its moral authority as any other agency in society. There is some definite dynamic of affiliation, that is, these younger Catholics still identify themselves as Catholics for the most part. But predictable beliefs and behaviors do not automatically flow from that affiliation.

This comparison is overdrawn perhaps, since many families still manage to communicate a strong sense of belonging and religious commitment to their children, and these people remain solidly Catholic in their attitudes and behaviors. A similar estimation of the commitment of Catholics can be seen in another structure of analysis. D'Antonio and his associates speak of three measures of the individual commitment of believers, calling them "nuclear Catholic, modal Catholics and dormant Catholics." Nuclear Catholics are those for whom the church is part of the nucleus of their life; modal Catholics are those who belong "modally," that is, according to their own mode or outlook; and dormant Catholics are those who do not participate on a regular basis but have not stopped thinking of themselves as Catholics.

Nuclear Catholics attend Mass at least once a week, say the church is one of the most important influences in their lives, and indicate that they strongly feel they would never leave their church. In a recent survey, 27% of a sample of Catholics gave such responses. *Modal* Catholics go to Mass at least once a month. They say that the church is quite important to them, as are other organizations. They say that they are fairly certain they would never leave the church. Of a recent sample of Catholics, 58% registered as "modal." *Dormant* Catholics say that they seldom or never go to Mass and indicated that the church is not so important in their lives. About 20% of Catholics surveyed fall into the dormant category.

Perhaps the most interesting aspect of this analysis is that dormant Catholics were clearly the youngest of the three categories and had strong male majorities. "They were the least likely to be married, and slightly more likely to be divorced or separated."[7] Further, the D'Antonio study indicates that even nuclear Catholics consult not only the teaching of the church's magisterium, but also their own conscience on such issues as divorce and remarriage, contraception, abortion, homosexual behavior and extramarital sex. There is clearly need for serious adult religious formation within the ranks of even the most strongly committed Catholics. One final footnote of interest is that the number of "dormant Catholics" represents the equivalent of the second largest "denomination" in the United States, with Roman Catholics being the largest, dormant Catholics being the second largest and Southern Baptists being the third.[8]

The Effects of Vatican II

A major cause for the shift in Catholic attitudes was the Second Vatican Council and the reforms which it introduced into church life. It is instructive to remember some of the central phrases that emerged from the debates and discussions of the council. Here are some key words: *aggiornamento, Lumen Gentium,* dialogue, inculturation/adaptation, collegiality, religious freedom, People of God, ecumenism.

The word *aggiornamento* was coined by Pope John XXIII to evoke the need for the council to bring the church up to date. The Italian word for "day" is "giorno." *Aggiornamento* therefore means to bring the church into the present day. With the goal of *aggiornamento,* there was an implicit admission that the church was out of touch with the contemporary world. A great emphasis of the post-Reformation church (the period is often referred to as the Counter-Reformation in Catholicism) was to insist upon the immutable and eternal quality of religious truth. This sometimes led to an overemphasis upon ecclesiastical authority. Even today there are some Catholics who would reduce all religious matters to the simple question of consulting the pope, convinced that God made the pope infallible precisely so that we would know exactly what to do in any circumstances. This oversimplification robs the church of its vitality, for it is not one person who is the dynamic element in the life of the church, but all the baptized.[9]

When the council went about the work of creating a Constitution on the Church, it began its text with the phrase *Lumen Gentium* and the opening words: "Christ is the light of the nations and consequently this holy synod, gathered together in the holy Spirit, ardently desires to bring all to all humanity that light of Christ which is resplendent on the face of the church, by proclaiming his gospel to every creature."[10] The council's shift from a preoccupation with the internal governance of the church as an organization of those in union with the Roman Catholic hierarchy to a proclamation of the mystery of the gospel to all peoples is one of the most characteristic shifts of the council. Likewise, when the document treats the nature of the church, it teaches that Christ instituted a new covenant to create "the new people of God" that is the church.[11] Later the council speaks of the church as a "pilgrim church" which carries the gifts of the gospel through the ages until the moment of the fulfillment of the church in the heavenly Jerusalem. Such expressions communicated a very definite attitude of openness and a conviction of the need for change.[12]

Another example of a central teaching of Vatican II is this passage from the *Declaration on Religious Liberty:*

> The human person sees and recognizes the demands of the divine law through conscience. All are bound to follow their conscience faithfully in every sphere of activity so that they may come to God, who is their last end. Therefore, the individual must not be forced to act against conscience nor be prevented from acting according to conscience, especially in religious matters. The reason is because the practice of religion of its very nature consists primarily of those voluntary and free internal acts by which human beings direct themselves to God.[13]

This is but one of many references in the documents of the council to the sovereignty of conscience in its religious anthropology. As a result of this and of other theological developments referred to in the previous paragraphs, Catholic Christians came to understand that not only must their own conscience and reflective understanding stand at the foundation of responsible religious behavior, but also that their own lives must be engaged in the work of the church's witness to the world.

In brief, we can note certain contrasts between the pre-conciliar religious culture and the post-conciliar culture. On the one hand, the pre-conciliar culture invited Catholics to be introverted, traditionalist, culturally passive and withdrawn from society, at least to the degree of protecting themselves from the dangerous influences of an unbelieving world. By contrast, the post-conciliar culture developed a more extraverted sense of Christian presence in the world, a passion for *aggiornamento* and culturally creative attitudes that impelled believers to become inserted actively within the institutions and operations that control the social forces of society at large. The post-conciliar church aimed at becoming missionary by becoming an involved witness within the social and political structures of a world in transition.

Recalling the observations about three generations of Catholics mentioned above, we can see that the challenges of Vatican II presented the possibility of disorientation and loss to each of the generations in different ways. Relative to the pre–Vatican II generation, the council represented a certain loss of identity, particularly through the reform of the liturgy and of some ascetical practices, such as "meatless Fridays." Traditionalist Catholics tend to refer (with romantic nostalgia) to the numinous quality of the Latin liturgy, as though those days presented opportunities for superior sanctification through the mysterious rites conducted in a dead language. (Such people seldom refer to the twenty-minute Masses during which priests rushed through the Latin Missal in a language unintelligible to the majority of the communicants.) Pre–Vatican II Catholics also lost a sense of coherence, I think, to the degree that everyone formerly had their place in a tightly knit hierarchy of roles and authority structures. This tight ordering of roles diminished with the growth of lay participation in roles of church education, administration and the animation of parish worship.

Vatican II Catholics have lost, above all, the naive expectations which they conceived in the decade following the council. Many of them would have desired that the reforms of the council could bring about a renewal that would be uniformly accepted and implemented in orderly fashion in a very brief period of renewal. Few realized how much cultural resistance would be expressed to the reforms of the council or how difficult and burdensome would be the actual work of creating the new texts and rituals needed to embody the liturgical and ecclesial structures for the Council's renewal.

Even post–Vatican II Catholics must face a certain kind of loss. This loss is associated with their inability to connect themselves with stories about the conflicts and gains of the great moments of the council's years of activity and the responses to it. Most of this generation were born after the council was completed. Most of them came of age at a time in which the council no longer had dramatic public significance. Not infrequently today's students do not realize that their professors are people who lived through the days of the council as a time of dramatic excitement. I have even heard some of our young priests today say to older clergy, "I have known nothing but the postconciliar church; I can't understand what you are so excited about."

Help from Developmental Psychology

It will be helpful to turn to a developmental understanding of the human life cycle in order to understand from another perspective the predicament of the church that I have been describing here. I want to refer to a metaphor developed by developmental psychologist Lawrence Kohlberg, who organized his study of stages of moral development in terms of three levels of moral reasoning that he called preconventional, conventional, and postconventional. (See Table 3.)

TABLE 3

Developmental Vision

PRECONVENTIONAL	
Ethics of the child	Constraint
	Deference to authority
CONVENTIONAL	
Ethics of the young adult	Takes society's point of view
	Participates in social process
POSTCONVENTIONAL	
Ethics of creative adults	Critical concerns
	Reformist stance
	Compassionate

In creating these categories, Kohlberg wanted to emphasize the degree to which each person must be initiated into an understanding of and feeling for social morality. Children must learn morality from a posture of gradual appropriation during a long period of apprenticeship during which there is much that they cannot understand. Kohlberg further wished to describe the sense of the inadequacy of conventional moral thinking for those who have seen through its limitations under critical situations. This vision of morality as related to cognitive development and to changing social position can help us to understand the divisions within the church today.[14]

Conventional Moral Reasoning

Let's begin with the conventional, the middle position. It is the easiest to explain. Conventional morality is the ethics of the young adult. It takes society's point of view. It is the vision of someone who participates in social process and feels responsible for maintaining the good order of society. The word "convention" refers to that which is taken for granted in a given cultural situation. So, for example, in North America it is conventional at table to use a plate with a fork at the left and a knife at the right. We recognize that children only gradually come to take this for granted, but often we fail to recognize that there are other cultures where a different protocol for the "conventional" exists. In India, for example, instead of a plate one uses a portion of a banana leaf and instead of a fork one uses the fingers of one's right hand. It would be insulting in India to insist upon a plate and a fork in a domestic situation where one is being invited to partake of what is culturally conventional for the people in that place.

Already this idea can be applied to life in the church. The intrusive quality of missionary activity in the eighteenth and nineteenth centuries, frequently inattentive to the dynamics of inculturation, led many people to become participants in church life without really feeling completely at home or responsible for the maintenance of the cultural structures by which the gospel was communicated. Often the missionaries required converts to abandon native dress, arts, and music as part of their "conversion" to Christianity. Even in our own country today, the question of whether or not adult Catholics are truly invited to become "conventional" stewards of the church's life, culture and holiness depends upon the degree to which their language, culture, attitudes and spirit are welcomed as fully worthy instruments of the expression of church life. Inattention to inclusiveness and cultural flexibility is not just a problem in the foreign missions; it is a predicament for almost every North American parish as well.

Preconventional Moral Reasoning

Preconventional morality is the ethics of the child. Children must be brought to internalize the expectations of the culture through deference to authority, the insistence of parents and teachers and, if necessary, constraint to make them conform. The presupposition is that those in a preconventional mode will not or cannot fully understand the reasons for the constructs of morality as they are established. Along with developmental factors, there are cultural and attitudinal factors that support a preconventional mode of thinking and acting.

For example, when lay people are given to believe that they have a secondary, inferior and not fully entitled role in the church's worship and ecclesial life, then they will experience themselves as being invited to maintain a preconventional stance. As noted above, this same implicit exclusion can be the result of linguistic and cultural factors, as when Asian or Hispanic or other immigrant groups may find themselves unable to express spontaneously their sense of God and worship in ways familiar to themselves through their own music, language and customs.

Postconventional Moral Reasoning

The third of these is postconventional morality. This could be called the ethics of creative adults, that is, people with critical concerns, a reformist stance or a compassion that leads them to judge as inadequate the conventional solutions to the problems of the most troubled parts of society.[15] We will argue a bit later that the concern to draw preconventional people forward into their full participation in social rights and responsibilities can move people of a conventional orientation to becoming postconventional. Generative concerns, in other words, tend to open up a spirit of compassion that leads people to put persons before principles.[16] Now let us imagine how these categories might help us to understand today's church.

Some Applications

Given these descriptions, perhaps we can understand how the Roman Catholic church in the pre–Vatican II days implicitly invited the laity to remain at a preconventional level of experience. In that world, only the ordained and religious seemed to be full participants in the church's life and holiness. The laity assisted at the liturgy of the eucharist as at a supernatural theater, celebrated in a language that was foreign and with rites that descended from past ages, utilizing gestures and vestments from a long-disappeared world. We forget that before Vatican II no lay person would read at Mass or enter the sanctuary (except for male children as altar boys to serve the priest and to make the Latin responses). Certainly no lay person would help in the distribution of communion. It was a priest-centered world. Thomas O'Meara has argued that that world knew only a "monoform ministry—that of the priest alone."[17] To maintain that the laity were subtly confined in a preconventional mode within the church is not to deny that they entered into conventional responsibilities and attitudes relative to their professional life, their work and their family relationships. It is rather to explain how Catholic religion remained a parenthesis in their lives, albeit an important one in that world view.

The reforms of the council basically sought the full and active participation of all the baptized not only in the liturgy of the eucharist but in their experience of the Christian community.[18] So a central goal of the council was to bring the laity into a fully conventional morality, a full participation in the church's life and service. However, that said, we can immediately begin to understand why it is that lay people who were for centuries treated in a preconventional manner find it difficult suddenly to enter into more conventional attitudes.

Unless we explicitly address the type of transition remarked upon here, we can expect that most lay people will imagine that the church continues to invite them to a preconventional stance, a limited partnership in ecclesial life. This explains in part their passivity at liturgy, their unwillingness to enter into the dynamics of a singing church and their holding off religion as marginal to their ordinary life experience. The real challenge for implementing the reforms of Vatican II is not finding better texts or better rites, but creating better ways to communicate the necessity of the full participation of lay Christians in the life of the church.

This scenario brings us to the postconventional. Priests or other pastoral ministers who simply keep business-as-usual going strong will not be the ones to help the laity to make this transition. What is needed are postconventional and generative ministers, people who can appreciate and understand the reticence of laity long treated like second-class citizens and who want to help them to enter into a full commitment to the life of the church. Such generative personalities need to be more concerned about the potential for growth of those whom they serve than they are about their own status. A generative personality is someone whose focus is the potential for fulfillment of their clients or neighbors. Generative ministers must get beyond their own personal identity issues and move into the most serious of all concerns at this time, namely, the building of a community that is described in Eucharistic Prayer III as people made "one body and one spirit in Christ" by the power of God's Holy Spirit.

Heteronomy and Autonomy

The three levels of moral reasoning that we have just examined are loosely based on the moral development studies of Swiss psychologist Jean Piaget, who died in 1963. In his studies of the morality of children, Piaget came to the conclusion that there are two forms of morality based upon two kinds of relations. He called the one heteronomy and the other autonomy.[19] The first represents the moral construct of children who depend upon an authority relation for their security but who also feel a relation of constraint. The second, autonomy, is the morality of the older person based upon peer relations and a mutual "co-construction of meaning" with others of similar competence to oneself.

The word "heteronomy" is similar to a word we frequently use, "heterogeneous," meaning of another kind. Heteronomy means a *nomos,* or sense of order or rightness, that is constructed by another *(heteros).* Children experience heteronomy when they find themselves in a unilateral relation of inferior to superior, of inexperienced to experienced. As an extension of this insight, whenever people find themselves in a "one-down" relationship, they are being invited into an experience of heteronomy—of having to comply without fully understanding. What is called heteronomy here is parallel to what we called earlier the preconventional.[20]

Autonomy is self-constructed meaning. Like the word "automatic," "autonomy" means a sense of right constructed or moved by the self. Piaget discovered that children arrive at an early form of autonomy when they work together in a mutual or bilateral relation with one another at about the age of six or seven. When children at play discover that they have to change the rules or invent new rules to continue their game in a satisfactory fashion, they are already discovering autonomy. Autonomy in Piaget's perspective means cooperation. It is the satisfying and successful interaction of peers in the development of something of spontaneous mutual interest to all involved.

The tremendously important insight of Piaget's theory here is that the form of address or form of relation with which we engage others will have everything to do with their sense of belonging, self-investment and understanding. For example, when the nature of a group's public communication is always that of an authority figure condescending to the incompetent, then we can expect the result of the group's heteronomous response characterized, among other things, by some lack of interest, conviction and satisfaction. Too often we fail to analyze that we expect adult believers to accept the church's rules or explanations when they are offered in the manner of a school-teacher addressing children. Respect for the intellectual and social autonomy of people is tremendously important here.

In a similar way, whenever we do engage in a dialogical and mutually constructed understanding of a social situation, we have already invited autonomy, characterized by the group's desire to be involved, their fuller understanding of the issues and their sense of ownership of the matters at hand. This has obvious implications for the issues we have discussed relative to the importance of the church in the lives of believers and the feelings of commitment that they may come to generate toward the church.

This analysis allows us to understand that a serious need for conversion exists at every level in the church. The reforms of the council and its call to *aggiornamento* represent a challenge to every one of us. This challenge to conversion can be described in terms of one of the council's deepest preoccupations, that is, a community's transition from an objective, material and static outlook to a new preoccupation with personal witness, a new relationship and a sense of openness to God's future. It was characteristic of the counter-reformation period to *reify* (a word meaning "to make thing-like") the mystery of faith. When the dominant dynamic of the authoritarian church was to insist upon complete uniformity of doctrinal expression and ritual practice, it turned everything into objects and texts.

Notice the tremendous contrast between a seventeenth-century world in which the Roman Catholic liturgy was celebrated in Latin everywhere in the world—from Japan to Canada, from the Philippine Islands to Russia, from Africa to Iceland—on the one hand, and the council's teaching on inculturation, in which the work of evangelization is incomplete until embodied in the culture of each people, on the other. The council's invitation is toward a personalization of faith in which the witness to the gospel is not judged simply in terms of correct words spoken about creeds and doctrines, but in terms of appropriately familiar gestures of families, communities, cultures and peoples awakening to the reality of God's love in language and rites that make them feel at home. In this sense, inculturation is the road to autonomy and to conventional morality.

From Maintenance to Mission

The present situation of the church is ambiguous. There is much to cause us alarm. The church has lost much of its taken-for-granted authority among even its own communicants in a world in which the secularizing power of the media and of other forces in the popular culture is enormously strong. Many Catholic young people seem to have experienced an impoverished education in the faith and to be relatively illiterate about the church's teachings and its attitudes in many areas of faith and morals. Those who have responsibility for running parishes, church institutions and dioceses can easily find themselves distressed by the sense that the life of the church is in danger. From a "maintenance" perspective, it can seem that all of our energies should be devoted to frantically striving to re-establish the dynamics of faith that were characteristic of a pre–Vatican II world.

But such a perspective overlooks the tremendous potential for renewal in the present circumstances of the world. What Vatican II tried above all to insist upon was the internal and spontaneous assent of faith of those called to believe in the gospel and to enter Christian community. The council invited the full and active participation of believers in the church's worship and social life; it described the missionary outlook of a church preoccupied not particularly with itself, but with the needs of the world. Yet we have disoriented people by trying to engage them in so challenging a vision of the church and the world without doing a fundamental reorientation of our catechesis about ecclesial life. The problem was not that we exaggerated the council's teaching. The mistake was failing to follow through on the genius of the council with effective catechesis.

The challenge that lies before us is to move from maintenance to mission. As *Lumen Gentium* and *Gaudium et Spes,* two of the monumental documents of the council, have insisted, the church's fundamental responsibility is evangelization: The church must reach out to the world in the spirit of Jesus. Yet we are blocked by our anxieties to maintain the familiar. With a maintenance perspective we seem inevitably to be inviting our young people to a nostalgia, perhaps a romantic nostalgia, about life as it was.

A mission perspective is really concerned about life as it can be in the spirit of Jesus. Notice the contrast. In a maintenance perspective, we will be preoccupied not to lose any aspects of the life or culture of the church as it was familiar to older generations. (This is not necessarily to maintain the church as it was at the church's foundation or in its early and most vigorous missionary period. Nostalgia tends to be linked to shorter memories). But, in a mission perspective, we will realize that we have hardly begun the work of *aggiornamento,* the work of reaching out to our times and people in such a way as to create a new moment of church in which we can trust the many languages and cultures of the world (not just the Latin language and southern European culture) to become worthy embodiments of the Christian message.

This is not to suggest that we have no serious problems to deal with. Clearly one of our greatest problems is the need for an evagelization of our own members. Those called earlier "dormant Catholics" ought to be the object of the church's major solicitude. But is it not feasible that one of the principal reasons that our younger people might conceive a new interest in the church is their coming to understand that God may be asking them to become missionaries for a church of the future? Have we ever told them that there is a role for them as autonomous, generative people within the church? This is their avenue to maturity of faith.

The purpose of my essay here has been to point out that although we find ourselves at a moment in the life of the church that is filled with ambiguities, there are reasons for hope. If we are chiefly preoccupied with recreating a moment from the past (the maintenance vision), we will find ourselves as frustrated as we have been at any time in the last thirty years. If, however, we can see the signs of the times as offering us a new moment in which the *kerygma* of Christ's good news can be brought into dynamic dialogue with our immensely creative moment of history, then perhaps we can find a new grasp on faith and evangelization.

This new moment will not be easy. The forces of secularization and materialism are strongly narcissistic, elevating individual self-interest above every other concern. Yet the power of the gospel is the saving power of the world. We must believe that there is a way for it to engage the future of humankind. The maturing faith of the church is a faith that tries to understand reality through the signs of the times and brings it to bear upon the work of *aggiornamento*.

Some Pastoral Consequences

What implications might this developmental analysis have for understanding the life of our parishes and our dioceses? Can this way of looking at Catholic life today help us to address our pastoral problems and possibilities in a better fashion? I hope that the answer will be "yes."

Perhaps the first step in such a reflection would be to ask, "Who within our circle of responsibility is relegated to the status of preconventional?" Who are the people who stand at the fringes of our social unit—be it diocese, parish or small Christian community? And why do they feel themselves to be there? A maintenance perspective might react, "Well, at least they're not a problem to us: They keep their place and take some part in church life. Why not leave well enough alone?" But a mission perspective will immediately realize that leaving people on the margins is failing in the very substance of the work of evangelization, failing to help people to incarnate—make evident with their lives—the reality of God's people.

Another step has had to do with our pastoral responsibilities: Have we done enough to make it clear that the church, in the name of the gospel, seeks a living faith that touches the everyday and not just the sacred hour of Sunday morning? Pope John Paul II has written of the need for a "re-evangelization" that will teach the laity how "to take up in their daily activities in family, work and society, an integrated approach to life that is fully brought about by the inspiration and strength of the Gospel."[21] As strong as is the pope's urging of the laity to become a dynamic force for good in the transformation of society, we cannot avoid facing the fact that great masses of Catholic lay people see the church exclusively as a part-time ritual obligation, not as a full-time apostolic responsibility. How often do we even try to preach about this fundamental truth? A maintenance perspective might protest: "Well, we have enough trouble just planning and providing for the Masses on Sunday; we don't have time for adult catechesis." But a mission perspective would immediately add: "The Mass is for mission—the very word comes from the *Ite, missa est,* a phrase reminding us of the sending out of the assembled participants at Sunday worship to their missionary witness in families, work, and the surrounding world."

I have often heard people say, "We tried to get our parish to support adult education, but the people don't come." But, of course, if people have been addressed as preconventional (and so as somehow marginal figures in the ecclesial enterprise), then they are not suddenly going to re-evaluate the church's role in their life just because someone suddenly comes up with the good idea of involving them more deeply. Further, if they have been addressed unilaterally for as long as they can remember, then they are not suddenly going to take seriously an invitation to dialogue from anyone in a position of church authority—priest or pastoral minister. It is going to take time, patience, repeated invitations, personal contact and dialogue, to make inroads against the habits of the past.

On the other hand, any dynamic that does actually engage people in the parish in dialogue, in bilateral exchange, has already done something to transform their structure of belonging. As noted above, it is peer relations and the mutual respect that dialogue signifies that create a new kind of morality—the autonomy that invites previously uncommitted individuals to stand up for what they believe. All pastoral workers have stories, I'm sure, about ways in which people previously uncommitted and disinterested have conceived a new involvement and caring about the church through being asked to assist or take responsibility for some dimension of service in the neighborhood or parish. Volunteers in soup kitchens can find themselves suddenly aware of their need to know and celebrate the mystery of Jesus with fellow Christians once they begin to serve in Christ's name.

There is, however, another topic altogether that must be at least mentioned here. That topic is collaborative ministry. As the picture develops of a fuller engagement of the laity's involvement in the life of worship and ministry, it becomes evident that no one person, ordained or not, can oversee all the details of community growth and service that will emerge. Scott Appleby has described the role of the priest in this new pastoral situation as that of the orchestra leader who must know how to keep the tonally distinct but individually rich voices of the whole group of players in vibrant interaction and effective harmony.[22] This seems an apt description. The role of the pastor cannot any longer be the monoform ministry of the ordained leader alone, but must be as well the mentoring ministry of the generative minister whose joy will enable the service of each member of the community.

In these and other ways, we can hope to overcome the lapses in catechesis and mentoring that have failed to enliven our communities in past decades. We can hope thus to acknowledge and address the particular grief and particular hope of our different generations of Catholics, and invite them all into common life and ministry. And we can hope together to rediscover the fuller meaning of our pastoral challenge: *aggiornamento*. This is our *kairos,* and in it we will find the maturing faith of the church.

1. See, for example, M.-D. Chenu, "La Fin de l'Ere Constantinienne" in *L'Evangile dans le Temps: La Parole de Dieu II* (Paris: Cerf, 1964), 17 f. Also Henri Fesquet, *The Drama of Vatican II* (New York: Random House, 1967).

2. William V. D'Antonio et al., *Laity: American & Catholic* (Kansas City: Sheed & Ward, 1996), chapters 4, 5. Jim Davidson et al., *The Search for Common Ground: What Unites and Divides Catholic Americans* (Huntington, IN: Our Sunday Visitor, 1997), chapter 7.

3. Ibid., 65.

4. Ibid., 76.

5. Ibid., 79.

6. See, for example, Ruth Wallace, *They Call Her Pastor: A New Role for Catholic Women* (Albany: State University of New York Press, 1992). A sample of this kind of testimony, about a lay woman pastor: "[She] is not afraid to get out and minister, to get out and work at things and not sit back and give orders to somebody else to do the work. . . . Priests we have had don't take initiative. They put themselves on a pedestal and let somebody else do the work. Right now we are getting more total community effort than we ever have because she is so active." (72)

7. D'Antonio, *op. cit.,* 133.

8. Ibid., 131 f.

9. See *Encyclopedia of Catholicism,* ed. R. McBrien (San Francisco: Harper Collins, 1995), 665: "infallibility is not 'omniscience,' knowledge about everything. Thus, the pope and the college of bishops can teach with infallibility only in the very restricted area of revelation."

10. *Vatican Council II: Constitutions, Decrees, Declarations,* Austin Flannery, ed. (Dublin: Dominican Publications, 1996), "Dogmatic Constitution on the Church," 1. All subsequent citations of conciliar documents are taken from here.

11. Ibid., 9.

12. Ibid., chapter VII, 48 f.

13. "Declaration on Religious Liberty," 3. See also "The Pastoral Constitution on the Church in the Modern World," 16: "Deep within their consciences men and women discover a law which they have not laid upon themselves and which they

must obey. Its voice, ever calling them to love and to do what is good and to avoid evil, tells them inwardly at the right moment: do this, shun that. For they have in their hearts a law inscribed by God."

14. Lawrence Kohlberg, *The Philosophy of Moral Development: Moral Stages and the Idea of Justice* (San Francisco: Harper and Row, 1981), 16 and passim.

15. Ibid., 17: Kohlberg's description runs as follows: "The postconventional level is characterized by a major thrust toward autonomous moral principles that have validity and application apart from authority of the groups or people who hold them and apart from the individual's identification with those people or groups."

16. Although Kohlberg does not use the concept of generativity in explaining his understanding of the postconventional, that is what I understand much of Kohlberg's concern to be, that is, identifying with and sponsoring the needs and interests of others who need assistance to arrive at their maturity. See Erikson's explanation of generativity (a term he coined) in Erik H. Erikson, *Insight and Responsibility* (New York: Norton, 1964), 130 f. Compare Don S. Browning, *Generative Man: Psychoanalytic Perspectives* (New York: Dell, 1973). See my "Readiness for Ritual" in R. Duffy, ed., *Alternative Futures for Worship, Volume I* (Collegeville: The Liturgical Press, 1987), 63 f.

17. Thomas F. O'Meara, *Theology of Ministry* (New York: Paulist, 1983), chapter 1.

18. "The Constitution on the Sacred Liturgy," 11: "[Pastors] must also ensure that the faithful take part fully aware of what they are doing, actively engaged in the rite and enriched by it." See Albert Rouet, *Liturgy and the Arts* (Collegeville: The Liturgical Press, 1997), chapter 3.

19. Jean Piaget, *The Moral Judgment of the Child*, trans. Marjorie Gabain (New York: The Free Press, 1965).

20. A good summary of Piaget's insights which stresses the role of relationships in transforming moral stance can be found in James Youniss, *Parents and Peers in Social Development: A Sullivan-Piaget Perspective* (Chicago: University of Chicago Press, 1980), 1–20.

21. *Christifideles Laici: Post-Synodal Apostolic Exhortation of His Holiness John Paul II*, 34.

22. See Jay Dolan et al., *Transforming Parish Ministry: The Changing Role of Catholic Clergy, Laity, and Women Religious* (New York: Crossroad, 1990); chapter 6, "The Emergence of the Orchestra Leader," by R. Scott Appleby.

Mary Frances Reza

Cultural Diversity in Worship: Will We Survive?

Seeds of Struggle, Harvest of Faith

The Archdiocese of Santa Fe is preparing to commemorate its Cuarto Centennial, the arrival of the gospel in New Mexico in 1598. The motto chosen is *Seeds of Struggle, Harvest of Faith*. The commission's mission statement reads as follows:

> To commemorate the 400th anniversary of the permanent estab-
> lishment of Catholicism in the southwestern United States, the
> Catholic Cuarto Centennial Commission dedicates itself to:
> - An examination of our past, an assessment of our present and
>   our dedication to our future;
> - Telling the stories of our struggles and triumphs;
> - Recognize our shortcomings and accomplishments;
> - Rededicate ourselves to the spiritual renewal of our people.

There are several events being prepared to mark the important moments in the history of our faith. As one listens to the different members of this culturally diverse commission each contributing their gifts, the history and the faith of the church in New Mexico unfolds. The dialogue between the gospel and the cultures in these past 400 years has guided the rituals and symbols that have become a part of our rich history. As we rededicate ourselves to spiritual renewal, we bring our personal, social, geographic and temporal locations. "We carry with us not only the realities of the 20th century,"[1] but also the common historical memory of a pilgrim people who have transmitted their values, customs, art, their music and religious expressions as they struggled to keep the faith alive.

Today, with people relocating to many smaller communities from all parts of the country, "[w]e are marked and affected by the times in which we live."[2] Our parishes can no longer mirror the homogeneity of parish membership in years past. For many people growing up in northern New Mexico, one's perception as a child was that only Hispanics were Roman Catholics. Today, unlike the past, some mission communities are no longer predominantly Hispanic.

> Far-reaching cultural and social changes took place during the latter half of the 19th century as more and more people of differing economic, social and ethnic backgrounds poured into New Mexico disrupting the relatively uncomplicated Pueblo Indian and Hispanic bicultural society. One of the most significant cultural developments was the disruption of the religious unity of the older groups. Although the pueblos practiced many of their tribal religious customs, they, like the Hispanos, were nominally Roman Catholic. Attempts to institute changes in local Hispanic church practices were made by excommunicating some of the native clergy. The new prelate recruited in European countries, especially France, to fill the vacant parishes and missions.[3]

In the midst of a prejudicial history, the seeds of struggle, imbued with Christian meaning, are very much a part of this sacred journey and are echoed in different ways throughout the country.

Increasing Awareness of Cultural Diversity

Cultural diversity is a concern in all structures of today's society: schools, industry and our church communities. When asked to present "Cultural Diversity and Worship: Will We Survive?" as a topic,

I found that the subtitle created some problems, brought many emotions to the surface. It certainly implies conflict and the fear or concern that prevails in all parts of the country. This mentality often filters into the church.

The bishops of the United States, in their pastoral statement "Together, A New People," note:

> Immigration is viewed with both optimism and apprehension.
> A national debate is under way on how welcoming the country
> is; how much diversity it can accept and at what pace.[4]

The news media daily reveal this apprehension. Some time ago they brought to light an incident in which people were being brought to work in a cargo ship to work in slave conditions. These people were being exploited, yet the focus became the "immigrant problem." Rather than focusing on the criminal activity that was taking place, the concern turned to Proposition 187. People feel threatened in their workplaces, in their neighborhoods. They live in a world they no longer control. Xenophobia then sets in, leading to attempts to limit immigration by nationality. The efforts to limit language use by creating government policies is having an effect not only in the educational system and the economy but also in our parish communities, influencing people's orientation toward minority groups.

Language has been a big issue in this country. The importance of a second language for all people, which has been a missing link in the priorities of our educational system, becomes the sole responsibility of those who do not speak English. Michael Krauss in *Earthwatch* (1992) writes: "Any language is the supreme achievement of a uniquely human collective genius, as divine and unfathomable a mystery as a living organism." English-only attitudes in worship have a disastrous effect on developing understanding of the Roman Catholic rite among non–English speakers. Those who lose their mother tongue in the place where they are living and in their faith community experience disorientation and bitterness. The new language will never be steeped in culture and faith as the first language is for all persons.

What is happening in our communities in this country impacts what takes place in the effort that is being made towards inculturation, how we celebrate multicultural liturgies and how we accept cultural diversity in our communities. It is important to reflect on the culture of the larger environment and its effect on our faith and culture relationship as we make an effort to respond to this "moment of grace."[5] As the pope said to the World Congress,

> The church has a leading educative role to play amongst the people, the leaders and the structures of society in order to enlighten public opinion and stimulate consciences. But she herself must bear witness to the quality of integration that she practices in her own bosom . . . They should work ceaselessly to build up a people, speaking the language of love, to be a ferment in the construction of human unity . . . [6]

Liturgy and Cultural Heterogeneity

Today there is a search for ideas and information that will help in the preparation of liturgies that reflect the diversity in the parishes and enable them to better serve culturally diverse assemblies. There are no simple answers; however, an effort will be made to address some areas that may be helpful. There has been much bridge-building by way of articles on inculturation, the history of cultural adaptation in our Christian rites, cultural diversity and worship, the availability of bilingual liturgical music and the excellent work done by the Institute of Hispanic Liturgy in the translating of liturgical documents. If made available in parishes, these resources are invaluable. What is lacking is a sincere dialogue within our parish communities. A misunderstanding of deep culture or value systems results in discrimination. There is a tremendous need to "bear witness to the *quality* of integration that she practices in her bosom."[7] "What is first and primary is the existence of a deep level of union in the Body of Christ before coming to the table."[8]

Cultural heterogeneity impacts our parish creating a diversity climate that influences our parish experience. How do people feel about their parish? What is their perception of their own situation within the church structure? Have they been called forth to serve? What is their perception of those in leadership? In placing emphasis on the physical dimension such as black, white, Asian, Hispanic, one ignores the individual person, intergroup dynamics or whether individuals who are appointed to represent a particular culture indeed identify with the cultural traditions of that group. Defining the diversity climate becomes the responsibility of all.

There is a need to bring the cultural resources of the community to bear on the preparation of liturgies, a willingness to identify what is taking place in the parish, to develop awareness, knowledge and skills. All of these take time, but are needed to become a culturally skilled professional. This too is an important ministry. A forum for an exchange of ideas and resources related to those who make up the parish family through sharing their beliefs and customs will encourage cultural awareness and bring to the surface the creative potential within the parish community. Such a forum fosters an appreciation of diverse ethnic backgrounds and clarifies for the parish community how diversity contributes to the church. This is an important challenge which is often delegated to the in-groups who allocate parish resources and become responsible for making the human transactions with the different cultural groups.

Many ask, "Where can I fit them in?" Providing places where they can fit into the liturgy is not only a poor framework but transmits to that particular group that they are either liturgically deficient or not capable of participating in the process of preparation. If there is a lack of understanding of the rites, the most effective way to develop knowledge is through full participation in the process.

I recently heard about a well-intentioned liturgy committee which invited Spanish dancers in full costume to process down the aisle during the presentation and preparation of the gifts. Though it was festive, the young girls were not instructed about what to do after they danced up the aisle. Looking at each other in dismay, they proceeded to face the assembly, forming a line in front of the altar as they waved their colorful skirts waiting for their next cue.

These dancers were placed in an awkward position, were embarrassed and deserved better instruction. The significance of the rite was lost. Rather than promoting the concept of entertaining, this procession of dancers would have had a greater symbolic meaning if the dancers, as representatives of the assembly, had participated in the preparation of the altar, the procession bringing forth the gifts or in the incensation of the gifts, the altar, priest and people.

Another example: Aztec dancers have a profound love for Our Lady of Guadalupe. Part of their commitment, their *promesa*, is making sure they have a place to pay homage and dance on her feast day. One group, after having been invited to participate as preparation before the liturgy began, was informed by the diocesan organizers that they would be limited to five minutes. When they responded with concern, they were reminded that their presence was only for "color."

Though these are isolated cases in different parts of the country, these hurtful experiences affect attitudes and feelings about our worshiping communities. Are we "working ceaselessly to build up a people?"[9] We sometimes fail to realize the nature and the amount of power that our church structure sometimes represents. As Catholics, our parish communities have become entry points, the bridge for the new families integrating and understanding the American society. For people whose cultural, social and economic status differs from the dominant parish community, the church often represents a power with little flexibility, with limited options. This is not only creating an unwelcome environment but creates a marginalized group that begins to disrespect the Roman Catholic church.

Understanding the effects of culture on human behavior is crucial. There are underlying values, beliefs and principles that guide our practices and behavior. "Culture is a system of standards for perceiving, believing, evaluating, and acting."[10] Culture expresses who we are and how we came to be who we are, what we value and what pulls us apart. A group culture is manifested in what members of the group think, believe, understand and do. Much is written about the fragmentation or tensions that exist in the church today. There is much work to do in recognizing learned prejudices.

The "Cycle of Oppression" can be a practical and useful tool in discussing some of the cultural diversity and fragmentation we face in our parishes. The cycle is expressed in this way:

> Individuals are born into a group membership, be it the dominant or subculture, then are taught an interpretation of history or misinformation, stereotypes, etc., by significant people in their

lives—such as religious, parents, teachers, etc. These are reinforced and sanctioned by culture, traditions, family, religious
institutions, etc. As a result, people "act out" prescribed roles.
They may take on the role of the oppressed or the role of the
oppressor; they thereby choose to maintain the status quo, repeat
the cycle, find it difficult to break it or have the courage to take
responsibility for themselves and for making change by becoming more aware of their roles, and unlearning misinformation.[11]

The Omnipresence of Stereotyping

We are all a part of this cycle of oppression in one form or another.
Depending upon our role or place in this cycle, we limit the gifts available in the parish family by sex, age, ethnicity, language, socioeconomic
level or exceptionality. Being born into a particular status or history
and taught our norms or stereotypes has created many forms of human
oppression. Using this model for discussion provides an insight into
personal attitudes and behaviors and, we hope, the realization that
different does not mean deficient. As church, we must become responsible advocates for all people who enter into worship in our communities and begin to ask the right questions. For example, how do we
treat people when they begin to prepare for the sacraments?

Christian communities throughout the country, "as guardians
of the mission of Jesus Christ, are accommodating the changing populations and shifting cultures" (National Pastoral Plan for Hispanic
Ministry, 9) that are moving into their parishes or are coming from
other parishes because they know they are welcome there. Though
Canon 518 states that "Personal parishes are to be established based
upon rite, language, the nationality of the Christian faithful within some
territory or even upon some determining factor," we know there is
another reality. Pastors who have taken the time to become immersed
in the language and culture of the people are overwhelmed with congregations that continue to grow on a daily basis and thus have had to
provide more Sunday liturgies to accommodate the numbers.

One such parish is St. Patrick's Church in Watsonville, California.
I had the privilege of witnessing and participating in a baptismal liturgy,

which had to take place on Saturday due to the number of Sunday liturgies. There were 50 infants baptized. Everyone was very comfortable and familiar with the rite. There was a sense of common identity, a sense of belonging to the community. The church was filled with families, extended family, friends and members of the community.

Children were the ministers of hospitality, making sure that everyone had a pamphlet for the order of worship with the music to be sung and they were very quick to collect them all after the liturgy. The presiding deacon gave an excellent introduction. The minister of music, Eleazar Cortes, rehearsed the music with the assembly. The presider invited the parents with their infants, the *padrinos* and *madrinas,* to go to the entrance of the church where they were welcomed and the Reception of the Children was celebrated. All were invited to enter the church.

As we entered, the assembly sang: *Agua viva que limpias, que lavas y purificas, reverdeces el tallo seco. Yo quiero agua viva.* The liturgy of the word was celebrated, and all participated in singing Salmo 118, *Este es el dia que actuo el Senor . . .* After the intercessions, the godparents, parents and infants processed to the font for the rite. As they processed, everyone responded to the litany of the saints. After each baptism, all sang *Bendito sea Dios que hoy te llama por tu nombre.* For the conclusion of the rite, they processed to the altar singing *El Senor es mi luz y mi salvacion.* The final hymn was *Somos una iglesia* as the infants were taken to be presented before the image of the Blessed Mother.

This was an excellent example of how each culture articulates a meaning of the sacraments. The celebration witnessed that it was "the common treasure of the whole church of Christ." It was moving to see grandparents wiping the tears from their eyes and whispering to the next person, *Que maravilla!*

The vitality of this faith experience—with full and active participation, hospitality and a variety of music which was indeed faithful to the rite—fulfilled the purpose of this sacrament, which "is to sanctify, to build up the body of Christ, to give worship to God. Because they are signs, they also instruct" (CSL 59). The teamwork and preparation of the ministers made this possible. Dorothy Tomaso, liturgist at St. Patrick's, spent much time working with the Spanish-speaking ministers, always making an effort to involve more people. As she prepared the bilingual liturgies, there was much support from the Hispanic community. A comment Dorothy made sums up how passionately she believes in her work. "I believe that—if we can sit together and worship in the house of the Lord and if we can journey together in a communion procession—we will be able to do it on the street and in the fields and wherever we happen to be. If farm owners and field workers can sit next to each other and greet one another in worship, they will be able to do it in the fields."

Pastors, liturgists and musicians have a tremendous responsibility in being good stewards with the gifts entrusted to them, providing the same teaching and training to all liturgical ministers. Preparing bilingual or multicultural liturgies takes time. A society or a church that expects an instantaneous change will be disillusioned.

> We learn to do the liturgy through repeated participation in it. More importantly, and on a deeper level, the readings, prayers, gestures work together over long periods of time to shape our ways of perceiving and living out our lives. Attitudes, values and ways of acting are subtly nurtured through the liturgy.[12]

The process of developing literacy in the Roman Catholic rite develops when there is an interaction with the parish community, an interaction in the process of planning parish activities, in the process of preparing liturgies and as full participants in the liturgical celebrations. Learning accumulates over a period of time within the church at prayer.

People immersed in this ministry and pastors with large immigrant populations all echo the same phrase, "Our cultural diversity is the hope of the church." Our cross-culture worship is a foreshadowing of the kingdom of God. "When you treat the alien who resides with you no differently than the natives born among you; have the same love for him as for yourself; for you too were once aliens in the land of Egypt. I, the Lord, am your God" (Leviticus 7:9).

As we enter the new millennium, our wisdom keepers, the indigenous people, have much to teach us as the changing face of the church challenges us.

Mary Frances Reza

Our people have always known that life begets death, which begets life and new beginnings are always marked by death of something old. It is death of the old which is necessary to bring something new . . . It is time when whole communities are going into healing. It is the time of the appearance of the White Buffalo. People are developing new ears to listen, they are asking for traditional knowledge and wisdom.

We focus on goal setting when we used to focus on process or how to get where we are going. We fear darkness when it used to be a place of healing. We serve our jobs when our work used to serve us. We think first, then feel second when we used to feel from our hearts first, then our minds would act on these feelings. We focus on the needs of today's generations when our decisions used to be based on the effects of seven generations.[13]

In Santa Fe, as we commemorate our Cuarto Centennial, we give thanks for our cultural diversities that make up the people of God. "Once you were not a people at all and now you are the People of God" (1 Peter 2:9). The customs and religious expressions have been transmitted through poetry, songs, the arts, all telling stories of the seeds of struggle in keeping the faith alive, a process of life and death that has encompassed changes that began in 1598.

1. Maria Harris, *Proclaim Jubilee: A Spirituality for the 21st Century* (Louisville: Westminster John Knox Press, 1996), 3.

2. *Against Forgetting: Twentieth Century Poetry of Witness* (New York: W. W. Norton, 1973), 40.

3. *The Historic Preservation Program for New Mexico*, Volume 1 (Santa Fe: State Planning Office, 1973), 40.

4. "Together, A New People," *Pastoral Statement on Migrants and Refugees* (Washington: NCCB, 1986). (See Pastoral Letters, Volume V, 4: "The Voice of the Church in the Current Debate," 336).

5. NCCB, Pastoral Plan, *The Hispanic Presence: Challenge and Commitment*, 1983.

6. John Paul II, "Pastoral Care of Immigrants," Address to the World Congress (October 17, 1985).

7. Ibid.

8. Mary Alice Piil, *Assembly* 23:3 (May 1997).

9. John Paul II, "Pastoral Care of Immigrants," Address to the World Congress, (October 17, 1985).

10. W. Goodenough, *Culture, Language, and Society* (Reading, MA: Addison-Wesley, 1971).

11. Adapted from Anne Bishop, *Becoming an Ally: Breaking the Cycle of Oppression* (Halifax: Fernwood, 1994).

12. Gilbert Ostdiek, *Catechesis for Liturgy* (Washington: Pastoral Press, 1986), 9.

13. Larry Kuuyux, an Aleut, shared these unpublished thoughts in a presentation at an educational conference.

H. Richard Rutherford, csc

Cremation American-Style:
A Change for the Better

Whenever one stops to ponder the changing face of the church at any point in its history, the way Christians care for their dead is a sure touchstone of the intensity of the changes taking place. Today we stand before a change of immense significance as we begin to incorporate the U.S. bishops' pastoral decision to permit the celebration of Catholic funeral liturgy in the presence of the cremated remains of our dead in place of the deceased body. This decision and the Roman indult authorizing its implementation recognize the widespread acceptance of cremation as an alternative to traditional funeral customs and, more significantly, the common cultural perception that sees no distinction between the body or the cremated remains of the deceased as the object of funeral liturgy. Does the bishops' decision usher in a change for the better? In the current cremation culture in North America, the answer, I believe, is an unequivocal "yes."

What do I mean by the qualification "current cremation culture"? Cremation American-style generally follows the pattern of direct or immediate cremation and disposition (usually by means of scattering, however creatively) of the cremated remains, with postdeath ritualization taking some form of memorial service without the ashes. North American Catholics and many other Christians have demonstrated that this manner of taking advantage of the cremation option is unsatisfactory. Christian funeral rites in the churches of liturgical tradition require a focus of ritual attention. If not the body, then the cremated remains!

In this climate, pastorally, the U.S. bishops had no other choice. Catholic Canada and four of their brother bishops as well as the ecumenical community had already declared in practice that funeral rites with cremated remains is "no big deal" and no different from traditional funeral liturgy with the body present.

Throughout Christian history, certainly, funerary ritual had to do with the body of the deceased. "Funeral"—derived from the Latin *funus* for funeral procession with the body—and "corpse" are inseparable notions. No wonder services after direct cremation and final disposition of the cremated remains are referred to as "memorial" rather than "funeral." Could our very language be telling us that such an event, however meaningful, is not the same thing as a "funeral"?

Whatever the circumstances, this pastoral decision to authorize funeral liturgies in the presence of cremated remains is a major profession of Catholic faith about the dignity of the human person and respect due to the earthly remains of baptized Christians. It stands in direct opposition to a cremation culture that, implicitly at least, preserves a secular view of death as the definitive end of life without future and its consequent disregard for any funeral rites with the body or cremated remains. Even though the Catholic bishops in the United States had little choice but to approve and thus regularize this change in funerary practice (the real *fait accompli* alluded to by Archbishop Medina Estévez in the letter of indult), their choice is—in his words— a "contribution to the shaping of future custom" and, in my opinion, a significant change for the better. Nevertheless, it is just a beginning, and its implications for liturgical practice will be part of the changing face of the church for a long time to come. Let us explore all of this more fully in light of contemporary culture and the explicit implications for the liturgy.

H. *Richard Rutherford*, CSC

A Changing Culture

Not too long ago *The New York Times* carried a front-page story recounting the chance discovery by archaeologists in Guatemala of still another mass grave containing the human remains of hundreds of victims of the revolutionary violence that marked that country's recent past. The accompanying photo revealed native Guatemalan women, the mothers and wives and sisters of the dead, kneeling in distraught prayer over the shallow grave of strewn skeletons (June 7, 1997). The article quoted one of the women deploring their helplessness in face of such violence and lamenting how in death their slaughtered men are thrown together in a common grave with no burial place of their own: "I just want to be able to give him a Christian burial. . . . I want to know where he is, so that I can leave flowers and candles, as is our custom" (page 5).

This is a culture we Christian faithful are familiar with. We understand the plight of these distressed women. We too want to know where our dead are buried and that their graves are cared for. We too know what it means to visit our cemeteries and remember our dead in prayer. This is our culture; this is the culture that gave us the *Order of Christian Funerals* as recently as 1989.

Yet it is a culture undergoing radical change. The extremes of the swinging pendulum offer little security, even at the time of death when consistent funerary rituals once provided a stable context, some peace of mind and the consolation of the faith. The culture in which those Guatemalan women lament the fate of their beloved dead and the horrors of mass graves is the same one that spawned the death squads who cut down their loved ones and buried them so scandalously.

Closer to home, our North American culture that spends millions annually on funerary ostentation and burial vaults guaranteed to withstand natural destruction is the same one in which a child born at a high school prom finds its near final resting place in a public dumpster, joining the many other unborn and newborn infants whose dumpster burials have made the news or remain undetected. Our newspapers report on practically the same page an airplane hangar stacked high with boxes of cremated remains abandoned by the person responsible for their respectful disposition and, at the other end of the swinging pendulum, "virtual cemeteries" where one can say farewell in cyberspace, sharing "memories and pain on the World Wide Web" (*USA Today,* June 19, 1997, page 12D).

This is the culture in which we today discuss cremation American-style and ponder how inculturating it into Catholic liturgical practice is a change for the better. To do so let us first examine the context characterized by the phenomenon I am calling "cremation American-style" and identify the Catholic beliefs and values that are touched by it. Next we must clarify the new situation ushered in by the recent indult. Only then, in my opinion, can we appreciate the full impact of funeral liturgy with cremated remains in place of the body.

Cremation American-Style: Aspects and Origins

Following the secular trends of "modern" nineteenth-century Europe, cremation in the United States began in the 1870s as an enlightened alternative to traditional, mostly religious, funeral and burial customs. In other parts of the Western world where cremation is common today, such as Great Britain and northern Europe, cremation continued as a secular substitute for traditional customs, on the one hand, while, on the other, traditional culture incorporated it simply as an alternative manner of disposing of the dead following the religious funeral with the body present.

Cremation in twentieth-century North America developed under different cultural circumstances. The past century saw the rise and cultural predominance of the "American way of death" with embalming and cosmetic restoration of the corpse and funeral parlors where the deceased can be laid out and viewed as life-like as possible. In contrast to Europe and the British Isles where these practices are not customary, funerals in North America are costly. A decade ago in the United States the average funeral cost $2400; today conservative estimates exceed $5000.

Already in the 1960s growing opposition to the high cost and perceived ostentation of this kind of funeral found a champion in Jessica Mitford. Her book *The American Way of Death* (New York: Simon & Schuster, 1963) gave Americans, Catholics among them, "permission" to look for simpler alternatives. Some established memorial societies dedicated to simplified funerals; some wrote do-it-yourself funeral manuals. For the majority, however, direct cremation became the option of choice, and "cremation American-style" was born. By this phrase I refer to cremation without any funeral ritualization between death and cremation; in other words, cremation as an alternative to the funeral. Instead of the traditional funeral, a memorial service was arranged sometime after cremation. Perhaps this is the origin too of the now familiar Catholic scenario where immediate or direct cremation takes place right after death and a "memorial Mass" follows some time later, a situation the bishops' decision and Rome's indult intend to correct.

On the West Coast, where this modern cremation alternative took shape, the movement quickly numbered people of all backgrounds, not merely secularized malcontents. In the years between the 1960s and 1980s Catholics chose some 20% of the direct cremations reported, and Jews another 20%. Previously uncommon organizations known as cremation societies blossomed into a new cremation industry.

In this context it is important to distinguish between a cremation society and a memorial society. Memorial societies define themselves as "nonprofit, nonsectarian, educational organizations that are geared to helping people make prudent, no-nonsense funeral plans" [http://vbiweb.champlain.edu/famsa]. Responding to the growth of such memorial societies and to the increased interest in cremation, some business people adopted the word "society" into the names of new commercial ventures promoting cremation. Best known among these is the Neptune Society of California, with its "membership" fee and final disposition at sea, and more recently the Internet Cremation Society on the World Wide Web [http://www.cremation.org].

Despite its beginning and early influence as an alternative to the American funeral, cremation has joined the list of services provided by the traditional funeral industry as "an acceptable method for preparing a body for its ultimate disposition" (*The Director*, November 1991, page 9), with appropriate goods and services for sale. As the decade draws to a close, some of those cremations (often with all the frills) cost as much as the old-fashioned funeral.

With its spread eastward in the 1990s, simple alternatives have given way to new and increasingly more expensive goods and services for those who choose cremation. For example, the Internet Cremation Society places ads on the World Wide Web for classic cremation urns side by side with containers for cremated remains in the form of a seated couple cast in bronze or matched jewelry boxes.

The *Cremationist* magazine advertises Blue Ridge Memorial Pottery, "a unique bond of the cremains of a loved one with the earthen elements of clay and glaze. . . . The finished pottery becomes an heirloom both elegant and personal." Concerned parish ministers are awestruck when asked to bless religious pendants "made from grandma's ashes, so all the grandchildren can wear a part of her memory." It is no longer a matter of grandma being *in* the urn on the mantle; grandma can now *be* the urn on the mantle. One wonders how long it will take creative religious goods manufacturers to offer cremation containers in the form of Michaelangelo's *Pietà* or statues of Mary or one's favorite crucifix!

Certainly we must be pastorally sensitive to the choices people make in these matters and, indeed, trivializing those choices is most inappropriate. My purpose for these illustrations and projections is not to trivialize but simply to describe the cultural reality within which we discuss our beliefs and values in face of death and the choice for cremation in North America. Who knows? Perhaps one day the *Pietà* may prove to be an appropriate cremation container for Catholics! For the present, however, that is not the intention.

A Brief History of the Cremation Indult

Nearly a quarter-century ago, in May 1963, the Holy See lifted the canonical prohibition against cremation. What was understood by cremation then, and even now outside North America, is a manner of final disposition of the deceased. Thus, where cremation was already widespread, it simply followed the full funeral liturgy with the body. In fact, the initial permission in 1963 did not authorize any liturgical rites in conjunction with cremation, neither accompanying the body to the crematory or prayers of committal. With the publication in 1969 of the *Ordo Exsequiarum* and of its U.S. edition, the *Rite of Funerals* in 1970, however, rites usually held at the grave were permitted at the place of cremation. All of this made sense in Europe and the British Isles, where crematories include gathering halls or "chapels" and conveyances by means of which the coffin is delivered into the actual cremation space or even into the cremation chamber (retort) itself. In that context committal rites were the appropriate liturgy for cremation.

Meanwhile in North America, however, Catholics found themselves in a different situation, "cremation American-style," in which it is not simply a matter of final disposition but generally speaking an alternative to funeral services with the body altogether. In other words, when North Americans select cremation they are opting usually for direct or immediate cremation following death, with the consequence that any post-death ritualization thus becomes some form of memorial, usually without the cremated remains present.

More and more, good practicing Catholics began asking, "If we are allowed to choose cremation, what's wrong with celebrating our ordinary funeral liturgy with the ashes instead of the body?" When the question found its way to Rome, the response was based on principles reflecting the European practice of cremation and the *Rite of Funerals* (*Notitiae* 13 [1977].) Although the response provided a valuable interpretation of liturgical principles, as we shall see, it only complicated matters in North America, where little more was heard than its prohibition of cremated remains at the funeral Mass.

During the 1980s, in response to pastoral demands, parishes across North America began including cremated remains at funeral liturgy. Often this happened without authorization or direction and caused quite a bit of pastoral confusion. By 1984 both French- and English-speaking bishops in Canada had secured permission from the Holy See to celebrate the full funeral liturgy with the ashes present. When they published the *Order of Christian Funerals* for use in Canada (1990), it included a provisional rite for "funeral liturgy in the presence of ashes." Although the 1989 U.S. edition of the *Order of Christian Funerals* (in preparation since the early 1980s and under scrutiny in Rome after approval by the U.S. bishops in 1985) included prayers for cremated remains at the Rite of Committal after cremation, it did not directly address the real issue. Quite simply, cremation American-style required a liturgy of its own, but the time did not appear opportune.

The Bishops' Committee on the Liturgy established a task group in 1989 to study the matter. By the end of 1991 the task group made its recommendations and drafted principles for a published statement by the NCCB. Meanwhile the annual percentage of cremations in the United States passed 20%, in some states exceeding 50%. Four dioceses with high cremation usage took the initiative independently to secure permission from Rome to include cremated remains at the funeral liturgy. Finally, at their June 1996 meeting, the bishops' conference decided to request the indult from the Holy See to celebrate the full funeral liturgy with the cremated remains present. The Congregation for Divine Worship and the Discipline of the Sacraments granted that permission on March 21, 1997.

The Message of the Indult

In the letter granting the indult, Archbishop Medina Estévez acknowledged the U.S. bishops' concern about the "increasingly frequent practice of cremation among the Catholic population" and its effects on liturgical practice and wrote on behalf of the Congregation for Divine Worship and the Discipline of the Sacraments as follows:

> In conformity with canon 1176, § 3, the custom of according burial to the bodies of the deceased is to be commended and encouraged.
>
> If, however, the family of the deceased or the testament of the deceased requests that the body be cremated or if this is required by civil authorities, the funeral may nevertheless be celebrated liturgically, provided that the cremation is not undertaken for motives in opposition to Christian doctrine (canon 1176, § 3).
>
> It is greatly to be preferred that the funeral liturgy take place in the presence of the body of the deceased prior to its cremation. Suitable texts should be identified within the existing liturgical books or prepared afresh which take proper account of the fact that the body is to be cremated rather than buried. . . .
>
> Experience has shown that on occasion request is made for the funeral liturgy to be celebrated in the presence of the ashes of

the deceased after cremation. In the light of an opinion expressed by the Congregation for the Doctrine of the Faith on 3 December 1984 (Prot. 99/18), and of the recent vote of the Assembly of Bishops, this Dicastery concedes a particular permission to the diocesan Bishops of the United States of America. By this, local Ordinaries are authorized in the individual cases which are brought to their attention to permit that the funeral liturgy, including where appropriate the celebration of the Eucharist, be celebrated in the presence of the cremated remains instead of the natural body. In each individual case the local Ordinary should give due consideration to the various aspects of the pastoral situation and to the spirit and precise content of the current canonical norms. It is necessary that care be taken that all is carried out with due decorum. (NCCB Committee on the Liturgy *Newsletter* 33 [1997]: 13–14)

With headlines and comments like "Cremation: A Change for Catholics," the news media and popular opinion billed the U.S. bishops' practical pastoral decision as if it were a request for the Catholic Church to "*reconsider its insistence* on the presence of the body at funeral Masses" (Associated Press, June 8, 1996, emphasis added). Yet the letter of indult authorizing this practice and all the literature explaining it, including the pastoral introduction and liturgical texts prepared as an appendix to the *Order of Christian Funerals*, insist that the "custom of according burial to the bodies of the deceased" remains the clearly articulated norm. The pamphlet *Reflections on the Body, Cremation, and Catholic Funeral Rites*, which the Bishops' Committee on the Liturgy prepared as a catechetical guide, affirms, "Although cremation is now permitted, it does not enjoy the same value as burial of the body. Catholic teaching continues to stress the preference for burial or entombment of the body of the deceased" (page 9). The introduction to the liturgical adaptations approved by the bishops in November 1996 explains the difference succinctly, "The Church clearly prefers and urges that the body of the deceased be present for the funeral rites, since the presence of the human body better expresses the values which the Church affirms in those rites" (OCF, Appendix II, 413).

This is the pastoral lead offered by the proposed adjustments to the *Order of Christian Funerals* and the spirit with which all in pastoral ministry are invited to use the indult.

> The Church's teaching in regard to the human body as well as the Church's preference for burial of the body should be a regular part of catechesis on all levels and pastors should make particular efforts to preserve this important teaching.
>
> Sometimes, however, it is not possible for the body to be present for the Funeral Mass. When extraordinary circumstances make the cremation of a body the only feasible choice, pastoral sensitivity must be exercised by priests, deacons, and others who minister to the family of the deceased. (OCF, Appendix II, 414–415)

Reflections interprets this "feasible choice" further, "While promoting the values that underlie our preference for burial of the body, we must exercise sensitive pastoral judgment concerning the choice that nearly 20 percent of our people are making in favor of cremation. Economic, geographical, ecological, or family factors on occasion make the cremation of a body the only feasible choice" (page 9).

Recognizing that an indult is always a statement by way of exception to current practice, as the term implies, we are not surprised that current canonical legislation about cremation and about liturgy with cremated remains is the norm. With the indult, in other words, full funeral liturgy with cremated remains present in place of the body of the deceased is now an authorized exception to the current canonical norm. This was a foot in the door, so to speak, but direct or immediate cremation remains an exception (however authorized) and so does its liturgy.

Is This a Change for the Better?

Change has occurred. Direct cremation is here to stay, at least for the foreseeable future, and American Catholics, like other Americans, now take it for granted. In light of the history briefly sketched above, cremation American-style now comes in two forms. Cremation societies generally follow the classic sequence: direct cremation, immediate disposal, memorial service. Funeral directors encourage the newer pattern: direct cremation, funeral services with the cremated remains, disposal according to the wishes of the client (the deceased or the family). In this case cremated remains substitute for the body.

How does this change affect Catholic beliefs and values? How is it a change for the better? These two questions are inseparable. To the extent that our beliefs and values at death are enriched through the experience of the cremation experience and indeed themselves enrich the developing cremation culture then we can say that the change will be for the better. Two criteria seem essential.

First of all, Catholic faith takes death seriously and affirms in its liturgy that death is real. Death happens to us, all of us, the whole of us. How does immediate cremation relate to the reality of death?

Where cremation fosters denial of this reality by avoidance of the ordinary recognition of death and the deceased, one would certainly question its value in Catholic practice. This death-denying aspect has been one of the standard arguments in bereavement literature against cremation. However, times and motives change. As one Catholic college student who experienced her father's death and cremation expressed it, cremation made the death and reality of the loss all the more real. It was so definitive that no one could mistake the ashes for anything but death, non-life. This assumes a role for the cremated remains in post-death rituals.

Several recent surveys and others in progress seem to show that cremation soon after death in itself is neither more death-denying or more affirming of death than extensive funeral rituals with the body. Those qualities of the experience seem to depend significantly on the nature of the loss experience and on the person of the bereaved. Whether services with the ashes present play a significant role in bereavement deserves substantial research in light of changes in Catholic liturgical practice.

A second criterion concerns the way Catholic faith has traditionally embraced the reality of death by professing its belief and hope in the resurrection of the dead. This is an incarnational faith, a sacramental faith in which the body of the deceased has played an essential role in the root metaphor of resurrection. How is this affected by immediate cremation? An important aspect of an answer to this question touches another, much more difficult question. Are the cremated remains the same thing as the deceased body?

Belief in the resurrection of the dead is in no way affected by the state of the corporeal remains, whether lost at sea, destroyed by fire, naturally decomposed or cremated—to mention the most common. This has been the clearly articulated teaching of the Catholic church throughout the entire history of the cremation controversy. (For a summary see Irion, 73–84.) Following the U.S. bishops' decision to seek the indult in 1996 Bishop Donald Trautman, then chairman of the Bishops' Committee on the Liturgy, stressed that the indult should not be interpreted as a change in this teaching. Nevertheless, he added that when cremation takes place following death, it is better to celebrate all the rites of passage with the remains present, not to exclude the remains from the funeral liturgy (Associated Press, June 8, 1996). The bishops' decision was a pastoral one. For the theology of resurrection there clearly is no significant difference.

Can the same thing be said for the liturgy? That is, can the cremated remains of the deceased body simply be substituted for the body in the liturgical expression of our resurrection faith? Liturgical symbolism must correspond to the reality it expresses, as the *Constitution on the Sacred Liturgy* stated so forcefully. Here the principles of the 1977 directive from the Holy See provide a clear perspective.

> It does not seem suitable to celebrate with the ashes present the rite which is intended to honor the body of the dead. This is not to condemn the practice of cremation but rather to respect the integrity of the signs within the liturgical action. In fact, the ashes which are an expression of the corruptibility of the human body are unable to express the inherent character of one "sleeping," awaiting the resurrection. The body, not the ashes, receives liturgical honors since it was made the temple of the Spirit of God in baptism. It is important to respect the verity of the sign in order that the liturgical catechesis and the celebration itself be authentic and fruitful. (*Notitiae* 13 [1997])

The faith claims expressed in the historic rites of the *Order of Christian Funerals* are grounded in the symbol of the deceased person, attended to liturgically through symbols related to the corpse. That is, we invest the body with what we believe about the person. Christians have always treated the body with reverence and kept its resting place sacred because we believe it has been one with the soul in life's spiritual journey. In the funeral liturgy we address the person, reflected in the body, who is believed to be participating now in the victory of Jesus' death and resurrection, carried by angels to the heavenly Jerusalem and welcomed triumphantly by the martyrs and all the saints even as the corpse is carried in procession to the church, the earthly symbol of that heavenly court, for burial.

This symbolism has its roots in the late antique and medieval body-soul anthropology (with its source in various forms of Hellenistic dualism baptized as a brand of Christian neo-Platonism) that could comfortably live with the expectation of a material resurrection of the dead and reunion of a raised material body and immortal soul on the last day of judgment. Hence the cemetery was experienced in everyday life as the "bedroom" of the dead *(koimeterion)* awaiting the resurrection. Although contemporary belief in the resurrection of the dead is not tied literally to a body-soul realism, the association between death and the body of the dead person, on the one hand, and the body and resurrection, on the other, is central to Catholic funeral liturgy. Similarly, the motif of procession to Christ *(ire ad Christum)* still captures the religious imagination of the bereaved church as do the baptismal references to the sacramental life of the deceased expressed in the sprinkling with holy water and placing the white pall over the casket.

Now to the question at hand: How is our incarnational faith in the resurrection of the dead affected, liturgically speaking, by immediate cremation? In my opinion American Catholics are to be applauded for persisting in the conviction that "memorial Masses" without the cremated remains present or after their final disposition were unsatisfactory as Catholic funeral liturgy. However, the pastoral decision to seek authorization of full funeral liturgy with cremated remains — although a change for the better — still urges us to follow through with liturgy appropriate to cremated as distinct from corporeal remains.

Cremation

The *sensus fidelium* is accurate: Cremated remains are certainly earthly remains. Yet they are no longer the body of the deceased. They are, in a sense, one degree of abstraction further removed from the living person. They are the result of a technologically accelerated process of decomposition (actually vaporization) by means of intense heat (1800° F) that reduces the human body to bone fragments, which are then pulverized into the desired consistency of a powder-like substance. Cremationists prefer not to call them ashes, which implies burning, a concept often found offensive to potential clients. They have coined the neologism "cremains." It is fitting, I believe, that American Catholic literature avoids this term, preferring instead "cremated remains" or "earthly remains" or simply the colloquial term "ashes." By whatever name, the reality does not evoke the image of the human body that is the focus of the spoken words and acted signs of the funeral liturgy in its present form.

Shaping Future Liturgical Custom

Are cremated remains perhaps more like relics of the body than the body itself? Without suggesting a return to our questionable history surrounding the relics of the saints, we remember that our funeral liturgy has its origins in keeping the memory of the martyrs and celebrating those memorials as closely as possible to their place of burial. We remember too that the church has embraced widely different cultural practices in its care of corporeal remains. One such custom was to exhume the bones of the dead to preserve them in special shrines called charnel houses; another reduced the exhumed bones to small fragments to keep them respectfully in small bone boxes or ossuaries.

What if today we were to view the cremated remains of dead Christians as such relics of the bodies of the baptized, to be laid to rest and preserved with reverence in the columbaria or cremation gardens of our cemeteries? What form would the spoken words and acted signs of our funeral liturgy in the presence of such relics take? One can imagine newly prepared rites that would include "the use of a worthy vessel to contain the ashes, the manner in which they are carried, the care and attention to appropriate placement and transport, and the final disposition" (OCF, Appendix II as proposed) and yet not replicate the funeral liturgy for the body. While this exploration is not entirely facetious, its chief purpose is to help us recognize the possibility of approaches to liturgy with cremated remains that are consistent with the funerary tradition of the church and the reality of cremation, as well as "respect the integrity of the signs within the liturgical action" (*Notitiae* 1977). Would this be a way the church in North America might enter the risky realm of genuine inculturation and perhaps make "its considered contribution to the shaping of future custom" (Letter of Indult, page 2)?

Meanwhile, the liturgical adaptations in the proposed Appendix II of the *Order of Christian Funerals* are a good beginning. Pastorally they take people where they are, accepting the reality that, as far as funerals go, North American public opinion generally equates the body and the ashes as the earthly remains of their deceased loved ones. So, the liturgical adaptations treat the cremated remains in the same manner as the deceased body as far as possible, including reception at the church door, sprinkling, procession, placement in front of the church where the coffin would otherwise stand and final commendation, all focusing on the container with the ashes. The only visible difference is the omission of the white pall, which is so closely associated with clothing the human body in a white garment at baptism that it would be a very forced symbol to apply it to ashes. I would argue that similar reasoning applies to sprinkling with holy water at the reception and even incense at the final commendation, both of which relate symbolically so directly to the human body as sacramentally engaged in the Christ life of the deceased that the symbols seem misdirected when used with cremated remains.

Nevertheless, I appreciate the potential of such symbols to be gestures of blessing, thus professing in ritual form the belief that "cremated remains of a body should be treated with the same respect given to the corporeal remains of a human body" (OCF, Appendix II as proposed) and that they "be accorded proper respect as befits the dignity of human person and of baptized Christians" (Letter of Indult, page 2). With respect for the pastoral liturgical choices which the

Committee on the Liturgy made in a spirit of compromise between prevailing scholarly positions, and particularly given the importance of preparing both liturgical adaptations and catechesis in a timely fashion, I am nonetheless convinced that they are but the beginning.

Beyond the liturgical ruminations above about relics, new ritual developments will surely follow as North American Catholics discover that appropriate respect for cremated remains does not mean any less reverence for the body of their loved one. Here too the *Order of Christian Funerals,* taken as a whole, should be able to surround our immediate need to provide funeral liturgy for cremated remains with the treasures of the vigil and related rites with the body as well as the rite of committal and opportunities for memorial at the final resting place of the ashes long after the funeral. Rather than assuming that the choice for cremation implies that the full OCF be celebrated with cremated remains, newly emphasized liturgical rites with the body might move closer to the time of death. Caring attention to the deceased body, expressed, for example, through a tender bathing and dressing of the deceased soon after death and surrounded by prayer and personal stories, gives new meaning to ancient Christian custom and to the revised rites in the *Pastoral Care of the Sick* and the related rites of the OCF. The reverence and respect for the body and its sacramental character in our faith life need not be diminished by the choice for immediate cremation and funeral liturgy with cremated remains, but in fact might be intensified. In this we might well follow the example of John Daniel, a secular humanist, who, while taking direct cremation and disposition of ashes for granted as appropriate to mark the definitive end of life, pays admirable respect to the flesh and blood remains of his mother in this moving scene from his autobiographical narrative *Looking After: A Son's Memoir* (Washington: Counterpoint, 1996, pages 204–205):

> Marilyn suggested that we wash my mother. She asked the nurse on duty to free the body of its IV and other paraphernalia while we waited in the hall, then the five of us went in and stood around her — Jim at her head, our cousin Betty at her feet, Marilyn and Paulann on her left, me on her right. We wet towels in a basin of warm water and gently wiped her skin, gently toweled her small breasts, her abdomen with its slanting hernia scar,

the sparse silver hairs of her pubic area, her silky upper thighs, her dry and purpled shins and forearms, her feet with their crooked and callused toes, her hands of graceful fingers, her peaceful face. We washed my mother, her accomplished body, the full flowering of her eighty-four years. Somehow she seemed young to me, a girl, but I felt her whole unliving weight when we lifted her to slip on one of her dresses from India, white cotton with raised white embroidery. We placed a string of sandalwood beads around her neck, and then a small leather pouch containing a few items from her bedside at home—a shell, a feather, a photograph of Sai Baba, a packet of his sacred ash. I read three poems she had asked me at one time or another to read upon her death: Tennyson's "Crossing the Bar," Christina Rossetti's "Song," and e.e. cummings' "anyone lived in a pretty how town." Then I read Robert Louis Stevenson's "Requiem," which she had occasionally recited from memory in her last years:

> Under the wide and starry sky
> Dig the grave and let me lie:
> Glad did I live and gladly die,
> And I laid me down with a will.
> This be the verse you 'grave for me:
> Here he lies where he long'd to be;
> Home is the sailor, home from the sea,
> And the hunter home from the hill.

Then we kissed her, and we left.

Rooted in the longstanding Catholic tradition that the death of a member of the church is not an isolated event, we reverence the body of our deceased brothers and sisters and their final place of rest as sacramental signs in a spirit of love and care and in support for those left behind. Thus the issue of cremation for Catholics—and an answer to whether celebrating the funeral liturgy with cremated remains in place of the body is "a change for the better"—is first of all, "How do we care for the body of the deceased and for the bereaved survivors?" and only then "How do we care for the cremated remains of the body?" Our "contribution to the shaping of future custom" will have less to do with liturgy pertaining to cremated remains than with how we treat the dying person and the body of the deceased as incarnational realities.

Thomas G. Simons

Where Is My Guestroom? Toward a Method for Assessing Catholic Worship

On the feast of the Body and Blood of Christ, the gospel relates the dialogue Jesus had with his disciples who were charged with preparing the Passover supper. Jesus sends the disciples with instructions:

> Go into the city and you will come upon a man carrying a water jar. Follow him. Whatever house he enters, say to the owner, "The Teacher asks, Where is my guestroom where I may eat the Passover with my disciples?" Then he will show you an upstairs room, spacious, furnished, and all in order. That is the place you are to get ready for us. (Mark 14:12–15)

These instructions remain the most basic criteria when a community is engaged in the planning of a new worship space or when assessing a current space for worship. At the same time, in our zeal for providing the right kind of space for the liturgy, we can become so preoccupied with the physicality of the place that we can forget the scriptural imperative found in Paul's first letter to the Corinthians (3:16), which is the second reading when we commemorate the Dedication of Saint John Lateran:

Thomas G. Simons

Do you not know that you are God's temple and that God's Spirit dwells in you? If anyone destroys God's temple, God will destroy that person. For God's temple is holy, and you are that temple.

The physical and spiritual sense of the church and the tensions that come with it intersect in the places we gather for public worship. This was the underlying point for this conference on the changing face of the church. One of the conference sessions focused on "Liturgical Housing: Reviewing Forms and Principles." Participants visited four different chapels on the Notre Dame campus which in a sense are rather typical of many parochial worship spaces today. All of the chapels had been built prior to the Second Vatican Council and had been renovated since that time in order to accommodate the liturgical reforms. Participants in the session assessed the various degrees of success and failure of each space and what principles need to be operative in order to bring about better renovation plans.

The way that liturgical spaces have been perceived over the course of centuries is significant. Stretching back prior to the Christian era, there was the tent-temple experience, in which God's chosen people experienced God's presence among them first in a tent that housed the Ark of the Covenant and moved along with them as they moved, then in the construction of the Temple in Jerusalem. Temple and city became house and home for those whose journey culminated in the city, which became their happy home. The destruction of the Temple in the year 70 altered this experience. The city remained the symbol and today the remnants of the temple wall are a focal point for many who lament the destruction of Temple, cult and priesthood.[1]

The beginnings of Christianity give witness to a similar evolution. For at least the first three hundred years of Christian life, there was no particular need to establish permanent places for the celebration of the liturgy. The home was the main model for a place of liturgical gathering for the assembly called church. The recognition of Christianity brought with it a need for larger and more varied places of assembly. Struggles with heresies gave rise to effects on art and architecture and the corresponding movement to dramatize the faith visually and spatially. The shift from house of the church to house of God became more marked and essentially was the image until the liturgical reforms of Vatican II. This basic question—"house of God" or "house of the people"—need not be mutually exclusive. As Pierre-Marie Gy, OP, points out, "The building is the house of God because the assembly is the house of God."[2] Gy states that "the Ekklesia is simultaneously and inseparably the Church of God, convoked by God in a universal and catholic manner, as well as the ecclesial assembly concretely gathered together in this particular place."

Thomas Slon, SJ, indicates that the question of "house of God—house of the Church" is now fundamental for designing church buildings and worship space:

> Adapting an older church building to the liturgical reforms is often difficult and frequently unsuccessful. This indicates the radical shift in the identity of the parish building. The older buildings were not meant to house worshipers. They were meant to house God, and this was consistent with the theology inherent in the liturgy and popular piety of the times.[3]

The renewal of the liturgy by necessity affected the spaces where we worship and we still struggle with the challenges and tensions that it has brought about. If we take seriously the conciliar renewal of liturgy and sacraments it will certainly affect our worship spaces. *Environment and Art in Catholic Worship,* published in 1978 by the U.S. Bishops' Committee on the Liturgy, prompted us to think collectively about the ways in which the church today sees itself spatially.

Reflecting the *Constitution on the Sacred Liturgy* (124), the Irish bishops in their national document on the building and reordering of churches address active participation as a major guiding principle and state that "the aim of facilitating optimum participation on the part of the assembly, both verbal and auditory, both bodily and spiritual" is key to any planning.[4] At the same time, a renewed worship space must look at the many forms of liturgy that will take place in the space, recognizing the primacy of the Sunday celebration of the eucharist. Noble simplicity, a term coined in the *Constitution on the Sacred Liturgy,* a welcoming atmosphere and the power of art are other key ingredients.

Inevitably, these efforts have brought about a corresponding concern about a loss of a sense of sacred in church environments.

Thomas G. Simons

Again, Thomas Slon, SJ, raises the question, "How do we see sacrality expressed aesthetically?" His response:

> For the architecture to contribute sufficiently to the sacred action, it must already give expression to the sacredness. It must be ready to receive and facilitate a ritual that is a sacred ritual, and sustain the sacredness as a memory of what has transpired and what will continue to transpire so long as the space is a place the community knows to be home. This is achieved through the aesthetics of the building.[5]

In many cases today, there are two main reasons for considering a renovation or reordering of an existing worship space. First, damage by destruction or natural disaster, or wear on a building due to time; second, an event such as the anniversary of a community or a change in pastoral leadership, which often brings about an examination of an existing place for Catholic worship. Whatever reason may ultimately lead to this review, the following are the kind of questions that should be part of a systematic assessment process:

1. What are the strengths and overall advantages of this worship space?

2. What are any weaknesses or neglected areas of this space?

3. Does this space reflect an awareness of and a response to the Church's liturgical principles?

4. If buildings and furnishings "talk," what does this space say?

5. Does this space foster a "climate of hospitality?"

6. How does this space convey a sense of mystery, of the holy, the transcendent?

7. Do you experience the gathered assembly as the most important symbol here?

8. How does this space symbolize Christ's presence in word, sacrament and assembly?

9. What about the placement of the reserved sacrament in this space? What are the eucharistic theologies or tensions existing in this space?

10. What about other sacramental symbols (holy water, candles, and so on)?

11. What about the design and care of liturgical appointments (for instance, cross, images, seasonal art)?

12. What is your assessment of "entry" or threshold into this space?

13. What about room for movement and processions in this place?

14. Does this space inspire devotion, both personally and communally?

15. Does this space embody a sense of our Catholic liturgical tradition?

16. Is visibility afforded in this space? Is there a visual connection with and among those gathered here? Are there good sight lines with altar, ambo, music ministry and so on?

17. Does this space reflect "noble simplicity" and make good use of natural elements (for example, furnishings that reflect genuineness and quality in crafting)?

18. Is the space illuminated well and are there sufficient options for variety in the lighting of this space?

19. What about the acoustical factors in this space? Is it "live" or "dead" in terms of sound? Does the space facilitate sung prayer?

20. What about the color or colors in this space? Do they please or offend? Do they clash or complement?

Another set of criteria and principles are offered by Rev. David Clark:[6]

Self-value: Within the liturgical environment, how do people feel? Or what to feel? Are they diminished? Is there a sense of ownership?

Sense of security: Is the place overwhelming or hospitable?

Sense of stimulation: Is the place visually stimulating? Acoustically alive and quiet? Are the textures boring? Is it "more" with people present?

Thomas G. Simons

Sense of structure: Is the place ordered? Is there form following function?

Sense of self-actualization: Can people express themselves? What helps or limits their expression and participation?

Sense of spiritualization: Are they stimulated to intuit, mediate, create, discern, reflect, imagine?

Proportion: How are the parts, the foci related to one another? Is there a sense of monumentality by appropriate proportions? Is there unity? Is it rhythmical or static? Is it separated from the outside world, or part of it? Are there transition spaces?

Scale: What is predominant? Is the human figure lost, overwhelmed and diminished? Is there emptiness? Concealment and revelation?

Suitability of materials used: What is the characteristic of the material? Is it natural or synthetic? Cold and hard, or warm and soft? Stone or wood? Textured or smooth?

Color and light: Is the space cool or warm in tone? Natural or artificial in lighting? Neutral or bold colors? Is there a play of light and dark? Tone and shadow? Are colors recessive or are they progressive?

Sound: Is there silence, aural and visual? Is the space conducive to speech or music?

Richard Vosko has also provided a reflection on the work of researchers concerned with people and their environments and the impact of physical space on human behavior. It is his contention that we need to pay better attention to these developments in order to assist us in our efforts to give shape to the most appropriate and beautiful spaces for our worshiping assemblies.[7]

We've all heard the familiar saying of Winston Churchill, "We shape our spaces and then they shape us." We are beginning to pay much more attention to the full weight and truth of this observation, not only in our efforts to build new places for Catholic worship but especially in breathing *new* life into older buildings for worship today. One of the fruits of the liturgical movement is that we are more sensitive to the environment for the liturgical celebration and to its effect upon participants in the celebration. Charles de Montalembert, the French Catholic liberal politician (1810–1878), once remarked to Victor Hugo: "You come to these places so that you might admire and reflect; we come to them so that we might pray and adore." May all our efforts at the renewal of worship spaces today fulfill the Christian ideal that they be places of prayer, that they be real guest-rooms, for all peoples.

1. For a more expansive treatment of this topic see *Re-Pitching the Tent: Re-Ordering the Church Building for Worship in the New Millennium* (Norwich, England: Centerbury Press, 1996).

2. See "Space and Celebration as a Theological Question," in *The Environment for Worship: A Reader* (Washington: United States Catholic Conference, 1980).

3. "What the Church Building Wants to Be," *Modern Liturgy* (May 1992).

4. *The Place of Worship: Pastoral Directory on the Building and Reordering of Churches* (Veritas: Irish Institute of Pastoral Liturgy, 1994).

5. Thomas R. Slon, SJ, "The House of God and the House of the Church," PH.D. dissertation, University of Scranton, 1996.

6. See *Liturgical Ministry 5* (Summer 1996).

7. See "Toward a Systematic Methodology for the Evaluation of Worship Environments" in the *Proceedings of the North American Academy of Liturgy 1995* (Valparaiso, IN: Valparaiso University, 1995).

The Spiritual Storyteller

There was a village that set up two tents. As evening came people arrived and sat in the tents to listen to a storyteller.

Each tent had a different storyteller, yet both storytellers told the same story.

One teller used the story to grab people's attention and hook them emotionally into a fundraiser that would greatly benefit that particular person.

The other told the story to help foster community, and to shed light on shared concerns.

The storytellers achieved their goals. The fundraiser for the first was highly successful. The second group came together as a community.

People who left the first tent went home thinking they were done. They had contributed to the cause. Maybe another day they might contribute again, but for now they were done.

People from the other group went home thinking they were just beginning. They had work ahead of them, but they were willing to pitch in. They were trying to improve their community.

Now two neighbors who had each been in a different tent came toward each other on the sidewalk. For many reasons these two *neighbors had not gotten along. They were both big people and the sidewalk was more narrow than usual because it had rained. Water and mud outlined the edges. One of the neighbors had to step aside for both to pass.*

The first who had been to the fundraiser felt that enough had been done on this night. There was no reason to do more, especially to yield to that person. "After all, I'm the one who went to the good tent."

The other neighbor who had been to the community builder thought that the challenges that had been discussed were already here. "Someone will have to yield. This time it will be me."

That person stepped aside into the mud, but somehow didn't sink down.

The two crossed, each giving a nice smile.

Telling Stories

My intent for this paper is to give insight to my readers about the interaction between storytelling and the Holy Spirit. My views on this subject are experiential. This is not a scholarly paper. It is my opinions that I have come to after twenty years of telling stories to people and of noticing the Holy Spirit alive in my life.

You can expect to find in this paper some discussion and over-view of storytelling and the Spirit, some anecdotes from my personal experience, lessons we learn from Jesus' storytelling, practical tips on mixing storytelling and the Spirit together and thoughts on the stories that need to be told by today's catechists.

But back to our opening story. In terms of control and intent the two storytellers are different. They both want to tell the same story, but for one the intent is merely to attract the attention of the people who are listening, and lure them in to a carefully controlled plan for the evening, a plan that person made for self-serving purposes. For the other the intent is to open up dialogue and discussion that is not exclusively in that person's control.

The two key words are control and intent. I believe that when the intent of the storyteller is to foster good among people the Spirit is readily available. On the other hand, when the intent of the teller is primarily self-serving there is an absence of the Spirit. When we try to tell something for the good of the people listening, as well as ourselves, we have to give up some control. The story may not always proceed as we have practiced, because we are not in control. God is.

Let's look at what I mean by Spiritual storytelling. By Spiritual, I mean that something is occurring that is coming from God, and that something opens hearts, clears thoughts, heightens emotions, enables the right words to be spoken, lets babies cry at just the right time, brings an audience together as a community. By storytelling I mean that there is a tale that is being communicated from one person to another or many others. Spiritual storytelling is not necessarily the telling of sacred stories. The stories do not have to be explicitly about God or about the most important things in our lives. They can be humorous or everyday stories. For Spiritual storytelling to occur there must be a connection that happens between people, a Spiritual connection, connected by the breath of God.

What does that mean? It's difficult to put into words, but it's similar to what happens in sports when someone reaches a heightened state of performance. Everything they do is right. It is sometimes said that they are in the "zone." In Spiritual storytelling it is as if both the listener and the teller are in the "zone." There is a heightened sense of understanding, a communion that happens between people. They are connected by more than just words.

I think Jesus was talking about this connection when he said, "For where two or three meet in my name, I shall be there with them" (Matthew 18:20).

The Presence of the Spirit

For storytelling to happen, there have to be at least two people present: the teller and listener. When the Spirit connects them it is a marvelous thing. But so often it doesn't happen. In everyday conversations, for instance, there are often two conversations going on, the first person's and the second person's. They may respond at the right times, but each is carrying on a monologue that has little to do with how the other person responds. When the Spirit is connecting two people, they are in a position of insight, intensely aware of how the other person is responding. This opens the door to compassion and empathy, to tolerance and understanding.

Now a person who is addressing a whole congregation or audience is not carrying on a conversation, but when the Spirit is connecting the group with the speaker, the speaker is aware of how the group is responding. The speaker pays attention to the effect the words have, noting what may need to be elaborated, what is already understood, what is enjoyable and what is uncomfortable. These are things that someone connected to the group perceives. They often cannot be planned out ahead of time. It is something that has to be done in the present moment, as the tale is being told, and in the present moment is where the Spirit is found.

Remember in the opening story that the first storyteller told the story to lure people to listen. There was a hidden agenda and it was purely self-serving. That does not bring out the Spirit. It does not connect the people and the storyteller on any kind of even ground. When people are connected by the Spirit they do not look down on their neighbor. There is grace between them and love in their hearts.

When we listen to a story that has a self-serving agenda for the teller as the primary use, not primarily to foster good works for God's people, then we go away feeling that we have already done our part, or perhaps we feel that we have to do something that will give us personal gain. On the other hand, when we have been connected by the Spirit, we leave feeling alive and ready to do our part. In the opening story, that is what happened to the two groups of people. One group left feeling they had already done their part. The other group left feeling energized and ready to go forward.

I want to briefly share a story that made me more aware of the Holy Spirit working in my life. I should tell my readers that I am a juggler by training, a tosser of clubs and balls. I weave stories into my presentations. I am often billed as an "entertainment social worker," other times as a "liturgical juggler." I didn't always have such lofty titles. They were put on me by other people. And I accept them. They came slowly over the course of twenty years of work. This particular incident happened at a nursing home.

It was the silliest thing I did in my whole presentation. I pulled out a kazoo, which is a horn that you hum to get to work. I announced, "I'd like to play the title cut off my first album. It's entitled *Earwax*. How many of you have it?"

A couple of the more good-humored and alert ladies raised their hands. The rest of the thirty or so people, mostly in wheelchairs wearing nightgowns or pajamas, sat still. There were lots of blank stares. There were some puzzled expressions as well.

One unshaven man peered out from glazed eyes.

I snapped my fingers in rhythm. "A one, a two, a one two three." I placed the mouthpiece of the trumpet kazoo against my lips and began to hum. Five seconds later the song was over.

"Thank you all," I said, taking multiple bows, even though hardly anyone was applauding. I knew the piece worked. People were laughing. I continued on with my show, not thinking about the effect my actions were having on the people. My goal was to make them happy. And it was working.

When the show was over I shook hands and smiled as the folks walked, shuffled and were wheeled away. As I passed one man in a wheelchair, I felt a tug on my arm. An unshaven man with long fingernails had caught me.

The old man's eyes met mine. There was a simmering fire behind his glazed eyes. The man licked his lips and said, "I, I used to, to play, the, the trumpet." The man let go of my arm. The one sentence seemed to have exhausted him.

A friendly smile was exchanged. I patted him on the shoulder and walked away. I hadn't gotten fifteen feet when the activities director swooped down upon me. "Did that man just talk to you?"

"Yes, he told me he used to play the trumpet," I replied.

The activities director leaned forward and said in a kind of whisper, "He hasn't spoken to anyone in the last six months."

"Six months," I repeated. It seemed there was a connection that had just been made by me and the old man that I hadn't recognized. After that I started paying more attention to the people at my performances. I began to look for those connections. A few years later I began to think of those connections as God bringing me together with my audiences.

Telling Stories Takes Two

Spiritual storytelling is a two-way street. The storyteller cannot do it alone. The listeners must actively try to listen, be open to nuance and help the teller get the story across. An appreciative, loving audience can help a teller who is having a bad night. A hostile, overly judgmental audience can destroy even the best story told by a great teller. Where is the Spirit during those times? The Spirit is waiting for acceptance. The Spirit does not travel into hearts that reject it. The Spirit flows into those who accept it. Sometimes that means trying to concentrate even when someone is not telling an engaging story. During those times, suddenly there can be flashes of insight. And other times we do not notice anything at all, except that we are tired and we wish the story was over, but at least we are trying to be open.

Jesus was connected to the people as he told his stories. Many of the parables he told were directly tied to questions that people asked. Because he paid attention to his audience, his words had even greater effect. We can follow in that tradition of trying to tell the stories that we feel people need to hear.

Where do we start? We start by observing and listening. Through this simple awareness of what is going on around us, God shows us what we need to say, and when we get ready to say it, the Spirit will be there to help us.

Even though the Spirit will help us to say what needs to be communicated, storytellers need to practice and plan what they intend to say. A college psychology professor once told me a good therapist must plan out a session as completely as possible, knowing exactly what he or she would like to happen, but once the session begins, go with the flow even if it's not what's planned. From the foundation of planning and preparation one is more free to recognize the help of the Spirit. Many times I have noticed after a story that it wasn't quite what I had planned, but because I had planned it, I was easily able to adapt it. The Spirit is more likely to be noticed when one plans ahead.

How do we distinguish improvisation from going with the Spirit? Improvisation is a tool that the Spirit can lead us to use. One can improvise without utilizing the Spirit. For instance, we might change something in our story just because we are bored with it.

Remember, the Holy Spirit in this instance is the positive connection between people. If our intent is to strengthen for the common good the connection between people then I believe the Spirit is likely to help us. We cannot accurately predict what the Spirit might lead us to say or do. And that means there is improvisation going on.

Nine Tips for Good Storytelling

Here are a series of tips that I think can help storytellers tap into the grace of the Spirit.

1. Pray for help from God before beginning a story.
2. Start with the attitude that the tale being told is God's tale.
3. Don't take all the credit if the story goes perfectly.
4. Don't take all the blame if the story goes poorly.
5. Spend time planning how to tell the story.
6. Tell the story; don't recite it.
7. Pay attention to people's reactions and moods.
8. Respond to obvious distractions, for instance, a bell ringing.
9. Be clear on the intent of the story.

Let's briefly go through this list. Jesus said, "If you have faith, everything you ask for in prayer you will receive" (Matthew 21:2). So it makes sense to pray for guidance and the power of the Spirit before and quite possibly during our stories.

God is in all things, and all stories are God's stories in some way. By acknowledging that, we acknowledge the big picture, the mystery of life. Our story then has a place. It is important to tell God's stories, and it can be fun, too.

You can't take all the credit for the story if it goes well, because you need a listener. The listener often has as much to do with it going well as the teller. And furthermore, the connector is the Holy Spirit. That's the force who brings the listener and the teller together. So we certainly can't take all the credit.

If the story goes poorly don't take all the blame. There are always factors that are out of our control. We can't know why the Spirit brings us together some times but not other times. It may be that God is teaching us something for important work in the future. Of course, there are times when the blame should rest with us. What are the factors that we could have controlled to make a more positive experience?

I am not a believer in planning every detail in the stories that I tell. But I do need to know what I am going to say and how I am going to say it. In other words, I need to practice. We all do. Practicing gives us the flexibility to go with the inspiration of the Spirit.

Storytelling is more than just reading, or spouting off a memorized tale. We are living creatures. If we live the details of the story as we tell it, then the story becomes alive. We need to feel the emotions of the story, the joy and the pain. For when the story is real to us, it is real to others. And when that connection happens the Spirit will be there.

We need to pay attention to our listeners' reactions. Occasionally a small change, like a pause before continuing, can make an immense difference in a how a story goes over. To recognize the Spirit and to give it a chance in our storytelling we must look to the people that we are telling the story to and see if we are connecting. If we are not, we need to slow down or speed up or change something so that there is a new opportunity to connect.

When an interruption occurs during one of our stories that everyone notices, we are best to respond to it in some way. For instance, if a bell goes off, listen to it and then comment on it or weave it right into the story. These interruptions can actually be blessings. They can help to create common experience between the teller and the audience. When ignored, the story's energy is diffused. A crying baby can be a good thing. The electricity going off can be a good thing. An unexpected burp can be a good thing. But then again, sometimes maybe not. In any case, we have to give up some control to benefit by these things.

Finally, we must be clear on what intent we give our story. Getting people to laugh together can be a fine purpose. The intent does not need to be of life-changing proportions. The Spirit dwells in the little stories of life as well as the big ones.

I believe if we use the nine suggestions I have listed, the Spirit will be alive in our storytelling and will connect us with our listeners.

Before sharing a concluding story, I want to make a few comments about the stories that need to be told by today's catechists.

The stories that need to be told are the ones that touch our own lives. To know what stories we need to tell we need to reflect on our own life. The things to tell will come to the surface. Some will be personal. Some will come from other sources. But no matter what the source, we must strive to move in the direction that God wants us to move.

In order to know what story to tell in a homily, or in a class, or at a conference, we must look at the context in which we will be telling the story. We must think about what would be the best story for the people we are addressing. What connections in our lives can we share with others? We must tell the stories that we are connected with, stories that touch a chord in our lives. I cannot state the topics that need to be addressed, because each of us needs to tell the stories that coincide with his or her life. We are all different. We all need to tell different stories, but they will all be God's story.

I finish with a story. Jesus said, "I tell you solemnly, unless you change and become like little children you will never enter the kingdom of heaven" (Matthew 18:3). So I finish with a story about a child. A story can do many things but my intent is to help you find the Holy Spirit in your storytelling.

Benjamin stood in front of his third-grade class. It was his turn to give a speech. It was the kind of speech where he had to walk up to the front of the class and stand by the teacher's desk. And everybody looked at him. His legs didn't want to go to the front of the class. They wobbled as he moved to the front. He began the speech he had carefully prepared. He had memorized all the words he needed to say.

"The honeybee is an amazing creature," he began. Benjamin's mouth was dry. His hands shook. They held a piece a paper with a drawing he had made of a bee.

As he continued he was aware that several of the kids in the back of the room were snickering at him. He heard Jack say, "Look, he's sweating."

A bead of perspiration slipped down his face. He thought, "God, I wish I didn't have to do this."

"*The honeybee hovers as it gathers nectar from flowers.*"

More laughter. This time not just from the back, but from the front of the room as well.

"*God, I wish I wasn't here,*" Benjamin thought. But then he got another thought that lasted just an instant: "*But the honeybee is an awesome creature. The class would like to learn about it.*"

At that instant Benjamin caught himself saying "*ah ah ah.*"

There was lots more laughter. But Benjamin had a new idea. He hadn't planned it. It just seemed to have come to him.

He changed the "*ah ah*" into a "*bzz bzzz.*" Benjamin began flapping his arms. Now the whole class was laughing, including Benjamin.

"*Everybody flap your wings,*" he called out. Most of the kids began to flap their arms. Even the teacher joined in.

"*Did you know that the honeybee can flap its wings more than ten thousand times in one minute? It goes so fast that you can't even see it.*"

Benjamin suddenly had the class's attention. He pulled out his drawing and pointed out the antennae on a honeybee and the six legs that made it a flying insect.

"*Did you know that the honeybee makes it back to its hive each night before dark? I guess after so much hard work flapping their wings all day, they are never late to get their rest.*"

As Benjamin finished his talk his class applauded. Several kids, including Jack, remarked that they never knew so much about bees.

The talk had not gone the way Benjamin had planned it. Somehow it had gone much better. Somehow how he had connected with his class.

James D. Whitehead and Evelyn Eaton Whitehead

Waking the Church: Grief that Frees Us, Dreams that Compel Us

Part One

There is something ungrieved in the church. Some enormous loss, some unspeakable lament lies hidden in our common body. Until we name our loss and honor it, we will not wake. Instead we will remain mired in the anger and lethargy and distress that mar much of church life today.

This lingering difficulty with grief puzzles us. As reflective adults, as experienced ministers, we should be experts in this emotion. Yet still it stumps us. We have studied the lessons of scripture, yearning for God's future as foretold in Isaiah 43:

> Behold, I am doing a new thing;
> now it springs forth,
> do you not perceive it?

And with the psalmist we have learned that this future often emerges from lament:

> This is the cause of my grief,
> that the ways of the Most High have changed.

Something ungrieved afflicts our church. We are called to learn anew the lesson of grief: that grieving is not a weakness, as our stoic ancestors would teach us, but a strength, a virtue. As a virtue, grief both afflicts and empowers us, freeing us for a future we had not expected. How shall we put on this virtue? How can we better dispose ourselves for the purification that God asks of us as church, and by so doing, prepare ourselves for the waking that God has promised?

In this essay, the first part of two on "waking the church," we will explore these mysterious dynamics of grieving. We will suggest a number of ways to re-imagine this intensely personal and necessarily communal lament that marks every human journey. We begin by offering one simple image to help picture our grief.

How We Hold Our Hurt

Grief is a physical, sweaty virtue. To equip ourselves for grief, we need to reclaim some of our bodily virtuosity. We must locate virtue back in the body. From the beginning we have called ourselves "the body of Christ." Over time, this common body became "a mystical body" — becoming more and more mystical, and less and less bodily. Faith, in turn, was pictured as an exercise of the will and intellect, safely buffered from the shifting tempers of the body.

We can reclaim some of our earlier vigor by remembering that faith is a way of holding. More than a mental assent, faith is a way we grab onto God and cling to one another. The adventure of faith begins when we recognize we are held and sustained by our Creator God— God as parent and protector. This is our first and most enduring embrace of faith.

Maturing on the journey, we enter a new, more adult embrace of faith as we become captivated by the life of Jesus. After a bad day at the parish, or a bad year, we are tempted to just walk away from it all. But we do not, because of the hold he has on our life. Saint Paul said it well, "In him all things hold together" (Colossians 1:17). We might define our faith, then, as "the bonds of affection and accountability that unite us in Jesus Christ."

And faith flows into action. In the parish we are drawn into volunteer work, perhaps even into a ministry that actually pays a salary! These activities lead us into new embraces: the necessary cooperation with several colleagues on a liturgy committee. Among the many folk we meet in the community, some of them—thanks be to God—we actually like! With them we learn the delightful embrace of friendship. As partnership matures in the community of faith, we move toward the very adult embrace of accountability. But how do we hold one another accountable; how do we hold our religious leaders accountable? New muscles are required in the body of Christ. And, in time, we meet the unavoidable embrace of conflict. If we are not too quickly frightened nor too easily scandalized, we learn that conflict is one of the ways we hold those whom we love.

Conflict can be one of the embraces of faith: The biblical accounts of Jacob wrestling with Yahweh and Paul arguing with Peter confirm this truth. In this realization—that the painful embrace of conflict may bear powerful graces—lies the bridge to the virtue of grief. Like conflict, grief is an embrace we would not choose. But like conflict, grief is a way of holding life that often releases grace.

Grief grabs us and we must decide to respond. A strong temptation is to hold our hurt away, to hold it down, to hold it out of sight. We do not want this loss; we cannot face this disappointment. So we look away, trying to deny our grief.

Holding our hurt in this unhealthy embrace, we privatize our pain. Most often we bury it in our bodies—whether our physical self or the common body of Christ. Psychologist James Zullo has described the unhappy result of this strategy: "We don't think about our feelings and get migraines. We swallow our feelings and get ulcers. We carry the weight of our feelings and get lower back pain. We sit on our feelings and get hemorrhoids."

When pain is private, we look for private remedies. We do not speak of it together or join in shared prayer. Instead we banish pain from our parish liturgies and diocesan meetings, searching instead for the pharmaceutical that will provide short-term relief. Even as we catch ourselves doing this, we know this is not God's design. This is not the grieving that will lead to waking and new life.

If we are tempted, as individuals, to hold our pain away, we are also tempted as an institution to deny the changes that are bringing us to grief. We see this denial especially in the "royal arrangements" in the church.[1]

Royal arrangements sacralize the status quo: We move from "this is how we do it around here" to "this is the way we have always done it" to "this is God's immutable will for us from all eternity." Many in the church are painfully aware of the royal arrangements that mark Christian life today: Christians divided into the status of clergy or laity; women systematically excluded from leadership roles in the church; the appointment of bishops and other leaders made with little or no consultation of the communities affected.

We craft such arrangements both in our hearts—private agreements we have with God about how our life should proceed—and in our church. With these royal arrangements we create patterns of believing that we define as God's will, hoping thus we can exempt them from challenge and purification. We can hear in such arrangements the human desire to construct an orthodoxy that will avoid the winds of change, that will never be brought to grief. Only reluctantly are we able to acknowledge that these arrangements are our doings, not God's. The day we can do this, we begin to wake the church.

A second way we hold our hurt is to cling to it in chronic complaint. Instead of privatizing our loss, we publicize it—repeatedly. We complain and blame, but nothing is healed. Perhaps the best example of this strategy lies again in scripture. Once our ancestors had escaped from Egypt, their exhilaration gave way to grumbling. The desert, devoid of food and shelter and a sense of direction, seemed not much of an improvement on captivity. So some of our tribe gathered at the doors of their tents and murmured against Moses and their leaders. They publicized their pain, at least in a grumble that would not quite reach their leaders. This strategy does vent some energy, but quickly it becomes circular. We complain rather than engage the problem, so nothing changes. We are not doing the work of the Lord.

But perhaps we should admit here, parenthetically, that sometimes complaining does seem to work—when it is joined with a certain kind of humor. Recall the writer and radio personality Garrison Keillor, whose work is a celebration of religious grief. His fictional town Lake Wobegon is, indeed, a petition: "woe begone." His very face and demeanor in performance is of a man at a wake. A central vignette in *Lake Wobegon Days* centers on a person returning to his native Minnesota to nail his own 95 theses to the front door of his Lutheran church.

Keillor's anecdotes lament the warping influence of religion on his early years. In one memorable passage he grieves the dampening of emotion in his religious upbringing that leaves him in this mood: "I am constantly adjusting my feelings downward to achieve that fine balance of caution and melancholy" (261). We recognize enough of ourselves to laugh. Yes, this is us; we acknowledge it, and in the complaint and chuckle, a measure of grieving begins. Laughter, if not too caustic or punitive, can wake us.

A third way to hold our hurt comes to us as a gift from the psalms: the invitation to hold our losses up to God in such a way that our pain turns into prayer. It is, to be sure, a messy, cantankerous prayer that is a cousin of complaint; it is what our ancestors called lamentation.

"Since I have lost all taste for life, I will give free rein to my complaints; I shall let my embittered soul speak out" (Job 10:1). "All you who pass this way, look and see: Is there any sorrow like the sorrow that afflicts me, with which Yahweh has struck me on the day of his burning anger?" (Lamentations 1:12).

Walter Brueggemann sums up the strategy of such prayer: the belief that "the daring speech of earth, when done with passion and shrillness, can change the affairs of heaven," and the hope that "pain brought to speech and made available in the community . . . is the mediator of new life."[2]

Graceful grieving is a question of holding, a very special kind of embrace. God has so designed us that if we hold our losses in a certain way, they may be transformed. Holding pain in an embrace that honors it even while resisting it, we begin a process of waking. Liturgical theologian David Power has said it best: "What is remembered in grief is redeemed, made whole, renewed."

We are blessed to have this experience; we know it is true. Yet we are also aware of losses that linger in the body of Christ, of pains that our institution chooses to ignore. So we see fellow Christians who privatize their pain, blaming themselves and looking for private remedies; we meet fellow Christians who excel at murmuring, uttering chronic complaints that expel energy but evoke neither grace nor healing.

So we continue our exploration into the mysterious dynamics of grieving. As we turn to a consideration of the social dynamics of grief, let us offer a brief definition of this emotion that can become a virtue:

> Grief is a salutary emotion, a necessary virtue that guides us through treacherous times. Its arousal ignites the dreadful feeling that something essential is perishing. The process of grieving prompts us to evaluate what we must let go. It stirs us to lamentation, with its cleansing if scalding effect. Finally, grief's energy impels us toward the future, uncharted but full of God's promise.

Social Change and Social Grief

The dramatic pace of change in our lifetime confronts us, personally and as a people, with significant loss. Unattended, these losses prompt behaviors that threaten to derail our shared life and erode our communal effectiveness. Well-attended, the shared experience of loss generates energy, healing and hope for the future. In this process, for groups as for individuals, grief is the door.

As Americans, we have for decades understood ourselves as an optimistic people who have faith in progress and confidence in the future. We have identified ourselves as a culture welcoming change. But today's widespread experience of the overwhelming pace of change brings these assumptions into question. Under the weight of the millennium's approach, many of us have felt our naive optimism give way to a richer awareness of the costs of change and the currency in which this debt is paid.

These personal realizations are echoed in the findings of social scientists. Social change starts in observable endings: leaders change, a group's goals are modified, communal priorities shift. New paradigms replace the established philosophies; earlier values are reinterpreted; time-honored institutions are dismantled or disintegrate on their own.

These public events carry with them hidden losses. Even if we agree with the changes, even if we helped to bring them about, still the shifts surprise us. We lose the security of familiar ways of acting. For some of us there is loss of pride and place: New social connections threaten the satisfaction and status we earlier enjoyed. All of us risk a loss of identity: Who am I, who are we, in this new dispensation? How will I contribute, what difference can we make, will anybody notice, does anybody care? Initially, then, social change often registers ominously—in the shock of endings, the threat of loss, the struggle—in the midst of some confusion—to find the energy to move on.

This struggle brings us to grief. The work of grief is to carry us, as individuals and as communities, from shock to responsible action. The gift of grief is energy released to help us embrace the future in hope.

Dynamics of Social Grieving

Our understanding of social grief draws on findings as disparate as family systems in distress, corporations in reorganization or merger, inner-city neighborhoods responding to urban renewal, and communities recovering from natural disasters—floods, hurricanes, earthquakes.

Across these diverse experiences, researchers have discovered that groups—like individuals—respond to change in expectable, even predictable ways. Their chief conclusion is that groups grieve too. Social grieving names a characteristic pattern of lament and loss manifested by groups experiencing significant transition or change.[3]

Most early studies focused on the negative effects of change. Social psychologists, for example, identified a pattern of disruptive behavior that frequently emerges in organizations facing change. They named this phenomenon *resistance* and interpreted resistance as a stance of active denial, an attitude that says NO to reality. But careful observers soon became convinced that naming this behavior *resistance* obscures something important. These researchers wanted to look again at groups caught up in change, tracking the social and psychological dynamics to see where they lead. Their work uncovered a constellation of feelings and behaviors typical in groups facing loss or change. Over the past two decades, students of change have started describing this experience as social grieving and charting its positive role in moving a group through change.

Today social psychologists and organizational consultants share the conviction that grieving is best understood not as a defense mechanism but as a coping strategy. In this understanding, grieving is a strategy for survival and growth:

- a positive tactic for regulating threat;
- a stance that supports the gradual absorption of loss;

- a pacing mechanism that "buys time" when a challenge threatens to overwhelm us.

Social grieving paces a group through change in ways that protect its continuity with a valued past—a heritage that is significant, a cherished shared identity, a proud common purpose.

Recognizing How Groups Grieve

In the swirl of activity that usually accompanies change, the losses that are involved can be obscured or overlooked or officially denied. But not for long. A cumulative sense of loss registers in the group's life, both in its emotional climate and in its communal behavior. As the initial shock of the change reverberates through the group, a kind of organizational paralysis sets in. A host of negative feelings quickly become contagious — confusion, anger, resentment, fear, regret. Reliable people start to mess up; procedures and systems that functioned well simply don't work anymore. People report a fog of unreality clouds everything; they feel suspended in time. Behavior in the group is alternately listless or compulsive, as people vacillate between numbness and panic. In the course of a day, or an hour, or a brief meeting, we swing between extremes—going through the motions as if nothing has changed . . . then falling into panic, with a sense that everything is threatened, all that we value here risks being destroyed . . . then looking away from the problem again and going on as before.

But after a while, as the reality of the change sets in, the organization's people characteristically move into a more reactive stage of pining and protest. Nostalgia sets in—a painful yearning for the past that romanticizes how things used to be. Attempts are made to get back to the previous state of affairs, to restore the earlier arrangements. Often this feels like an advance, at least we're doing something! But the efforts are not well thought out and tend to be futile.

Experiencing this futility, the pining often turns to angry protest directed at those seen as responsible for the change. There is a sense of betrayal: "We've been lied to; promises have been broken; someone must be to blame." The likely candidates, of course, are internal—the group's leadership, past or present; people older or younger than our age cohort; or simply those with whom we disagree! But external villains are also easy to find—the hierarchical church or the federal government, in any of their multiple manifestations, quickly qualify as targets. But immigrants and other foreigners, or gays and lesbians, or any group we sense are "dangerously different" might qualify as well. In both pining and protest, the group has energy, but it is used to deny the change and to defend against the loss.

Unchecked, this reactive stance propels a group toward disorientation. As facts accumulate, reinforcing the inevitability of the change, the shaky consensus based on denial disintegrates, leaving people feeling alienated from one another. Group behavior becomes disorganized: Our defensive efforts have proved useless in restoring the past. But no reliable criteria have yet emerged to help us act together effectively for the future. People feel frustrated, confused, vulnerable: "There is nothing we can do; nothing worthwhile can come of this; things will never get better." Task performance and effective communication break down further. Colleagues withdraw from one another and leadership becomes aloof, as people retreat into personal isolation.

We've traced the symptoms of denial in organizational grief: shock—reaction—withdrawal—disintegration. But this downward spiral is not inevitable. The work of grief is to carry the group from shock to responsible action. Honoring the group's distress releases its energy for healing. The group's resources of hope and commitment return, even if at first these seem only fleeting: "Sometimes you see it, sometimes you don't."

Much about the process of resolving grief, personal or communal, remains mysterious. Coming out of crisis, people often report an amnesia toward much of what happened in the heart of the distress. But nevertheless we have some clues to what goes on as social grieving does its work—moving our group toward its future, safeguarding our connections with the valued past, pacing us through a gradual absorption of necessary loss.

An early indication of social grief resolved is a group's growing sense of itself as agent—not just a victim—in the transition. The focus of the group's energy shifts from defending against change to making the change user-friendly. Moving beyond nostalgia, members start to envision positive alternatives. Change signals things will be different; some differences could make things better around here; we can help shape that preferred future. As our imaginations flex, we begin to envision a future in which my best self, our best selves, can thrive.

Resolving social grief reestablishes a sense of continuity. We are able to weigh the pros and cons of the new arrangement, to acknowledge that the change has not destroyed all that is of value in our shared life. We can recognize the parts of our past—personal and institution—that *will* accompany us into the future, even if in a purified form.

Resolving communal grief restores energy. Recognizing that the future is not all bleak renews our awareness of personal and institutional strengths. Some of these resources we have had all along, but lost sight of in the midst of the crisis of change. Other resources come as strengths cast in the conflict itself, gifts of our struggle together to face the demands of change.

Helping Groups Grieve

Grieving is tricky business. The transition from shock to responsible action is not guaranteed; the process can bog down along the way. How do we avoid that—as individuals, as groups? If the symptoms outlined above trap organizations in grief, how does an institution break the spell? By honoring, rather than ignoring, the human side of change.

Honoring the human side of change involves helping people clarify, helping people learn, helping people be accountable and helping people find support.

Helping People Clarify

Confronting significant change, we need help identifying what is ending—for this group, for our shared task, for ourselves. We need to know what is being asked of us, both in the transition and in the new order of things. And we need help to appreciate what is not ending, the parts of our past that will accompany us into the future.

Helpful Action: Establish strong lines of communication and keep the messages clear. Provide information continually and consistently. Acknowledge the risks and indicate how these will be minimized. In many groups, it is important to confront rumors early by providing ongoing opportunities for people to ask questions and dispel misinformation.

Helping People Learn

People facing change need help learning how to survive and thrive. We need information about the shape of the organization's future. We can learn new ways of acting, better suited to the new circumstances. We can gain skills enabling us to succeed at new tasks. We can develop attitudes that help us respond effectively to what is happening to us and around us.

Helpful Actions: Navigating change requires both formation and information. Respond quickly to requests for information and practical assistance in support of change. Offer programs to expand people's skills and confidence. Provide learning opportunities that teach and model the future.

Helping People Be Accountable

In a time of significant transition, people easily feel unmoored, set adrift without access to their own characteristic strengths. Paradoxically, one way to help is by holding people accountable. Accountability anchors us in both our resources and our responsibilities. So as leaders, as colleagues, we can let people know that this group expects mature behavior. In fact, this group needs you at your best. Holding us accountable, a group announces its confidence that together we will survive. We can make it through this challenging passage together, if not with ease at least with honor.

Helpful Actions: Develop among us the procedures that support personal accountability: clear expectations, appropriate job descriptions, workable schedules, congruent rewards and sanctions, candid feedback, competent supervision.

Helping People Find Support

People don't need to navigate change all by themselves. Going it alone is not the best way to go. Research evidence over the past fifty years confirms what most of us know from personal experience: Peer support is the most powerful factor helping people deal effectively with the significant demands of loss and change. Supportive companions—whether personal friends or work colleagues or partners in faith—validate our pain even as they model ways to move beyond it. Seeing how people like us are managing the transition, we discover new options for ourselves. More than experts and outsiders, peers can help us safely explore possibilities the future might hold, and offer us realistic encouragement along the way.

Helpful Actions: Foster—for ourselves and others—workable networks through which people can both give and receive positive support in times of transition. When a group is facing organizational losses, such as institutions closing or units consolidating or personnel leaving, initiate supportive responses early and continue to promote their availability. Realizing that public changes often raise unresolved personal issues for an organization's members, we can take steps to insure that people have access to formal counseling resources. And we can take care to insure that those who take advantage of these resources are not shamed or penalized for dealing directly with their issues of grief and loss.

Responses like these, undertaken by the group's leaders or initiated by active members, do not guarantee an organization's successful emergence through the stresses of significant change. But they do enhance the possibility that the volatile dynamics of change can be harnessed to pursue the group's benefit and the members' best hopes.

Part Two

In Part One we examined the dynamics of grief as these are often manifest in a group or organization's life. As we saw there, social grieving generates an "outward" energy, focused on active construction of a future in which what is best is us may thrive. In this chapter we will explore the "inward" energy of cultural grieving, tracing the painful experience of collective loss that accompanies significant change and the healing responses that render these losses memorable, meaningful and thereby bearable. And we will examine the critical role of ritual in these dynamics of personal and social transformation. We start with a look at how change affects identity.

Let us recall the convictions that have brought us this far. The experience of change involves the shock of endings, the recognition of loss and the effort to mobilize energy for a new beginning. Embracing change demands reconciling with what is ending, recognizing how—and how much—the past continues into the future, and responding with hope to what lies ahead. And this process seldom proceeds in a straight line. Confronting significant transition, people move back and forth among beginnings, endings and the losses involved. These losses register in us personally and communally, bringing us to grief.

Re-Centering the Self

Significant change shakes us up. Both "who I am" and "how I make sense of life" are undermined. Even if we survive these initial tremors, the aftershock assaults us: We confront how fragile are the certainties we've staked our lives on.

Psychologists describe this dynamic as de-illusionment—an initially frightening, ultimately maturing process, that challenges our expectations of "how the world works." Carl Jung named this process individuation; cognitive psychologists, such as Sharon Parks, James Fowler, Carol Gilligan, discuss it as an emergence from imbeddedness. Peter Homans uses the image of re-centering of self.

Whatever the name of the process, there is agreement about the cost it exacts. Change strikes a hard bargain, even when we wholeheartedly embrace the shift. To move safely into the future, we must let go the security that comes in the status quo. But the staying power of the status quo derives less from the roles and rules enforced "out there" and more from our inner allegiance to familiarity. Change moves us beyond conventional expectations, disrupts our established identity and threatens our assumptive world.

Negotiating significant change exacts a painful distancing from the received wisdom that has formed and fostered us. Let us restate that more precisely, to fit our experience in the church. For most of us and for many of the people among whom we minister, negotiating significant change in the church has exacted a painful distancing from the religious worldview that initially formed and fostered us. In Paul

Ricoeur's evocative image, we must pass through the desert of criticism. Setting out on this journey is seldom the result of coolly reasoned choice; instead we feel ourselves torn from the web of meaning that earlier sustained us. Thrown to the margin, we are forced to view our once familiar world now as outsiders. We are rendered homeless. But moving to the margins also brings new perspective. This distance gives deeper insight into both personal religious experience and the religious heritage we share.

Personal Experience

Change forces us to scrutinize our accustomed ways of thinking, because customary explanations no longer work. Early on, we tend to judge our own experience as significant—that is, correct, trustworthy, orthodox—to the degree it fits the common consciousness of the communities we belong to. As the gap widens between these received categories and what is happening to us now, the locus of authority starts to shift. The claims of personal experience become more credible. We start to pay more attention to the evidence of our own lives, even when this sets us outside the common consciousness.

This maturing inwardness re-centers the self. It also upsets and energizes the community. As more aspects of our religious lives are accountable to personal discernment, variation in individual thinking and feeling becomes significant. The once-conforming assembly now bristles with diversity. Conflicts arise in the household of faith, initiated not in defiant acts of disobedience but in the struggle to be faithful to one's adult conscience and call.

Religious Heritage

Maturing personal consciousness also transforms our relationship to tradition. Grounded in our own experience, we hold our faith heritage differently. The myths and symbols that shape Christianity—that have shaped us—come under critical examination. Now we are mindful of both their limits—as historical constructions influenced by subtle dynamics of class and race and gender—and of their lasting richness: the continuing contribution, to us and to all humankind, of the Christian witness to God's active presence in the world.

This transformation requires an intervening moment of critical distance. As we struggle to come to terms with our religious past, we stand outside the tradition and look at it anew. This struggle carries us to the brink of deeper faith; it also initiates us into the movement of cultural mourning.

Robert Kegan reminds us, grieving and mourning are not really painful in themselves. In fact, these dynamics reunite us with life and honor its movement. *Pain registers our resistance to the movement of life, of which we are essentially a part and to which we are finally obligated.* Any resistance that sets us against the movement of life will cause us pain.[4]

Commitment to this movement of life requires a special kind of courage—more receptive than the active mastery that characterizes the American adult ideal. There is a letting-go, a giving over, that softens the edges of our usual vigilant control. This receptivity allows us to turn toward the future, even though it seems filled with threat or, worse, empty of hope.

And it is in this absence, hollowed out by the "loss of an old coherence with no new coherence immediately present to take its place,"[5] that meaning will again emerge.

Creation of New Meaning

Cultural mourning is a healing response to the painful experience of collective loss. And the fruit of successful mourning is creative continuity—the creation of new meaning, the generation of new values but always built on vital continuity with the past. From his own work on collective loss, historian Peter Homans concludes: "no individual, no group, no society, no culture has ever broken totally with the past. No matter how severe the break, vestiges and important elements of what what thought to be totally rejected become the basis of the creation of new meanings."[6] Effective grieving reestablishes these links to both personal and communal past, enabling us to carry the core strengths of the past, now transformed, as resources for our future.

Paul Ricoeur, Homans' colleague at the University of Chicago Divinity School, offers a metaphor that helps us understand how this happens. Ricoeur has reminded us that symbols carry a "surplus of meaning." A symbol's evocative power derives from this surplus; it "means" more that any one of us can appreciate. Symbols, images, metaphors carry significances that are never fully disclosed by any generation of interpreters. Cultural change undermines current interpretations. The meanings previously assigned to the central beliefs and communal images no longer serve. These may not be wrong but they do not persuade. These assigned interpretations do not move us, do not convince us, no longer make sense. Even as the institution continues to proclaim these truths, we sense the community has lost faith in their significance.

This loss compels the faith community to explore the surplus of meaning in religious beliefs and values. But probing the Christian core in pursuit of its surplus of meaning both invigorates and disconcerts the church. We have only to recall the controversies that swirl among us as the defining symbols of Catholic belief and practice are reexamined:

grace	church	trinity
justice	ministry	incarnation
eucharist	religious life	salvation
reconciliation	priesthood	the kingdom of God

In a pastoral statement issued in preparation for the Extraordinary Synod of Bishops in 1986, the bishops of the United States used other words to speak of this compelling contemporary demand when they acknowledged that the church stands in need of "a new symbolic and affective system." The faith community's capacity to generate such new structures will demand and depend upon effective cultural grieving.

To wake the church to God's future we will need to commit ourselves to both conscious planning and communal grieving. Planning helps a group face the demands of change by focusing our attention on the future. And much of the Catholic community's efforts over the past thirty years have been focused on planning efforts for the structural side of change—establishing new roles and rules, implementing fresh policies and procedures. These planning efforts must surely continue. But the parallel effort of communal grieving must be consciously supported as well.

James D. Whitehead and Evelyn Eaton Whitehead

Communal grieving helps a group face change by enabling us to hold our past in new ways. Here the strategies are different, less dependent on the rational skills of analysis and planning and more on extra-rational resources:

- recognition—acknowledging both loss and gain;

- remembrance—*anamnesis* recalling God's graceful patterns of the past as surety of the Spirit's continuing presence with us;

- recommitment—pledging ourselves to God's future (seen only through a glass darkly) in responses of both fidelity and hope.

In all these efforts, we recognize the significance of ritual.

Religious Leaders and Rituals of Grieving

Liturgists know that religion has a special calling in regard to emotions like grief. By design, religion addresses suffering, helping us face failure, loss and pain while leading us through them. At its best, religion functions as a school of the emotions. Gospel memories, stories of saints, devotions and prayers all show us how to feel, what to do with our delight and our depression, how to handle our gratitude and our grief.

Theologian William Spohn reminds us that scriptural stories "do not directly dictate what to do," but by evoking our emotions in distinctive ways, "they frame perception and encourage certain scenarios."[7] Religion's vocation is to provide a practical guide to life, training us in fruitful rhythms of emotion, how to feel as deeply and fully as Jesus felt, how to live a passionate life. If religion fails at this lofty vocation as often as it succeeds, this only reminds us that religion bears our fingerprints as well as God's.

Liturgists are also keenly aware of two special ways that religion serves us in periods of high emotion: how sanctuaries and rituals allow us to hold our grief in graceful ways.

Sanctuaries

Religious leaders provide us with sanctuaries: safe places to feel the full terror or delight of their lives. A sanctuary, whether a church building or hospital room or counseling office, serves as a haven, a protected space. In the psychological imagery of D. W. Winnicott, sanctuaries are "holding environments" — privileged places where our usual composure is no longer necessary, where we can afford to acknowledge our worst fears and our most threatening hopes.

A person's home may be overflowing with children and pets and chores, or the office may be too public a turf to allow us to register genuine feelings. But in a sanctuary, people find the space to feel as bad as they feel. The Spanish author Miguel de Unamuno remarked, "The chief sanctity of a temple is that it is a place to which (people) can go to weep in common."[8]

Theologian Jonathan Z. Smith has observed that ritual vessels are holy because of what we do with them; they enjoy no pre-existing sacredness. Our actions bless them and make them holy. This is true of the healing sanctuaries in our American culture. An extraordinary example of such a sanctuary is the Vietnam Memorial in Washington. You know the story: the post-war refusal of our country to acknowledge its losses and its failure. We had never lost a war and did not know how to respond. As a people, we resolutely refused to grieve.

Then this national memorial was commissioned. The architect Maya Lin, a young Asian American woman, designed a most unlikely site: no threatening bayonets, no striving heroes. But her creativity released the country's thwarted need to grieve. At this secular shrine, cut into a hill like a gash in the earth or the entry into a crypt, people reach out to touch a name on a stone wall. Emotions are honored and released; private pain is transformed into public prayer. The angular wall is an odd shape for a sanctuary, but it works. This site has become a holy place where painful emotions are honored, and as a people we begin to wake from the nightmare of that war.

The AIDS quilt is a second example of an unlikely sanctuary. Before the quilt appeared, AIDS deaths were most often kept secret. Vague causes of death were listed in obituaries. Shameful deaths were hidden from our national view; our common grief was thwarted. And, again, the human imagination conjured up a sanctuary — a portable sanctuary — that could allow a public grieving. Part of the genius lay in the image of a quilt: a warm protector with memories of childhood and family comfort. A quilt consoles as it holds us. And it is communal property: Individual names share space on this broad blanket.

People came to this movable feast, this wake, to acknowledge and honor lives that had been lost.

These examples remind us that sanctuaries come in many shapes. They shake our naive conviction that the church building alone provides our sanctuary. They remind us that sanctuaries are holy because of how we act in them.

A sanctuary can, of course, be converted into a hiding place. We can structure liturgies that provide us with ready-made emotions and with scripts for how we should feel. In such a sanctuary, we are spared the challenge of registering our own unruly feelings. A piety of "offering it up" may lead us to hold our pain away, rather than holding it up to God in a troubled, rancorous prayer. By design, a sanctuary is meant to be a haven without becoming a hiding place. It is not simply a container, but more like a crucible — empty enough and resilient enough to hold and transform our emotions.

Rituals

Sanctuaries gain this transforming power when we enhance them through the dramatic actions of rituals. Rituals are bodily gestures that call attention to some part of life. Rituals provide us with ways to hold our powerful emotions. As Thomas Driver has remarked, "Ritual controls emotion while releasing it and guides it while letting it run."[9]

Ritual and sanctuary provide boundaries within which we give fuller rein to our feelings. These communal boundaries, provided by the fellow believers who stand with us, are strong enough to protect us in a time of great loss. Here we can fall apart, because we will be held. An important function of ritual, then, is to honor our emotions: Here we can feel as bad as we feel.

Ritual's second gift is to fold our loss and pain into a larger narrative. The force and uniqueness of our loss — no one else can know the pain I feel at the death of my child or the loss of my clear identity as a Catholic — leads us to privatize the pain. We may even feel we are going crazy. The gift of a communal ritual is to hold us, reminding us of the larger story we, on better days, have believed: Jesus has come this way. He fell and failed and died a terrible death. For him grief became the door to life. This story, gently recalled, folds our pain into a larger narrative, holding our loss until it is warmed by that story. Even now, in this terrible time, we are following Christ. Could our present troubles be part of the plot? Is the grief that afflicts the church the door to new life? This folding of our pain into a tradition of life and death begins to heal us.

Recent research on post-traumatic shock syndrome reminds us of the healing force of narrative in general. Psychologist Jonathan Shay in his *Achilles in Vietnam* recounts the destructive cycle of "thwarted grief" that struck many participants in the Vietnam war.[10] The soldiers and nurses who were witnesses to sudden, horrendous deaths were given no chance to acknowledge their feelings or honor the victims. Frenetic activity on the front and hospital were alternated with brief periods of R & R taken away from communal support. The hope was that rest and recreation would somehow dissipate the stress of these powerful feelings. When these members of the military completed their tour of duty, they again left the comrades with whom they had shared these experiences and returned to a world that could not comprehend their losses. In time this pain, utterly ungrieved and privatized, surfaced in symptoms of insomnia, alcoholism and domestic violence. These traumatic memories, untethered from their context and unhonored, flared up in nightmares and destructive behaviors.

When these patients were given the chance to share their traumatic recollections in a supportive setting (one might say, in a sanctuary), the memories began to lose their power. Instead of being simply experienced as night traumas, memories began to be rewoven into life stories. Such "narrative enables the survivor to rebuild the ruins of character." This sharing—certainly a ritual—lifts these memories, formerly isolated in nightmares, into the light of day, "thereby reestablishing authority over memory."[11] Through this process, horrendous scars are transformed into honorable wounds.

The third gift of ritual is to provide the pacing that leads us through a painful loss toward a renewed life. Grief stops us in our tracks, freezes us or bends us into circles of chronic complaint. Rituals of lamentation allow us to slow down but keep going. They invite us to brake our movement enough to honor the loss, but not to simply halt. The simplest example is the funeral procession. When we walk with measured pace in a public display of grief, we slow down but we keep moving.

A more complex example arises from recent research on burial rites in ancient China. Stanford scholar Lee Yearley has discussed how these rituals intentionally provoked an oscillation of denial and acceptance.[12] After death the body was not moved from the house for several days, allowing the relatives to pretend the person may only be sleeping even as they admit their loved one is dead. (We repeat this pretense with the Western practice of embalming. Our loved one looks so peaceful, as though she is just sleeping.)

In ancient China, when the person was buried a lute was placed with the corpse, as though to provide music. But the instrument was left intentionally untuned, admitting it would not be played. The deceased person was dressed in festive clothes, but these clothes did not have the usual buckles and belt. These missing accessories acknowledged what the clothing was permitted to deny. Grieving rituals, in their genius of pacing, permit us to both hold on and let go at the same time. This oscillation, done with patience and persistence, brings us through our grief toward life.

Something Ungrieved in the Church

The question remains: What is the unspoken loss that saps our energy and debilitates our common life? How can we grieve if we cannot even admit what we are losing?

Karl Rahner, in an influential address in 1979 on the emerging world church, noted that since Vatican II the church is "still groping for (its) identity."[13] At the heart of this groping, too rarely admitted, is the terrible question that grief raises: Will we survive? If we let go the religious identity we have worn proudly for centuries, who will we be? Behind this question lies troubling experiences: Catholic parents of our generation watch their children show little interest in the religious institution still central in the parents' lives. This generation experiences the threatening absence of vocations to priesthood and religious life. Are we the final generation? Is this how it ends?

The grief of an identity crisis is that we lose our accustomed self before we discover a new identity. This gap generates the terror of change; this gap is also the crucible in which the new is fashioned. In this crucible which is our life as church today, we glimpse three aspects of Catholic identity that have come to grief.

Most of us here were born into a religious identity that was clear, exclusive and austere. Catholic identity was clear in doctrine and devotion: We knew what we believed and had a catechism to prove it. We knew how to behave, and moved easily and sometimes automatically through the practices and pieties that composed our identity as Catholics.

Our identity was also exclusive: We were God's chosen people, as Jews once had been, as Muslims and Buddhists were not. The "we" of Catholicism was often set against all of "them" in the world of non-Catholics. Our very identity depended on these "others" who served as boundaries and backdrops to Catholic faith. Our rejection of them gave the fine edge to our identity.

Our identity was also austere in our shared caution about the sensual and the sexual. Despite our patrimony of sacramental touch and taste, of anointing oil and broken bread, of liturgical pageantry, we had crafted an identity that harbored deep suspicions about the body, about women, about pleasure.

Since Vatican II, Catholics have sensed the Spirit inviting us to surrender this clarity, exclusiveness and austerity, and risk a richer identity. Three shifts in our shared life reveal both the grievous threat we face and the risky but exciting future to which the church is waking.

The changing shape of the ministry of hospital chaplain in the past thirty years exemplifies the fruitful blurring of a once-clear identity. Thirty years ago Catholic chaplains were almost exclusively priests. The ministry offered in Catholic hospitals was well-defined and sacramental in the narrow sense: Holy communion was distributed each morning; the sacrament of Extreme Unction was offered to the dying; pastoral visits were made by priests who were highly visible in their clerical attire or religious habits, but not especially trained for this work.

Today hospital chaplains are predominantly non-ordained persons, drawn from lay and religious women and men. These diverse ministers seldom wear distinctive clothes. Thanks to clinical pastoral education and other improvements in counseling, these ministers provide a vastly improved (that is, more graceful) ministry. While the

James D. Whitehead and Evelyn Eaton Whitehead

chaplaincy ministry has lost its clear boundaries, it has blossomed in richness and effectiveness. The controversies generated by this blurring of ministerial identity raise healthy questions: Are these people really representatives of the church? Why can they not administer the sacrament of the sick? and function as signs of new life awaking?

An example of religious identity becoming less exclusive is happening at this moment in Adelaide, Australia, and replicated in many other places as well. The archdiocese of Adeliade is promoting a move of the seminary across town to new quarters that will be shared with Anglican and Uniting Church seminaries. In the change the traditional identity of "a Catholic seminary" will die and be transformed into "a school of ministry." The new setting will welcome not only unmarried men studying for the Catholic priesthood but Catholic laity involved in ministry and others preparing to serve the Anglican and Uniting Church communities. In this new context, pre-existing boundaries between genders and between denominations will be blurred. By economic necessity and by theological conviction, the local church is being led to acknowledge more actively that in our Christian calling we are more similar than different.

This physical move is, nonetheless, a profound loss for many people, heralding as it does the demise of an exclusive vision of priesthood. Grief is palpable in the diocese. But the community is experiencing more than loss; in this death something previously unimagined is being born. In this shift in identity, we begin to perceive that these "others"—women and laity and Protestants—need not compromise our priestly integrity, but may, in fact, fulfill it.

The third example of our shifting religious identity lies in the realm of devotion. As Catholics we have a proud and austere tradition of discipline. A part of this heritage is our commitment to fasting: saying "no" to certain parts of life in order to defend the "yes" that charts our commitment to the gospel and our fidelity to Christ. The reforms of Vatican II ended the discipline of Lenten fasts and Friday abstinence; to many it suddenly seemed that fasting was foolish, an archaic affectation to be jettisoned in a post-modern age.

But a human instinct reminds us that fasting and feasting are a natural and necessary rhythm in our life; we do not thrive when either of these dynamics is wounded. And our Christian memory recalls this rhythm shaping the life of Jesus and his followers. So we remain convinced that fasting is a necessary part of our identity at Christians. But this discipline, like every other part of life, survives by changing. Today we are challenged to fast not from meat on Fridays, but from the deceptions of a society in thrall to consumption, celebrity. We are called, as Christians, to fast not from sexual pleasure but from the addictions that abuse this gift of God's creation. People will flock to a church that regains its voice about the graceful rhythm of fasting and feasting.

In these and all the other losses that are part of a profoundly changing Catholic identity, we are losing what we had assumed was essential to our faith. Grief protests: Will we survive? But institutional grief has another more subtle complaint. We know that we are all sinners and in need of constant purification; we confess ourselves *ecclesia semper reformanda*—a church always in need of reform. But, almost unnoticed, we may have come to believe that certain parts of our institution are exempt from change. If these arrangements were directly crafted by Christ, then they may escape the need for re-examination and purification. Yet if God's own son was not exempt from the paschal mystery, what part of our institution will plead this privilege?

As the fires of Vatican II burn down and the century ends, we are introduced, in the words of philosopher Martha Nussbaum, to "the inner life of mourning" which concerns "nothing less than how to imagine the world. The struggle against grief is to strive toward a different view of the universe."[14]

As Catholics, can we risk recasting our identity as less clear, less exclusive, less austere? As we struggle to imagine what this even means, we face the double challenge carried in the image of "waking the church." We must honor the passing of something noble and holy of our past, as we arouse the church to its new life.

Both these waking activities will be carried out, as has always been the case among us, in privileged places and symbolic actions. And you are the people who will create the sanctuaries and rituals with which the church will wake to its new life.

James D. Whitehead and Evelyn Eaton Whitehead

1. We are referring here to Walter Brueggemann's ideas about the "royal consciousness" in his *The Prophetic Imagination* (Philadelphia: Fortress Press, 1978).

2. Walter Brueggemann, *Interpretation and Obedience* (Minneapolis: Fortress Press, 1991), 198.

3. Our understanding here of the dynamics of social grieving owes much to the work of our colleague, J. Gordon Myers, PhD.

4. Robert Kegan, *In Over Our Heads: The Mental Demands of Modern Life* (Cambridge: Harvard University Press, 1994), 265.

5. *Ibid.*, 267.

6. Peter Homans, *The Ability to Mourn: Disillusionment and the Social Origins of Psychoanalysis* (Chicago: University of Chicago Press, 1989); for a helpful introduction to Homans' perspective on cultural mourning as the context of creative meaning-making, see "The Ability to Mourn: A Conversation with Peter Homans" in *Criterion: Journal of the University of Chicago Divinity School,* volume 30, no. 2 (Spring 1991), pages 2–8; the quotation here is taken from page 8.

7. "Jesus and Christian Ethics," in *Theological Studies,* 56 (1995), 92–107, esp. 104.

8. *The Tragic Sense of Life,* trans. J. E. Crawford Flitch (New York: Dover, 1954), 17.

9. *The Magic of Ritual* (HarperSanFrancisco, 1991), 156.

10. Jonathan Shay, *Achilles in Vietnam* (New York: Atheneum, 1994).

11. Shay, 188 and 192.

12. See his *Facing Our Frailty: Comparative Religious Ethics and the Confucian Death Rituals,* Gross Memorial Lecture, 1995 (Valparaiso, IN: Valparaiso University, 1996).

13. See "Towards A Fundamental Theological Interpretation of Vatican II," in *Theological Studies* 40 (1979), 716–727, esp. 717.

14. *The Therapy of Desire* (Princeton, NJ: Princeton University Press, 1994), 384.

Joan Workmaster

Sunday Worship in the Absence of the Eucharist: Short-Term Solution or Long-Term Problem?

The dialogue that has been under way for more than two years in the diocese of Rochester, New York, has done more than hold our leaders accountable. It has asked all members of the church to step forward and take some responsibility, in so far as they are able, for the development of new and creative ways to do ministry in our parishes and faith communities. In effect the dialogue has said that while leaders cannot "tell the people the eucharist is the center of their lives and then refuse to provide them with the very things that make eucharist possible,"[1] the people cannot just accept what is taught and do nothing to collaborate with their leaders to provide those very things that make eucharist possible.

We have struggled with issues around eucharist vs. communion, the need to celebrate eucharist vs. the importance of maintaining the community, the size of parishes, the number of Masses, the numbers in attendance, the proliferation of Masses to fill the need of every parish organization's agenda. As we've waxed and waned, we gradually realized that we simply could not take the route of a short-term solution. How that all came about for our diocese is what I would like to share with you in the hopes that some or all of it may be helpful to you and your ministry in the local church.

Joan Workmaster

The Diocese of Rochester

It would help you to know a bit about the diocese in which the issue emerged. Rochester is a medium-size diocese just a little over a hundred years old. There is one large metropolitan area, the city of Rochester, and several smaller cities — Elmira, Auburn, Ithaca and Corning. There are many small towns and villages with a number of parishes in rural areas. While Catholics comprise only 24.5% of the total population, the influence of the church in the geographical area of the diocese is much greater than that small percentage would imply, due mainly to strong Catholic health facilities, a strong presence of Catholic Charities offices and the leadership of the bishop in social justice and ecumenical issues.

Bishop Matthew H. Clark, the eighth bishop of the diocese, was installed in June 1979. We currently have 171 active priests serving 161 parishes, hospitals, campus ministries and correctional facilities. It is possible that, if the situation falls in certain ways, a parish or faith community might be without eucharist on a Sunday.

Priests and Parishes

Diocesan leadership has already tried clustering parishes within geographical proximity and, in the last two years, four parishes have been assigned pastoral administrators and sacramental ministers. Of the four administrators, two are religious women, one is a permanent deacon and one is a layman. The parishes with administrators have been quite successful, but the clustering has not worked as well as expected. This is probably due to the fact that in most instances the parishes clustered, while within walking distance of each other, do not share similar cultures and ways of praying.

We share many of the same joys and problems that all dioceses of our size have. While we have, in large measure, a well-educated body of pastoral leaders, we also have the nagging feeling that for all the education we do have we could be further along with liturgical reform and renewal. There are small pockets of resistance, both on the right and the left. The overwhelming majority of the population of the diocese, however, walks that middle ground trying to remain faithful to the gospel message.

The Process of Making Decisions

Rochester is a place where the grassroots speak often and audibly. The people in the pew are never far removed from decisions that need to be made. This is principally the result of the Synod which ran for three years, 1992 to 1994. Preparation for the Synod started in 1990 and the first sessions were held in parishes in September, 1992. The General Synod took place October 1–3, 1993, when representatives from all the parishes and faith communities in the diocese gathered together to examine the parish and regional reporting and set the future priorities of the diocese. The final work of prioritizing and setting the goals was finished in the fall of 1994.

Bishop Clark asked from the very beginning that all the dialogue through the time of the Synod be done according to the following five values: to be a collaborative church; to call forth lay leadership; to utilize fully the richness of our diversity; to be open, trusting and respectful in our dialogue with one another; and to engage in ecumenical and interfaith dialogue and cooperation. These values will live far beyond the Synod. They are invoked by the bishop at every turn of every major diocesan dialogue.

The grassroots discussion around six themes dealing with life-long faith formation, social justice issues, gender issues and the various needs of people of all ages resulted in the establishment of four major Synod goals and a five-year commitment on the part of the parishes, assisted by the diocesan ministries, to integrate action steps around the goals into their planning for worship, catechetics and social ministry. These goals form the backbone of what the diocese is all about: to form Catholics in beliefs, traditions and moral values throughout life; to advocate for a consistent ethic of life; to recognize and value the dignity of women in church and society; and to promote the formation and growth of small Christian communities.

Understanding that the liturgy is foundational to all Synod goals, but most particularly to lifelong faith formation, Bishop Clark asked the Priests' Council—as they began their work year in September 1994—to give some reflection to their needs as they acted as presiders at and chief catechists of the liturgy in their particular communities. There were many issues raised but overshadowing everything was the question of what are we do as the number of priests dwindles and the number of Catholics rises. How will we provide for Sunday eucharist in these circumstances? Clustering parishes did not seem to be working well. How many parishes can we legitimately shut down? Are we to become a diocese of circuit riders? How many parishes can one pastor care for? Can't we just substitute a communion service when we cannot celebrate eucharist? What about the Sunday obligation in church law? And always at the heart of all the practical questions was the one that no one really wanted to deal with: What happens in the long term if some communities end up celebrating communion services more often than they do eucharist?

In December 1994 the Office of Liturgy entered the conversation at the bishop's request. Of course, everyone wanted to know what we were going to do for them that would solve the problem. We all quickly understood there was no quick fix or easy answer. By the time we had reached the Convocation of Priests and Pastoral Administrators in April 1995, everyone realized that it was time to do some major work. The bishop suggested at the end of the convocation that we devote the next year to a dialogue about this topic that would conclude at the Convocation of 1996 with a set of guidelines that the diocese could use to determine how we would solve the dilemma. It was a unanimous decision to follow this path. Thus began the saga that has just completed its first major phase this month.

Wider Topics for Discussion in the Diocese

We began work in earnest in September, 1995. At that time and derived from the discussion of the previous year, we identified four major questions that would form the heart of the bloc and council meetings for the year. Those questions were:

1. Given your belief in the centrality of eucharist in the life of the community, what skills and understandings are essential to be an effective presider today?
2. Someone wanders into Sunday eucharist at your parish. What would lead them to believe (or find it hard to believe) that for this community full and active participation by all the people is the aim to be considered before all else?[2]
3. What practices reveal parishioners' understanding eucharist as a sacred action in which they play a vital role, helping them to live a eucharistic life during the week?
4. What aspects of the community celebration now reinforce a more limited understanding of eucharist as only the sacred species to be received?

Along with the discussion questions all priests and pastoral administrators received copies of *The Liturgy Documents* and *The Dilemma of Priestless Sundays* by James Dallen. In addition, as we went through the year, the Liturgy Office provided two brief research papers on "Exposition and Adoration of the Blessed Sacrament" and "Communion Services as Alternative Celebrations."

The discussion was extremely difficult. There were moments when we felt that we would never get beyond the need for warm, welcoming hospitality ministers. There was much difficulty with language. Certain terms, such as communion and eucharist, were being used to mean the same thing and different things. To help with this, a liturgical glossary was drawn up. There were many questions that could be answered by the documents, but no one was reading them. At Bishop Clark's request we drew up a reading list of the more important and applicable parts of the documents and he presented it to the clergy and the pastoral administrators as their suggested Lenten reading. We hoped in this way to prepare them for the dialogue that was scheduled to take place at the April Convocation.

Eucharist and Ministry

What no one understood for a long time was that we were asking our priests, in particular, to talk about and dissect something that was at the heart of their identity. For each one of them, whether conservative or liberal, this conversation was talking about who they were, what the most important element of their daily lives was all about. If they did anything consistently, day after day, they celebrated the eucharistic liturgy. What we were talking about could change what they did and how they did it. This dialogue was asking them to have some flexibility about the central core of their being. Everyone knows how hard this can be.

It was not until these thoughts and fears were spoken at the table that we began to deal with the issues at hand. We were almost ready to enter the 1996 Convocation. There were those who were convinced that we would just put the issues on the table, arrive at consensus and write guidelines. There were others who felt that we were not ready to do that but were willing to see how far we could get.

The process had been developed to engage the participants in large and small group discussions. These discussions revolved around six issues:

1. What do we understand by "full, conscious, and active participation"?
2. How does Sunday Mass form our communities into a eucharistic people?
3. How is the quality of Sunday Mass affected by the number of Masses and the number of people present at each Mass?
4. When a priestless Sunday occurs, shall we send the people to a neighboring parish or shall we provide for some form of alternative celebration, that is, communion?
5. Consider the appropriateness of a eucharistic celebration at all weddings and funerals and the relationship of wedding and funeral Masses to weekday Masses.
6. How shall we catechize about our decisions here?

We never had to worry about the last question because it became evident early on that we were not ready to make any decisions. There was little consensus theologically or pastorally. What was evident was that the priests and pastoral administrators were really talking to each other. The small groups were actually the eleven regions of the diocese and the conversation going on in each of those rooms was deep and respectful. There was an excitement about what was happening. In the

history of the Convocation this was the first time that the membership had done this large amount of preparation and were now actively
participating in the work rather than passively listening to speakers.
Nevertheless we ended the Convocation knowing that we had not
arrived at any conclusions other than that we needed further study
and definition of the issue. It was at this time that the focus began to
shift away from talk of the shortage of priests and toward just what
did we mean when we spoke of the centrality of the Sunday eucharist.

The Pastoral Letter of Bishop Clark

The following summer months as we discussed the outcomes of the
Convocation, Bishop Clark made the decision that it was time for him
to write a pastoral letter addressing the centrality of Sunday eucharist.
A task force was formed headed by the Liturgy Office to assist in the
preparation of the letter. Published in October 1996, and entitled
"From East to West, A Perfect Offering," the letter first focuses on
eucharist as the central event and action of reconciliation for the
church and on the importance of this event and action occurring at the
Sunday gathering. The bishop offered this event and action as a defining characteristic of our Catholic faith. "In this eucharistic action,"
he wrote, "we are fed and nourished so as to go out into the world to
be the presence of Christ, to live Christ's dying and rising in our worlds
of family and friends, work and play, neighbor and stranger."[3]

The bishop called for a dialogue, not restricted to clergy and parish staff, but open to all the people of the diocese. He asked for that
dialogue in the spirit of the Synod values and raised nine issues that
he felt needed to be addressed. Those issues ranged from the need to
understand that nothing can ever replace the eucharist, not even the
reception of communion, to the quality of our Sunday celebrations,
the number of Masses, the appropriate use of alternative celebrations,
the recognition of the value of the local community, the development
of appropriate eucharistic devotions and finally the recognition of
what an individual priest can be expected to do within the norms of
the church. The bishop intended to center us on the meaning of the

eucharist as a way of life and identity, rather than planning extensively for how we would live without it.

Study Guides for Parishes

Along with the publication of the letter, four study guides were prepared for parishes to assist them in the discussions the bishop had called for. Over the course of the fall and spring, especially during Lent of 1997, our diocesan parishes involved themselves not only in the discussion of the pastoral letter through the study guides, but also in other unique and creative ways. Some of our parishes looked to materials such as Susan Jorgenson's *Eucharist!*[4] and Gilbert Ostdiek's *Catechesis for Liturgy*[5] in a search for some experiential things to do with their small groups. Other parishes looked at this period of time as a way to catechize the daily Mass groups and those who were devoted to exposition and adoration. The results of these discussions and experiences were sent to the Office of Liturgy and eventually found a place in the document that we are about to publish.

Along with the parish discussions, the Priests' Council and blocs continued their dialogue on five topics that they gleaned from the pastoral letter: the church and the eucharist; the role of the assembly; the role of the presider; the nature of the Sunday obligation and alternative celebrations. Each month from November to March saw discussion on one of these topics and we began to develop what we called "whereas" statements. These statements attempted to define as succinctly as possible current theology and pastoral practice on the topic. From the discussions, editorial changes were made and then we began to create a list of "therefores" for each topic. All of this work included what we were hearing from the parish discussions as well. Also, other groups in the diocese, such as the pastoral associates, were also holding meetings in which the topics were discussed and feedback given to the Office. While the work was difficult, this time around we were ready for dialogue that really explored the issues. We were able to hear one another and make the necessary adjustments while adhering to the norms of the church.

We arrived at the April 1997 Convocation with a document that consisted of good "whereas" and "therefore" material on all five topics and we were ready to come to some conclusions on the material. We were looking for answers to four questions: What can you live with? What do you absolutely disagree with? How would you change it? and finally, What is missing? Through an intense process that involved large and small group work, language and text changes that were deemed necessary by the whole were made and the material was remanded to two readers for a final editing. The key point in this document is that Sunday celebration of the eucharist is the norm and it will only be in the most extreme of emergencies that anything else will happen. We have agreed that we will not settle for Band-Aid approaches. We have committed ourselves to ensuring that a Band-Aid won't be necessary. For some that means examining several areas such as how to make better use of facilities, how to make better use of personnel, how to bring parish and faith communities together to worship together (this means much work to be done on the quality of the celebration). For others it may mean challenging the current system.

Following the editing at the Convocation, the pieces dealing with the role of the presider and the nature of the Sunday obligation were returned to the Priests' Council and blocs for a final sign-off. The other three topics on the church and the eucharist, the role of the assembly and alternative celebrations were taken to the diocesan Spring Ministry Day to be given a final editing by people who comprise parish staffs.

Spreading the Word

Throughout this entire period of dialogue, especially during this last year, there have been a number of supporting activities going on that helped everyone focus on the various aspects of the discussion. The staff of the Liturgy Office as well as members of the Diocesan Liturgical Commission and faculty from St. Bernard's Institute have been active in the diocese giving presentations on the centrality of the Sunday eucharist. In addition, Nathan Mitchell and Bob Duggan gave major presentations at Spring 1996 and Fall 1996 Ministry Days. Jim Moroney from the Bishops' Committee on the Liturgy gave the major presentation at the August Keuka Days in 1996 and Bernard Cooke will be the major presenter at this year's Keuka Days. The Keuka Days traditionally attract parish volunteers as well as some staff.

This year, the Spring Ministry Day was used to engage parish staffs in the work of the final editing. Again, in a process of large and small group dialogue, the participants had the opportunity to pull the documents apart and consider all the components. As at the Convocation we asked them the four questions: What can you live with? What do you absolutely disagree with? How would you change it? and finally, What is missing? The response was incredibly fine and the document left their hands not substantially changed but considerably strengthened.

The material will be ready for publication on June 25. Along with the guidelines it will include an enlarged liturgical glossary and a sheet of Frequently Asked Questions. With the glossary and the questions we are able to address some of the issues that need explanation but cannot be included in the document itself.

Ongoing Catechesis

Are we finished? Not at all. We still struggle with the tension between the value of the gathered community and the desire to always celebrate eucharist. We are only too aware of the need for some substantial catechesis on many issues such as the shape of alternative celebrations, the careful planning required for them, the need for training in leading prayer, how this fits into the RCIA and music. Most importantly all our parishes need assistance in integrating these guidelines on the centrality of the Sunday eucharist into the diocesan strategic planning for the millennium that is just beginning. Between now and 1999 all of our parishes and faith communities will be expected to participate in strategic planning both at the parish level and at a cluster level. These guidelines on eucharist are foundational for measuring the vitality of the parish. Bishop Clark has said on many occasions that it is his understanding that how we celebrate eucharist and how that celebration forms us as a eucharistic people is of first importance. We have made the commitment that eucharist on Sunday is our norm and that we will do whatever is necessary to creatively plan for the future to ensure that Sunday celebration of the eucharist will take place in all our parishes. We have agreed as a diocesan community that we do not wish to risk the loss of our eucharistic identity. Only time will tell if we will be successful. For the present, we have asked the Spirit to guide us and this is the direction we will take, not because of a mandate from our bishop, but because we the people, who have the most at stake, have taken up the challenge.

1. Nathan Mitchell. Talk given at FDLC Region VII Fall Meeting, November 13, 1996.

2. *Constitution on the Sacred Liturgy,* 14.

3. *From East to West, A Perfect Offering.* Pastoral Letter of Bishop Matthew H. Clark, Bishop of Rochester.

4. Published by Resource Publications, Inc.

5. Published by Pastoral Press.

Nathan Mitchell

Sunday Celebrations in the Absence of Eucharist

In a pastoral letter published in June of 1995, the bishops of Kansas addressed the challenges connected with "Sunday Celebrations in the Absence of a Priest." "We, the bishops of Kansas," they wrote,

> have come to judge that Holy Communion regularly received outside of Mass is a short-term solution that has all the makings of becoming a long-term problem . . . Such practice could well contribute to the erosion of our many-sided belief in the Eucharist. *It is for this reason that we restrict such services to emergencies only.*[1]

The bishops explained their decision by outlining a number of "disturbing implications" that flow from the practice of replacing Sunday Mass with a communion service. Chief among these is "a blurring of the difference between the celebration of the Eucharist and the reception of Communion."

In an article related to the Kansas bishops' statement, Father Jim Dallen alluded to *The Shape of the Liturgy* (London: Dacre Press, 1944), the seminal work of Dom Gregory Dix, who argued that what first brought Christians to the eucharist was not "sociability or learning or an emotional thrill, nor even . . . eucharistic communion."

Instead, they came to *do* something; "They were convinced that *doing* eucharist was essential to the survival of the Body of Christ, because eucharist was more verb than noun."[2]

Eucharist: More Verb than Noun

In a nutshell this difference between verb and noun is indeed the difference between "celebrating eucharist" and a "communion service." For the phrase *"celebrating* eucharist" suggests a distinctive kind of *doing,* one that flows from a distinctive kind of *being.* This kind of being is the gift of belonging to the church, which happens in what is classically called "baptism." It creates a distinctive way of *living,* which is classically called "church," the body of Christ, the people of God.

A communion service is statically focused on an object already produced, an event already done, an action already completed. Whatever its other values may be, a communion service does not "create" church, does not draw it into existence. Thus, a communion service, in and of itself, cannot unite the church to the sacrifice of Christ in such a way that his act of *sacrifice* — his paschal *transitus* to new life in God's presence — now becomes its own act of sacrifice, its own passover to new life in God's presence.

The Language of Sacrifice

Here we touch the heart of the reason that Roman Catholic tradition insists on understanding eucharist in *sacrificial* terms. Many years ago, Father Clifford Howell wrote a short book, *Of Sacraments and Sacrifice,* that did much to update our understanding of eucharist in light of biblical research and new thinking about the sacraments. Today many Catholics have grown uncomfortable with the language of sacrifice as applied to the Lord's supper.

Part of the discomfort with the language stems quite legitimately from our modern recognition that the word "sacrifice" has been used to mask terrible atrocities, to legitimate violence and repression and to minimize the systematic abuse of women and minorities. "Sacrifice" of this sort is, of course, utterly indefensible—and it is small wonder that postconciliar Catholics are skittish about using such a troubled term to define or describe our central act of worship.

On another level, however, the language of sacrifice and "self-surrender" has a legitimate place in our understanding of human life and in our experience of God. For at its deepest level, sacrifice implies not the violent *taking* of life, but the *renewing* of life at its physical, psychological and spiritual sources. The broken language of sacrifice tries to speak about that most life-giving of all actions: the giving of our own bodies as food for each other. This is, perhaps, most evident when we see a child at its mother's breast, for in this act the mother is saying, in effect, "Eat of my body, drink of me . . ."

At the heart of sacrifice lies *exchange*—an action, a doing wherein all that I am becomes another's, freely given and freely received. When applied to the eucharist, then, the term "sacrifice" has more to do with how *we*, through God's gracious initiative and self-bestowal, become present to and participate in Jesus' obedient surrender to "death on a cross" (Philippians 2:8) than with convoluted explanations of how that once-for-all historical event is somehow repeated or re-presented. In short, the language of eucharistic sacrifice intends to illumine *our* side of the street, to clarify what it means to say, as we pray in the eucharistic prayer, that "*we* give thanks and praise . . . *we* remember . . . *we* offer to you . . ." It aims at showing how we, the people of God, made so in baptism, are empowered to "have that mind in us which was also in Christ Jesus" (2:5).

We were empowered to offer sacrifice precisely because of that "wondrous exchange," which is also the core of Jesus' own sacrifice, when in the mystery of the incarnation God chose humanity as the only definition of the divine. God chose to be be known, henceforth and forever, only in and as our neighbor. Sacrifice isn't about changing God or changing Christ, or even about changing bread and wine into something else; it's about changing *us*. And so the proper definition of sacrifice is not the violent taking of life, but the renewal of life, the re-sourcing of life, the return of life to its generative sources. The word "sacrifice" describes the action whereby all that I am—body, soul and spirit—becomes another's, a gift of person freely bestowed, freely received.

We can still hear an echo of this ancient sense of sacrifice in the old English marriage formula, as in the Book of Common Prayer of 1549, when the groom places the ring on the bride's finger: "With this ring I thee wed; this gold and silver I thee give; with my body I thee worship; and with all my worldly goods I thee endow." Here, obviously, sacrifice is not a violent taking, but an act of worship, an act of complete self-bestowal and surrender: "With my body I thee worship, and with all my worldly goods I thee endow." Such is the sacrifice of the eucharist.

Eucharist in Parishes

In their 1995 pastoral the bishops of Kansas wrote that "the *parish* is *the usual place* where all the faithful gather for the Sunday celebration of the Eucharist." Quoting the *Catechism of the Catholic Church* (2179, 2182), the bishops go on to remark:

> [T]he parish initiates the Christian people into the ordinary expression of the liturgical life; it gathers them together in this celebration; it teaches Christ's saving doctrine; it practices the charity of the Lord in good works . . . .
>
> Participation in the communal celebration of the Sunday Eucharist is a testimony of belonging and being faithful to Christ and to his Church. The faithful give witness by this to their communion in faith and charity. Together they testify to God's holiness and their hope of salvation. They strengthen one another under the guidance of the Holy Spirit.

Clearly, the phenomenon of "Sunday celebrations in the absence of eucharist" is not a theological or pastoral abstraction. Its impact on parishes is immediate and deep. Thus what is really at risk in the proliferation of communion services is the continuing vitality of individual parishes that are forced to "fast" from full eucharistic action, from eucharist as *verb*, sometimes for weeks at a time. Also at risk is the church's traditional understanding of pastoral ministry at the local level. Ministry—especially, though not exclusively, that of priests—reaches beyond preaching the Word and celebrating the sacraments. At the heart of the local parish, pastoral ministry is traditionally understood as a complex, many-layered act of building community.

Vatican II understood the church not as some kind of supernatural welfare state holding entitlements to grace for the submissive and the well-behaved, but as *sacramentum mundi*—as a diverse, combative, inclusive, vigorous, multivalent and effective symbol of all that the world of humanity is meant to be, meant to become. *All* who serve the parish are co-workers, collaborators in the church's mission to become God's human face in the world. For again, the church exists not to serve itself, but to serve the "liturgy of the world." This is what Karl Rahner once described as that "terrible and sublime liturgy, breathing death and sacrifice, that God celebrates . . . throughout the free history of men and women . . . throughout the whole length and breadth of this colossal history of birth and death."[3]

The church exists for the world's sake, for the liturgy of the church exists for the sake of the "liturgy of the world." Borrowing this image from Rahner, we erect a small sign, a humble landmark that points to the world as the place already possessed, at its roots, by God's gracious presence, grace and self-bestowal. In short, our task is to make conscious, public and visible what God is always and already doing at the heart of the world. This is the whole point of ministry, and this is precisely what is threatened if we allow ministry's significance to shrink down to the clinical ministrations of a few circuit-riding clergy on Sunday morning.

In sum, we can't allow priests and other ministers to be reduced to mere "sacramental functionaries," circuit riders who suddenly appear on the scene, "confecting" sacraments and "dispensing" grace, and then departing for an indefinite period of time. Christian ministry is inherently local, indigenous, residential, collegial, collaborative, *plural*. As my teacher Aidan Kavanagh used to say, it's not really accurate to say one is "consecrated" a bishop; rather, one is received into a *college* of bishops. Similarly, someone is not "ordained" a priest (priesthood, after all, is a consequence of baptism), but rather, as a consequence of baptism, someone is received into a *college* of presbyters.

The rites themselves already tell us this, for at least three bishops are expected to be present to impose hands at an episcopal ordination; other presbyters are to be present to impose hands at a presbyteral ordination. All ministry in the church is collegiate, collaborative, plural. It happens publicly in "colleges," not privately in closets. It requires that people and ministers live together in a common search for mystery and meaning, for justice and truth. Such ministry cannot continue if sacraments are assigned to circuit riders who have no more connection to the parish, the local community, than a ritually anonymous one-hour layover.

Alternative Futures for Ministry and Liturgy

The leaders of the church, then, like the bishops of Kansas, must meet to consider the life of the church: If eucharist cannot be celebrated, is a communion service the only option available?

Today many pastoral ministers seem to assume that the only alternative to the full celebration of Sunday eucharist is the dreaded communion service. But is this really the case? In a recent article, Arthur Canales proposes an interesting alternative: the celebration of the Hours — Morning Prayer or Evening Prayer, for example — on Sunday, without communion. He points out that:

> The goal of offering a community an opportunity for Sunday worship with deacon/lay presiders is to enable the community to gather on the Lord's Day to hear the Scriptures proclaimed, contemplate God's word, make intercession for the church and the world, pray with the universal Church, sing praises to God, become edified by the sermon preached, exhort the brothers and sisters in Christ, and encourage the assembled community to live out the gospel message.[4]

These goals can, Canales argues, be well met in a celebration of the liturgy of the hours. Such celebrations can also connect well with the tasks and goals of parish ministers whose job is to catechize the people of God about the significance of Sunday, the essence of eucharist, and the distinction between celebrating Sunday eucharist and receiving holy communion (46).

Ultimately, of course, "the best catechetical methodology is to learn by actual participation, that is, through liturgical catechesis, experiencing the rites, rituals, and symbols in the liturgy of the hours." In this light, celebrating the Hours well may be the best possible catechesis, not as an end in itself, but for moving people toward an eventual Sunday eucharist. The author concludes:

> In the final analysis, the liturgy of the hours without distribution and reception of holy communion is the best possible practice at this time for Sunday worship with deacon/lay presiders. This is so because it focuses on community praise and thanksgiving, fostering faith, with a view toward eventually celebrating Sunday eucharist, and it does not exacerbate current problems with Catholic identity, liturgical spirituality, and eucharistic theology (46).

Even if one is reluctant to accept his solution, Canales has a point worth pondering. I am well aware, of course, that particularly after the seventeenth century in the Church of England, Morning Prayer became *the* typical Sunday celebration in parishes, with eucharist relegated to rather secondary status as an occasional—say monthly or quarterly—action. Our present dilemma does force us to grapple with the whole question of eucharistic frequency—how often, why, and for what reasons do we schedule Masses, including the "Masses of convenience."

Ritual Differences

Our dilemma also forces us to deal with centuries of "over-eucharistizing"—the knee-jerk habit of "celebrating Mass" on every possible occasion, for every possible pretext. In her demanding and important book *Ritual Theory, Ritual Practice*, Catherine Bell notes that one of ritual's basic definitions is "a way of acting that distinguishes itself from other ways of acting." She thereby draws attention to ritual difference, ritual distinctiveness. In the case of the Mass, for example, a variety of ritual markers have been used, over nearly two millennia, to distinguish eucharistic dining from other human occasions of food, table, meal.

This happens by distinctions, limitations, that mark this ritual as different from others. In the eucharist, for instance, we limit the kind of food to bread and wine, while ordinary human meals involve many more selections. And we limit amounts—a morsel of bread, a sip of wine, not enough to sustain life. And we limit frequency—once a week, once a day—not the ordinary human practice of several mealtimes per day.

It would be possible, Bell notes, to alter the ritual markers in the eucharist or to choose different ones altogether. For instance, a rich, plentiful abundance of bread and wine, rather than meager quantities, could have been chosen to symbolize ritually the boundless festivity of the Lamb's high feast. Or again, the pattern of frequency could be altered—once a week *only*, for instance; or, perhaps, Sundays only, never on weekdays; or once a year *only*, since Jesus' command to repeat his actions at table did not include a calendar.

The point here is simply that our present dilemma may also include a hidden blessing—it may force us to determine more precisely what we hold as central in our theology and pastoral celebration of eucharist.

The Meaning of Presence

The last issue is the elephant in the room. Swirling beneath, above and around this whole debate about Sunday celebrations in the absence—of priests, of eucharist—is a more fundamental issue of liturgical theology and our theology of ministry. Namely, our dilemma prompts to re-consider how we understand *presence* in its many varieties: God's presence to us; our presence to God; Christ's multiple presences in the assembly—in the Word, in gatherings for prayer, in ministers, in celebrations of sacraments, in eucharistic bread and wine. Each of these presences is real and yet each of them is also distinctive.

Nathan Mitchell

If we're going to resolve the dilemma of priestless Sundays, we are going to have to consider seriously what we stand to gain or lose if our tradition of Sunday eucharist is changed, compromised or forfeited altogether. Eucharistic theology in the West has been shaped principally by two sets of questions. The first set of questions is christological; it asks, basically, "How does Christ become present to bread, present to the communicant?" And "How are the presiding priest's identity and powers related to that presence?"

The second set of questions is ecclesiological. It asks, "How do we believers, baptized into Jesus' death and destined to share his resurrection, become present to God, to the mysteries of salvation?" In other words, how do we become "church"? It is my conviction that neither one of these sets of questions can be adequately answered in isolation from the other. Even Thomas Aquinas, that icon of respectability among Roman Catholic thinkers, understood that in the eucharist Christology is ordered toward eccclesiology, that the presence of Christ in the sacramental elements is not an end in itself, but exists for the sake of something else, namely, the "unity of the body which is the church" *(unitas ecclesiastici corporis)*. In other words, the point of celebrating eucharist is not to create an object, but to produce an outcome. The body of Christ is not merely on the table but at the table.

The Real Implications of Our Dilemma

Below are six implications of the present discussion about the absence of the priest and the absence of the eucharist. We need to consider the consequences of the choices we make for the church that we will become in the future.

First, let us not forget that this is a problem we as church have created. There is no shortage of talent, pastoral ministers or theological acumen in our church. There may well be a shortage of ordained clergy, but this is a problem that doesn't need to be one. It's a problem we've created for ourselves.

Second, our churches are changing day by day. Changing demographics, economics, social mobility, urban decay, and suburban development have drastically altered the identity of Catholic parishes. It's no longer possible, in every case, to identify the parish, as a unit of pastoral care, with a particular territory or locale. Moreover, it's possible today to have parishes without clergy, something that would have been absolutely unthinkable 35 or 40 years ago. Furthermore, almost every diocese in the United States has had to face the fact of parish closings and mergers—either because of clergy shortages or more often because of urgent fiscal factors. Over the past ten years, for example, the diocese of Pittsburgh, with nearly 770,000 Cathoics, has dissolved 163 of 333 parishes, closing 39 of them and merging others into 59 new parishes.

It's no longer obvious what actually defines a parish. A century ago, parish boundaries were determined largely on the basis of geography, ethnic identity, the neighborhood or physical distance—people in cities usually walked to church. Today, definitions of parish aren't so easy. Is a parish simply a collection of like-minded people who shop at the same suburban malls, send their kids to the same schools, hire the same brokers and attorneys, fill their portfolios with the same stocks and mutual funds, celebrate the same values of consumerism and affluence, belong to the same clubs, and share the same socioeconomic status, the same prejudices and politics, the same fear of diversity and change?

Maybe Catholic parishes today need busing. Maybe the people of "Our Lady of the Rich and Powerful" need, regularly, to share altar, pulpit, hospitality and resources with the people of San Carlos or St. Benedict the African—and vice versa. Maybe the challenge today is not how to build community but how to welcome differences, strangers, in our midst.

Third, concerning Masses of convenience. In the "good old days," Masses of convenience proliferated. Sometimes this proliferation resulted from real pastoral exigencies—a suburban parish of 5000 families had to manage with a gymnasium church that could hold, at best, 300 people per Sunday service. As time passed, however, the liturgical schedule was often rigidly retained, even as pastoral conditions had changed. In the Irish-American parish to which my family belonged, for instance, it made pastoral sense, in the late nineteenth century, to schedule a 6:00 AM Mass on Sunday morning, so that Irish immigrants who were employed as domestics could "fulfill their obligation" before going off to cook and clean all day for their wealthy Protestant employers. By the early twentieth century, however, those immigrant conditions had faded, yet the number of Masses remained steady. This encouraged the view that "you go to church when it's convenient." Proliferating Masses also permitted people to avoid services they felt were too long. Some parishioners preferred the quick, silent low Masses at 6, 7:30 and 9, the Masses of convenience, rather than the 10:30 high Mass, which was followed by Benediction. In Richmond, Indiana, the city near where I grew up, three parishes still exist, but they now share a single pastor, a single school, and in each place only one Sunday eucharist is celebrated.

Fourth, we as Catholics have to consider what kind of parish fits our understanding of church as the people of God. At a time when many Catholics are stressing the value of small basic communities, many Protestant groups in large American cities are forming huge mega-churches. I mention this simply as a fact, not as a model for emulation. But we need to think about what this says about the religious sensibilities at work in our culture. The ecclesiology of Vatican II is still being concretized in the world, and this is realized in the choices parishes make about liturgy, personnel, buildings, ministry and so on.

A fifth consideration is about what can we learn from recovery groups. Many people today seem to find their most satisfying experience of church not through affiliation with an ecclesial body, but through participation in recovery groups—for example, Alcoholics Anonymous, Alanon, NA, OA and so on. Many of these people would probably tell you that in these groups they find

- profound acceptance, community and belonging;

- an inclusive, welcoming environment where diversity and difference are affirmed and appreciated rather than feared and despised;

- caring, supportive companionship where honesty, openness, and teachability are norms rather than exceptions;

- a group of people willing to face fearlessly the terrible truth about themselves, their angels and demons, their mistakes *and* their potential;

- a group that is willing to love you when you can't love your-self, but is also and equally willing to tell you to quit whining and start taking responsibility for your life and your choices;

- a group that actually believes in redemption and knows that every person on this planet stands in need of mercy;

- a group with no hierarchies, no oracular authorities, no religious professionals, no prestigious status, no privileged priesthood, and where nothing counts but trusted mutual service;

- a group that is entirely self-supporting through its own contri-butions, that accepts no outside donations and that conducts no capital gifts campaigns.

This is a pretty impressive list of what Christians might call pastoral values. I wonder why we in the church can't seem to learn from the experience of such recovery groups.

A final factor is that we need to hold our leaders accountable. Little can or will change in our church unless and until we ordinary members insist that *everyone*—ourselves *and* our leaders—be held fully accountable for the decisions we make. If we talk the talk, we have to walk the walk. If we tell a woman she must have that baby, then we have to be willing to work tirelessly to guarantee that this child will have food, care, medicine, love, nurture, education and eco-nomic opportunity. If we tell a mother she's got to get off welfare, we can't then refuse to help her find a job that pays a living wage. We can't tell people that eucharist is the center of their lives, and then refuse to provide them with the very things—ministry, service, pas-toral care—that make eucharist possible.

Assembled as the body of Christ at the table, we can and indeed must accept the challenges of celebrating, living and being the eucha-rist in our ecclesial bodies, in our social bodies, in our physical bodies. With and as the leaders of the church in our dioceses and our par-ishes, we can face the concrete gifts and problems of the present with courage, with strength, with integrity and with faith.

1. "Sunday Eucharist: Do This in Memory of Me," in *Pastoral Music* 20:3 (February–March 1996): 41; emphasis in the original.

Nathan Mitchell

2. "Sunday Worship in the Absence of a Priest: What Is at Risk?" *Pastoral Music* 20:3 (February–March 1996): 39.

3. "The Mass and the World," *The Tablet* (13 March 1971): 267.

4. "Celebrate the Hours on Sunday, but without Communion," *Pastoral Music* 20:3 (February–March 1996): 42–46, here 44.

Authors

John L. Bell is a member of the Iona Community, Glasgow, Scotland. He is an international presenter on worship and spirituality, and is the producer of ten collections of original and world songs for worship.

Michael Clay is pastor of Saint Thomas More parish in Chapel Hill, North Carolina, and author of *The Rural Catechumenate*. He has served as a presenter in dioceses throughout the country, addressing pastoral issues about Christian initiation, including the initiation of adults in small parish communities.

Timothy Fitzgerald is a presbyter of the diocese of Des Moines and is associate director of the Notre Dame Center for Pastoral Liturgy. He is author of *Baptism: A Parish Celebration* and *Confirmation: A Parish Celebration*.

Austin Fleming is a presbyter and pastor in the archdiocese of Boston. He is author of *Parish Weddings* and *Prayerbook for Engaged Couples*.

Diana L. Hayes is associate professor of theology at Georgetown University. A systematic theologian with emphasis on black liberation and womanist theologies, she is the author of *And Still We Rise: An Introduction to Black Liberation Theology* and *Hagar's Daughters: Womanist Ways of Being in the World*.

Theresa F. Koernke, IHM, is assistant professor of theology at Washington Theological Union in Washington. She serves as a theological advisor to the U.S. Bishops' Committee on the Liturgy and to the Faith and Order Commission of the World Council for Churches.

Carolyn Osiek, RSCJ, is professor of New Testament studies at Catholic Theological Union in Chicago. She is the author of *Beyond Anger: On Being a Feminist in the Church* and co-editor of *Silent Voices, Sacred Lives: Women's Readings for the Liturgical Year.*

Nathan D. Mitchell is associate director of the Notre Dame Center for Pastoral Liturgy. He is writer and editor of *Assembly* and writes the "Amen Corner" for *Worship*. His published works include *Cult and Controversy* and *Eucharist as Sacrament of Initiation.*

Lois Paha, OP, is director of the Worship Office for the diocese of Austin, Texas. She is a writer and presenter; she serves as an instructor in the diocesan ministry program.

Paul Philibert, OP, is director of Notre Dame's Institute for Church Life. A teacher and researcher, he is the author of *Living in the Meantime: Concerning the Transformation of Religious Life.*

Mary Frances Reza is a teacher, director and composer. She was a consultant for the hymnal *Flor y Canto,* and is a presenter in Hispanic music and liturgy. She serves as a board member for the Instituto de Liturgia Hispana.

H. Richard Rutherford, CSC, is professor of theology and pastoral liturgy at the University of Portland. He is the author of *Death of a Christian* and a consultant to the Bishops' Committee on Liturgy for the *Order of Christian Funerals* and Catholic funerary practice, including cremation.

Thomas G. Simons is pastor of Saint Francis de Sales parish in Muskegon, Michigan, and a speaker and facilitator for the National Forum on Environment and Art in Catholic Worship (Form/Reform). He is the author of *Holy People, Holy Place.*

Thomas Sparough, also known as the Space Painter, is a full-time juggler, storyteller and large group facilitator who specializes in making scriptures come alive.

Bishop Donald W. Trautman, recipient of the 1997 Michael Mathis Award, is bishop of the diocese of Erie, Pennsylvania. As chair of the U.S. Bishops' Committee on the Liturgy from 1993 to 1996, he directed the bishops' preparation and consideration of a revised lectionary and sacramentary.

Evelyn Eaton Whitehead and James D. Whitehead are consultants in education and ministry, contributing to programs of ministry education, leadership development and adult formation in faith. Their numerous books include *Shadows of the Heart: Spirituality of the Negative Emotions.*

Joan Workmaster is director of the Office of Worship of the diocese of Rochester, New York, and coordinator of diocesan dialogue about the future shape of the diocesan church, its ministries and its sacramental life.

These books published by Liturgy Training Publications are compilations of presentations at the annual conferences of the Notre Dame Center for Pastoral Liturgy:

Children in the Assembly of the Church
with presentations by
> John Brooks-Leonard
> Paul Philibert, OP
> Mark Searle
> Gertrud Mueller Nelson
> Linda Gaupin, CDP
> Joan Patano Vos

The Renewal That Awaits Us
with presentations by
> Anscar J. Chupungco, OSB
> Nathan D. Mitchell
> Mary Collins, OSB
> Mark R. Francis, CSV
> Sylvia L. Sanchez
> Michael S. Driscoll
> Thomas F. O'Meara, OP
> Theresa M. Koernke, IHM
> Catherine Vincie, RSHM
> Helen Marie Raycraft, OP
> Julia Upton, RSM
> J-Glenn Murray, SJ
> Archbishop Emeritus James M. Hayes
> Gertrud Mueller Nelson

Traditions and Transitions
with presentations by
> Bishop Donald Trautman
> Godfried Cardinal Danneels
> Kathleen Hughes, RSCJ
> Richard P. McBrien
> Mary Coliins, OSB

Rosa María Icaza, CCVI
R. Scott Appleby
Edward Foley
John Hibbard
James Schellman
John Allyn Melloh
Kathleen Norris
Alan J. Hommerding
Richard S. Vosko
Jan Michael Joncas
Victoria M. Tufano
Catherine Dooley, OP
Toinette M. Eugene

These books are available from your bookstore or from Liturgy
Training Publications.